E X P L O

Los Cabos & Baja California Sur

A Great Destination

2ND EDITION

Los Cabos & Baja California Sur

A Great Destination

Kevin Delgado

The Countryman Press
Woodstock, Vermont

OPPOSITE: *Tourists crowd onto Lover's Beach.*

Los Cabos & Baja California Sur: *A Great Destination*

978-1-58157-121-9

Interior photographs by the author unless otherwise specified
Maps by Erin Greb Cartography, © The Countryman Press
Book design by Joanna Bodenweber
Composition by PerfecType, Nashville, TN

Published by The Countryman Press, P.O. Box 748, Woodstock, VT 05091
Distributed by W. W. Norton & Company, Inc., 500 Fifth Avenue, New York, NY 10110
Printed in the United States of America

10 9 8 7 6 5 4 3 2 1

The Adirondack Book

The Alaska Panhandle

Atlanta

Austin, San Antonio
 & the Texas Hill Country

Baltimore, Annapolis & the Chesapeake Bay

The Berkshire Book

Big Sur, Monterey Bay
 & Gold Coast Wine Country

Cape Canaveral, Cocoa Beach
 & Florida's Space Coast

The Charleston, Savannah
 & Coastal Islands Book

The Coast of Maine Book

Colorado's Classic Mountain Towns

Costa Rica: Great Destinations
 Central America

Dominican Republic

The Finger Lakes Book

The Four Corners Region

Galveston, South Padre Island
 & the Texas Gulf Coast

Guatemala: Great Destinations
 Central America

The Hamptons

Hawaii's Big Island: Great Destinations
 Hawaii

Honolulu & Oahu: Great Destinations
 Hawaii

The Jersey Shore: Atlantic City to Cape May

Kauai: Great Destinations Hawaii

Lake Tahoe & Reno

Las Vegas

Los Cabos & Baja California Sur:
 Great Destinations Mexico

Maui: Great Destinations Hawaii

Memphis and the Delta Blues Trail

Michigan's Upper Peninsula

Montreal & Quebec City:
 Great Destinations Canada

The Nantucket Book

The Napa & Sonoma Book

North Carolina's Outer Banks
 & the Crystal Coast

Nova Scotia & Prince Edward Island

Oaxaca: Great Destinations Mexico

Oregon Wine Country

Palm Beach, Fort Lauderdale, Miami
 & the Florida Keys

Palm Springs & Desert Resorts

Philadelphia, Brandywine Valley
 & Bucks County

Phoenix, Scottsdale, Sedona
 & Central Arizona

Playa del Carmen, Tulum & the Riviera Maya:
 Great Destinations Mexico

Salt Lake City, Park City, Provo
 & Utah's High Country Resorts

San Diego & Tijuana

San Juan, Vieques & Culebra:
 Great Destinations Puerto Rico

San Miguel de Allende & Guanajuato:
 Great Destinations Mexico

The Santa Fe & Taos Book

The Sarasota, Sanibel Island & Naples Book

The Seattle & Vancouver Book

The Shenandoah Valley Book

Touring East Coast Wine Country

Tucson

Virginia Beach, Richmond
 & Tidewater Virginia

Washington, D.C., and Northern Virginia

Yellowstone & Grand Teton National Parks
 & Jackson Hole

Yosemite & the Southern Sierra Nevada

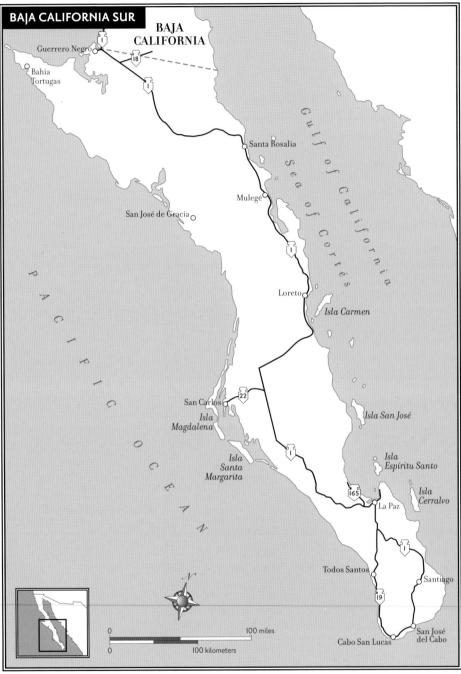

BAJA CALIFORNIA SUR

BAJA
CALIFORNIA

Guerrero Negro

Bahía
Tortugas

Santa Rosalia

Mulegé

San José de Gracia

Gulf of California

Sea of Cortés

Loreto

Isla Carmen

San Carlos

*Isla
Magdalena*

Isla San José

*Isla
Santa
Margarita*

*Isla
Espíritu Santo*

*Isla
Cerralvo*

La Paz

Todos Santos

Santiago

Cabo San Lucas

San José
del Cabo

P A C I F I C   O C E A N

N

0   100 miles

0   100 kilometers

Contents

Acknowledgments

I arrived in San Diego, California, as a 17-year-old country boy who had spent his entire life within a few miles of a small Wyoming town. Despite the fact that I was just one generation removed from my Mexican roots, my provincial life experiences had made that fact all but irrelevant, and at the time, even San Diego seemed an exotic and frightening otherworldly place. When several months later, while waiting tables in a restaurant, a co-worker invited me to go with her and her friends across the border for a night of dancing, I reluctantly agreed to go only because I had been looking for some way to get to know her better. Although trips to Tijuana's Avenida Revolución have long been a rite of passage for underage San Diegans, to me it seemed like utter madness. This was my introduction to Baja California in the early '90s: a bar-lined street, packed with hucksters and rowdy American teenagers. That evening, after several beers and a couple tequila shooters, I was willing to say anything to impress that co-worker of mine. I told her that I had actually been thinking about taking a trip farther down into Baja or maybe even living in Mexico for a while. You can imagine my surprise when her reaction was, "Take me with you!" As it turned out, we lived together in Mexico for a time, thanks to her persistence. And together we fell in love with the whole country, from Oaxaca to Mexico City to La Paz. Even when life took us to New York City, it was hard to forget the allure of Mexico. Writing this now, I realize that it was that co-worker who busted open my provincial shell and showed me the world. Thank you so much, Mary.

I am forever in the debt of the cast of characters whose stories and insights have contributed to this book. Thanks especially to Mike Brady for all the rides to and from the border and for the all of the travel and photography advice. Thanks to John Harten, Greg Zsulgit, and the other Yampounding Sherpas for your wisdom and for dragging me along on all of those adventures. Thanks to the Jason MacBeth and Andrew MacBeth for your generosity and fishing expertise. I am thankful for the kindness, support, and assistance of the hoteliers, restaurant owners, tour operators, and others whom I visited during my research. Thank you to Betty, Monica, and Robert, as well as to Penny and Todd for keeping an eye on the kids, and to Daniel, Summer, Riley, and Isabel for your patience; to my parents, for always giving me a chance; to my brothers and sisters (Mickey, DJ, Lori, Barbie, Davie, Teddy, Brian, Penny, Darren, Ryan, and Sean), for making me who I am; to my old buddy, Brian Schwartzkopf; to Mona Klausing, just for being there; and, noteably, thank you, Simon Lozano and Craig Sodaro for teaching me to write. Without you, I would likely still be a poor excuse for a waiter.

Introduction

On the surface, the southern region of the Baja Peninsula is almost a world unto itself. The capital city of La Paz has a population of fewer than 200,000 people and is separated from the principle regional city of Tijuana by 946 miles of rocky desert. The Sea of Cortés separates the region from the Mexican mainland with a thousand miles of open water. This state is so isolated that many people from the Mexican interior wonder what language is spoken here or if they need a passport to visit. In fact, because most visitors come from California, it is quite easy to get by with English.

Early inhabitants of this region were simple nomadic fishermen who lived in harmony with their natural surroundings. During the colonial period, the conquistador Hernán Cortés sent five expeditions to the region in search of a passage that would link the Atlantic and Pacific Oceans. On the fifth expedition, Cortez established the settlement of Santa Cruz at the present day site of La Paz. However, the Spaniards found living conditions difficult in this arid region, and the native inhabitants refused to submit to their rule. The colony of Santa Cruz was abandoned after only two years.

The area remained largely forgotten for more than a century. Then in 1695 Jesuit missionaries established the Misión Nuestra Senora de Loreto. From here, the Jesuits began establishing missions from Cabo San Lucas north to present-day San Diego, San Luis Obispo, and San Francisco. Also, as Spain established trade routes between the Philippines and Acapulco, sailors began to dock in the calm waters of the Sea of Cortés. The Spanish influence continued to grow on the peninsula and by the 19th century, most of the present-day communities had been established. In 1888 the Mexican government divided the territory of Baja California into northern and southern parts. Although Loreto and La Paz had once been the administrative and economic centers of the region, the pull of the United States began to draw people northward. Today the northern region of the peninsula has a population of almost 3 million people while the southern region is home to fewer than 500,000.

Although it has quickly become famous as one of Mexico's best tourist destinations, the region remained in obscurity until the 1970s. In fact, before the 1,060-mile-long Mexican Federal Highway 1, or Transpeninsular Highway (Carretera Transpeninsular), opened in 1973, southern Baja California was one of the least traveled regions in the world. Even after the highway opened, development came slowly. The two-lane road had no shoulders and rapidly became rutted and washed out by winter rains. Serious development did not begin until the 1990s, and even then it was uneven, concentrating mainly in the area of Los Cabos and some spots on the gulf side. As a result, travelers can still find long stretches of secluded beaches relatively close to areas rife with amenities. Furthermore, southern Baja's rich environment offers a wide variety of unique experiences such as whale watching in the Sea of Cortés, horseback riding in the Guerrero Negro Desert, and swimming in a resort hotel pool.

The area around Los Cabos at the tip of the Baja Peninsula is certainly the region's most famous tourist destination. The twin towns of Cabo San Lucas and San José del Cabo are an adult playground famous for golf, deep-sea fishing, and health spas. The towns have very different personalities, showcasing the magnificence of the area in divergent ways. Cabo San Lucas offers an upper-class resort atmosphere and lively nightlife, while San José del Cabo is a more traditional Mexican town lined with modern beach resorts and elegant shops.

Take an easy 135-mile drive up the Gulf Coast and you will find the city of La Paz, a tranquil city famous for sport fishing and scuba diving. It is the second largest city on the Baja Peninsula but retains the feel of a small Mexican colonial town. A number of beautiful gulf islands are located nearby in calm blue waters.

Farther north, you will discover Loreto, one of Baja's best-kept secrets. Like other towns to the south, there are plenty of beaches, natural beauty, and opportunities for adventure such as sea kayaking, hiking, and sport fishing. Matched with its rich history and the fact that it is not surging with tourists, Loreto is an extraordinary destination.

Take an hour's drive into the inland desert, and you will come to the town of Mulegé, literally an oasis in the desert. The Río Mulegé, which flows through town, is the only freshwater river on the peninsula. Nearby in the high red mountains, Baja's long history is demonstrated by ancient petroglyphs on the walls of canyons. The origins of these paintings trace back to before Baja's first-known inhabitants.

Southern Baja exists as a natural masterpiece. Enjoy all it has to offer, and it will beckon you back again.

1

History

There's no getting around it, Baja California Sur is one of the most beautiful places you are ever likely to visit. It has gorgeous desert vistas bookended by a backdrop of jagged mountains and a pristine white-sand coast. On the peninsula's Pacific side, waves crash against the shore, creating a setting that is ideal for surfing. Across the peninsula, the Sea of Cortés laps against the sand with warm, calm water that is clear, blue, and inviting. It is hard to spend time in this place without thinking of the buccaneers who once used this rugged landscape to hide out. While Baja has several tourist areas with plenty of amenities, it is not hard to find secluded beaches that haven't changed much since the time of the Spanish galleons. Since that time, Baja has had an interesting history filled with all sorts of characters. Despite this, the southern half of the peninsula has been accessible to the average outsider for only about 40 years.

NATURAL HISTORY

Baja California Sur is the southern half of the world's fourth-longest peninsula (after the Antarctic, Kamchatka, and Malay peninsulas). It is separated from the Mexican mainland by 155 miles of open sea at the widest point. This landmass was once connected to mainland Mexico. However, like the coastal region of the state of California to the north, Baja California lies on the North Pacific Tectonic Plate, while the rest of the continent is part of the North American Plate. These two landmasses abut each other along the geological periphery known as the San Andreas Fault, which extends through the Sea of Cortés north along the coast to the region around San Francisco, where it curves into the Pacific Ocean. For millions of years, the Pacific Plate has moved in a northwesterly direction at about a couple of inches per year. By about 5 million years ago, this movement had created basins that allowed the formation of the Sea of Cortés along the fault zone. In fact, this body of water once extended northward as far as Palm Springs, California. However, silting from the Colorado River delta eventually created the northern boundary where it is today, well south of the U.S.-Mexico border.

The Cape

The peninsula's most unique geography is found in the south along the southern cape. Here, the Sierra de la Laguna mountain range is much lusher than in the peninsula to the north because these highlands receive significantly more rainfall while the coastal areas

OPPOSITE: *Turkey vultures sit atop saguaro cactuses along the central cape.*

are much more arid. Furthermore, all lands south of Todos Santos—almost a full fourth of the entire peninsula—lie below the Tropic of Cancer. This tropical latitude combined with moist uplands and dry lowlands creates two distinct types of flora. The arid tropical forest contains plants commonly found in other parts of the Sonoran Desert, though they grow more densely due to the increased moisture of the region. Much of this vegetation is normally associated with the tropical thorn forests of coastal Colima and Guerrero on the Mexican mainland. Some plants that are unique to the Cape include the Tlaco palm, wild plum, and the supposed aphrodisiac herb damiana. The other type of flora is the Cape Oak-Piñon Woodland found high in the southern mountains. These high-altitude forests are composed of Mexican piñon, *madroño,* and *palmita.* There are areas of wetlands along the shallow bays and lagoons throughout the cape. Prominent examples include the mangrove forests of the Bahía de La Paz and the marshes near Todos Santos. They are generally composed of salt marshes of eelgrass, saltwort, and other salt-tolerant plants or mangrove forests. Because of the highly variable level of salinity, water depth, and temperature the plants and animals vary considerably from area to area. However, you are sure to find enough waterfowl to please the most fickle birdwatcher.

Mountains

The Baja California peninsula has a group of mountain ranges, or sierras, that run down the center like a spine, veering in a northwestern direction. These mountains are actually part of a mountain system that stretches all the way to the Aleutian Islands of Alaska. The mountains that dominate in Baja California Sur are known as the Sierra de la Gigante Mountain Range. The western side of these mountains has a gradual slope relative to the eastern slope, which is generally steeper. These are volcanic mountains, with the excep-

The Sierra de la Gigante Mountain Range runs like a spine through the southern peninsula.

tion of the Sierra de la Laguna Mountains on the cape, which is a granitic fault-block range. This southern mountain range receives up to 40 inches of annual rainfall, which creates runoff that flows into a system of arroyos, or streambeds, which allow substantial fruit and vegetable farming in the interior of the peninsula.

Deserts

About a quarter of Baja California Sur can be classified as desert, averaging less than 10 inches of annual rainfall. These lands are actually an extension of the Sonoran Desert, which stretches south from California and Arizona into the northwestern region of the Mexican mainland.

Isla Espíritu Santo.

However, Baja's mountainous interior traps moisture off of the Sea of Cortés, resulting in a more verdant flora than is generally found elsewhere in the Sonoran Desert. In the southern stretches of the Gulf Coast Desert, tropical storms and rain runoff from the mountains result in many more trees and flowering cacti.

Islands

The Sea of Cortés contains many islands and islets, the largest of which are Isla Espiritu Santo and Isla Cerralvo near La Paz. Most of these chunks of land broke away from the Baja Peninsula as it moved away from mainland Mexico due to plate tectonics. They are therefore considered land-bridge or continental islands rather than true oceanic islands. These islands are arid due to their low elevation and meager rainfall. However, their isolation has resulted in a large number of endemic plant and animal species. In fact, at least half of the 120 cactus species on these islands are endemic.

The Sea of Cortés

The Sea of Cortés is the biologically richest body of water on Earth, sustaining more than 900 species of marine vertebrates and more than 2,000 species of invertebrates. The 700-mile-long sea has an average width of around 95 miles and has one of the sheerest sea bottoms in the world with underwater canyons and valleys running along the entire length, reaching depths of more than 2 miles. The zone below La Paz is oceanic, with trenches and submarine canyons more than 12,000 feet deep. At the tip of the Cape, the Sea of Cortés meets the Pacific Ocean and their particular currents mix to produce dangerous rip currents, making swimming during the winter potentially treacherous.

CULTURAL HISTORY

Despite its remote location, Baja California Sur has figured into the stories of some very colorful and famous characters throughout the centuries. None other than the conquistador

Misión Señora de Loreto.

Hernán Cortés was one of the first Europeans to set foot on this land, only to be followed by such an eclectic group as Sir Francis Drake, John Steinbeck, and Desi Arnaz. Although Westerners were initially interested in this land because they thought it might be an island inhabited by treasure-hording warrior women, it didn't gain any true strategic importance until the Spanish established a trading route between Acapulco and the Philippines in the 16th century. However, it wasn't until the 20th century that outsiders truly came to appreciate this region for its natural beauty and abundant sea life. And even then, the entire region remained inaccessible to most outsiders until the early 1970s, when the Transpeninsular Highway was opened. Today, the entire region maintains a secluded character that makes it an ideal destination to get away from it all.

Earliest Inhabitants

Baja California Sur has had human inhabitants since as far back as 10,000 BC. These early residents of Baja were likely fishermen and gatherers who collected seeds, roots, and berries. They took shelter in caves and the remnants of their civilization can still be found today in cave paintings a short distance from La Paz. The folklore of the Cochimí tribe that settled around present-day Mulegé maintains that they were the descendants of a race of giants who created the now-famous cave paintings in the nearby hills. The Cochimí also practiced healing arts, for which they used special clay. These arts have been passed down and are still practiced by some of the Mulegé villagers today.

Conquistadors and the Warrior Women of California

One of the first Europeans to visit the southern half of the Baja Peninsula was the famous Aztec conqueror Hernán Cortés, who arrived in May 1535 well after gaining fame and fortune as the conqueror of the Aztecs of central Mexico. Cortés had been so moved by rumors of an offshore island to the northwest that he sent a letter to the king of Spain in which he related reports of a land "rich in pearls and gold" that was inhabited by warrior women. These reports were likely inspired by a 1504 novel by Garci Rodríguez de Montalvo that read, "Know that on the right hand of the Indies is an island called California, very close to the terrestrial paradise and is inhabited by women, without any man among them." Baja California was thought to be this island, ruled by warrior women who used men only to procreate and who had huge stores of gold and pearls. In reality, this region was inhabited by wandering bands of hunter-gatherer fishermen who had no stores of riches. Cortés made landfall near present-day La Paz and called the area Santa Cruz. He attempted to use it as a base from which to conquer the rest of Baja—the first of many efforts to subdue Baja by force that failed due to the region's harsh desert conditions.

Over the next two decades, Cortés commissioned several expeditions to the Baja Peninsula but never discovered his tribe of Amazon women. His navigator, Francisco de Ulloa, circumvented the peninsula in 1539-40. He named the sea the Mar de Cortés and it henceforth appeared on maps with that name or Mar Vermejo. However, in the early twentieth century, the Mexican government officially renamed it the Golfo de California (Gulf of California). Despite this, the sea has continued to more commonly be referred to with its older name. Furthermore despite the findings of Francisco de Ulloa in the mid-16th century, the belief that Baja was an island persisted for decades.

Spanish Galleons and Marauding Privateers

In 1565 a small ship called the *San Lucas,* captained by Andrés de Urdaneta, successfully sailed east for the first time from the Philippines to the California coast, establishing a Spanish trade route from Asia. Over the next several centuries, Spanish galleons carrying the richest treasures ever to be transported on the high seas left the Philippines en route to Acapulco and ultimately made their way back to Spain. Ships would sail this route only a couple of times a year at most. Although the trip from Acapulco to Manila was a relatively easy one, the trip back was considered one of the longest and most dangerous voyages a sailor could make, often taking upwards of seven months to complete. A great number of people would die of malnutrition and disease during this trip, and on at least one occasion, not one person was left alive onboard. However, the European demand for Asian silks, spices, gold, and other goods was so high that the lucrative profits from these voyages justified the danger.

The first North American landfall from these return voyages was often made around Cabo San Lucas, which eventually made the southern cape of Baja, along with the bay of La Paz, a popular spot for British and Dutch privateers to wait for these vulnerable and treasure-laden galleons. (Privateers are distinguished from pirates only in that they were licensed and even financed by their respective governments to attack and pillage the ships of enemy nations.) In November 1587 the British privateer Sir Thomas Cavendish captured the Spanish galleon *Great Saint Anne,* prompting King Phillip II of Spain to order the establishment of a small fort at Cabo San Lucas to rid the area of marauders. This fort helped to open the Baja Peninsula to exploration. Pearls were discovered in the Sea of Cortés, and settlements started to spring up all along the interior coast. However, the harsh desert environment soon forced the abandonment of these settlements.

It wasn't until 1596 that Sebastián Vizcaíno would give the area that Cortés had called Santa Cruz its modern name, La Paz, meaning "The Peace," in an effort to lure settlers.

A sea cave on the east coast of Isla Espíritu Santo may have served as a pirate hideout.

However, supply problems and a fire soon forced the abandonment of Vizcaíno's settlement. The entire Baja Peninsula subsequently remained free of permanent Spanish settlements for the next hundred years until the village of Loreto was established to the north in 1697. During that time, Spain continued to send ships along its famous Manila trade route from the Philippines to the northwest coast of America south to Acapulco and back again. In the 16th and 17th centuries English, Dutch, and French privateers and pirates used the Bay of La Paz as a staging ground to launch raids on the Spanish galleons laden with super-cargoes of silk, spices, and gold. Francis Drake and Thomas Cavendish are just a couple of the famous buccaneers who took refuge in the waters of La Paz.

Establishing Baja's Missions

Loreto was established the first capital of all of the Californias until 1830, when a fire destroyed the town's infrastructure, prompting authorities to move the capital to La Paz. This move sent Loreto into obscurity, a fact that allowed it to retain the peaceful atmosphere that still exists today. Walking along the cobblestone streets, you will see shaded courtyards set behind ancient wooden doors and cracked stucco walls. It is clear that the centuries have done little to change the town's charm and character. Loreto's most conspicuous feature is the mission of Nuestro Señora de Loreto, located west of the main street, Calle Salvatierra. This first mission of the Californias was established in 1697 by the Jesuit missionary Juan María de Salvatierra, though it has been rebuilt many times due to earthquakes and floods. From here, Father Junipero Serra set out on his 18th-century expedition that led to the establishment of 17 other California missions from the tip of Baja all the way north to San Francisco.

In May 1699 Jesuit missionary Father Francisco María Piccolo arrived in the mountains

The Island of California

In the 16th century, European cartographers adopted the assumption that California (today known as Baja California) was a large island completely separated from the North American continent rather than a peninsula. This misconception continued in one form or another all the way into the 18th century, despite the fact that several explorers had proven otherwise. Early one, this misconception was tied with a legend that the island was a terrestrial paradise. This idea was first put forth in the early sixteenth century romance novel *Las sergas de Esplandián* by Garci Rodríguez de Montalvo, in which he described California as an island inhabited by treasure-hording warrior women. In the 1530s, Spanish explorers led by the famous conquistador Hernán Cortés made landfall near present-day La Paz and named the land after this island described in the popular novel by Rodríguez. This led to the initial assumption that the California was in fact the very same island. However, by the end of the decade the fact that California was in fact a peninsula was proven by the navigator Francisco de Ulloa and subsequently confirmed by Hernando de Alarcón, who ascended the lower Colorado River. Therefore, maps published thereafter in Europe correctly showed California as a peninsula. However, the idea that California was actually the famed island of women continued to be propagated for the next century as various explorers searched for a northwest passage through North America. This image became the standard on maps throughout the 17th century and occasionally into the 18th. This issue was finally put to rest by such Baja explorers as Juan de Ugarte whose explorations in the 18th century settled the question beyond all doubt.

The Sea of Cortés was occasionally thought to be a strait separating the Baja Peninsula from the mainland.

Nuestra Señora del pilar de Todos Santos.

southwest of Loreto, where he found a freshwater spring that the native Cochimí referred to as Viggé Biaundó. Father Piccolo soon began construction of a chapel at the site, about 5 miles north of the town of San Javier's present location. However, in 1701 the chapel was abandoned due to an ongoing Indian revolt. In 1702 a Honduran missionary, Father Juan de Ugarte, arrived in the area and established a new chapel at the site where Misión San Javier stands today. He proceeded to construct dams and aqueducts to preserve the little available water. Ugarte also introduced cattle breeding to the local Cochimí as well as small-scale agriculture and the establishment of the first pack animal road to Loreto. Ugarte went on to succeed Juan María de Salvatierra as head of Baja California's missions, through which he helped to establish a mission at La Paz and the completion of *El Triunfo de la Cruz,* a ship that he sailed to the head of the Sea of Cortés to determine if Baja California was indeed an island. He returned to the mission that he had founded at San Javier and died there in 1730. Between 1744 and 1758, another Jesuit missionary, Father Miguel del Barco, oversaw the construction of the mission at San Javier that stands today. The construction was an incredible feat fraught with the hardships of transporting materials to an isolated location and complications wrought by a shortage of specialized craftsmen such as bricklayers and carpenters. There were long periods in which Barco had to suspend construction due to labor and equipment problems. Throughout this period, the local Cochimí population suffered the ravages of European diseases. Despite the new agricultural and engineering techniques that they had learned from the missionaries, their population continued to dwindle, and by 1817 the mission had been deserted. Today it has been restored and declared a historic monument by Mexico's Instituto Nacional de Antropología e Historia (National Institution of Anthropology and History), or INAH. Walking along the grounds, one cannot help but be amazed by the mission's mere existence in such an isolated place, let alone by its beauty.

Baja California's Road to Statehood

Las Californias was the initial European designation for the Spanish territory comprised of the modern Mexican states of Baja California and Baja California Sur, as well as the American state of California and part of the state of Nevada. Because the border of this region was so ill-defined, it at times contained the additional territories of present-day Arizona, New Mexico, and Utah. The entire territory was administered by the Viceroyalty of New Spain. The name is plural because the region was divided into Alta and Baja (upper and lower) administrative areas until 1848, when Alta California was ceded to the United States at the end of the Mexican-American War. The region was initially colonized by Jesuit missionaries, who arrived with the intention of converting and modernizing the native tribes of the region. After these missions were established, the native people began to organize in communities around them and Hispanic residents from other parts of northern New Spain began to arrive. The first, secular European city in the Californias was Loreto, which also became the first capital of the territory. Loreto was also the site of the first successful mission, which was established in 1697. This process was initially carried out during the 17th century on the Baja Peninsula and later repeated in the late 18th century from present-day San Diego to San Francisco. In 1767, the missionaries from the Dominican order were sent to Baja California to replace the Jesuits, who were expelled due to their reputation of political maneuvering and economic exploitation. Around this time, the Franciscans were chosen to carry out missionary activities in Alta California. The dividing line between orders established in 1773 later became the western end of the U.S.-Mexico border. In 1804, the Spanish crown established separate governments for Baja California and Alta California because the later territory was quickly growing in population. With Mexican independence in 1821, these regions became mere territories because of their small populations. Mexico permanently lost the northern California territory in the Treaty of Guadalupe-Hidalgo, which ended the Mexican-American War. Baja California was recognized as a Mexican state in 1953; however, the region of Baja California Sur was not granted full statehood until 1974, three years after the completion of the Transpeninsular Highway.

When the Jesuit missionary Juan María Basaldúa arrived on the Baja Peninsula in 1705, he founded the Mission Santa Rosalia de Mulegé. However, the existing structure that sits on the south side of the river from the main town of Mulegé only dates back to 1770. The mission was moved to this elevated location after a flood damaged the original structure. The dam below the mission was also built by the missionaries and Indians for the irrigation of crops. This mission is not as impressive as others in the area, although its elevated position provides nice views of the town and estuary. This building continues to function as the town's Catholic church, despite the fact that mission operations ceased in 1828.

In 1724 the Jesuit missionary Father Jaime Bravo established a farming community at present-day Todos Santos (All Saints) to take advantage of the fertile ground and underwater springs. His goal was to provide supplies to the nearby community of La Paz. He also established a church and called it Todos Santos. The town was a success and within a few years, Bravo was shipping hundreds of burro loads of provisions east to La Paz. Within a quarter of a century, the population of the town had outstripped that of La Paz. Todos Santos reached mission status in 1749 and was renamed Nuestra Señora del pilar de Todos Santos.

In April 1730 a Jesuit missionary named Nicholas Tamaral founded the mission of San José 20 miles to the northeast of the fort at Cabo San Lucas. Together, the two settlements became known as Los Cabos (The Capes). Tamaral's purpose was to convert the Pericú people who inhabited the area. He chose a spot overlooking the Rio San José, 3 miles north of where the town is currently situated. However, because this spot was swarming with mosquitoes, Tamaral quickly moved the mission of the mouth of the estuary. The Pericú tolerated Tamaral until 1734, when he issued an injunction condemning the prac-

The tranquil Malecón in La Paz belies the city's tumultuous history.

tice of polygamy, long a tradition in Pericú society. After Tamaral punished a Pericú shaman for violating this decree, the natives rebelled, burning the mission and killing Tamaral. The Spanish returned to the area in 1737, establishing a presidio manned by 30 soldiers to quell the rebellious natives. The nearby Rio San José served as an important source of fresh water for the military outpost as well as for Spanish galleons arriving from the Philippines. This establishment had an impact on the native population and within 30 years, nearly all of the Pericú had died in skirmishes with the Spanish or from European diseases. Those who survived were moved to missions farther north. Due to a lack of a steady water supply, the Los Cabos region at the southern tip of the peninsula remained largely undeveloped for nearly 250 years. However, San José remained an important military post. During the Mexican-American War, U.S. marines from the U.S. frigate *Portsmouth* occupied the presidio for a short time. However, the Mexican Navy, led by José Antonio Mijares, laid siege to the Americans and ultimately forced them out. San José's town square and main boulevard is named after Mijares to commemorate this victory.

Eking into the Modern World

The town of La Paz has had a tumultuous history. As European diseases decimated the region's Native populations, Mexican ranchers and fishermen from surrounding areas gradually took up residence along the bay. In 1811 these new residents founded a town and called it La Paz, as Sebastián Vizcaíno had several centuries before. In 1829, after Loreto was destroyed by a fire, the capital of Baja California Sur was moved south to La Paz, where it has remained ever since. In March 1847, during the Mexican-American War, an American warship landed in La Paz and imposed surrender over its inhabitants. Afterward, a battalion from New York known as the "baby regiment" was stationed in the city to keep the peace but left after the Treaty of Guadelupe-Hidalgo ceded the southern portion of the Californias back to Mexico. Soon afterward, however, the American general William Walker invaded La Paz and declared it to be part of an entirely new country that he himself was creating, which he called the Republic of Sonora. He had been dissatisfied with the treaty and hoped to add another state to the United States to counter the growing abolitionist movement. His expedition was short-lived, though, as he left abruptly on hearing that an army was on its way to liberate La Paz.

In 1840 Todos Santos was secularized, but the town continued to thrive due to sugar cane production. By the end of the century, the town was supporting eight sugar mills. However, after World War II sugar prices fell sharply, and the freshwater spring that fed Todos Santos dried up. The town appeared to be dying, and by the mid-'60s, all the mills in town had shut down. Todos Santos remained an insignificant dot on the map until the 1980s, when the natural spring suddenly began flowing again, allowing a large quantity of crops to once again be grown here. Also in the '80s, the road between Cabo San Lucas and San Pedro was paved, and suddenly tourists began to pop up. The road also brought in artists who were drawn to the town by its authenticity, solitude, and mysterious manner. Over the last decade developers and American expatriates have picked up on the town's colonial charm and have polished it just a bit. Its historic feel is so well-known that Mexico's National Institute of History and Anthropology has declared the town a national monument, and restoration guidelines are strictly enforced.

To the southeast, the region's mining industry gave out in the late 19th century, when San José lost much of its population. By 1940, when the town church was rebuilt, only a few farmers and fishermen remained in the area. San José remained a forgotten backwater until the second half of the 20th century, when sportfishermen began to discover what the cape region had to offer. Since the '70s, the Mexican government has sponsored several tourism development projects along San José's seashore. Residents, too, have done plenty to develop the town by restoring its 18th-century architecture, preserving its colonial character.

For many years La Paz was a center for pearl fishing. In fact, the city is the setting for both John Steinbeck's novella *The Pearl* and Scott O'Dell's novel *The Black Pearl.* In the late 1930s the industry was wiped out due to disease and overfishing. Later, the city banked its economic security on being a duty-free port as well as agricultural trade with the Mexican mainland. The city also developed as a vacation destination for Mexicans from the mainland and wealthy Americans, but it remained inaccessible to most Americans until the Transpeninsular Highway was completed in 1973. Baja California Sur was given statehood in 1974, and La Paz was made the state capital. Linked by air, highway, and ferry to mainland Mexico and the United States, the city has continued to grow, particularly over the last decade.

The Tourism Boom

In 1917 an American fishing company moved into the area and built a floating platform to catch tuna. This more or less established Cabo San Lucas as a fishing village. By the 1930s Cabo San Lucas had a population of about 400, when sportfishermen began to discover the area. It would remain largely inaccessible to most people for another 40 years; still, word continued to get out about the abundance of fish to be had off the coast of Baja, and in 1948 several American celebrities, including Bing Crosby, Desi Arnaz, and John Wayne, invested in a small hotel on the East Cape called Las Cruces. This kicked off a small development boom of hotels from La Paz to Cabo San Lucas. But the area remained accessible only to long-range yachts, small planes, and off-road vehicles. It wasn't until the Transpeninsular Highway opened in the 1970s that development really got under way in Cabo.

By the mid-1970s the population of Cabo San Lucas had grown only to about 900, when FONATUR, Mexico's tourism development agency, began to pour money and resources into the region. Development included a freshwater pipeline, a 300-slip marina in Cabo San Lucas, and an international airport in San Jose del Cabo. Initially, clientele were mainly sportfishermen attracted to Cabo's many tournaments. In recent years Cabo has attracted an extremely broad range of visitors, from golfers and beach lovers to families and eco-tourists. Today Cabo San Lucas has a permanent population of around 40,000, many of whom are expatriate Americans. This growth has brought a stable infrastructure and development of services that ensures a good standard of living for visitors and residents alike.

Despite its auspicious beginnings, Loreto has been little more than a dusty desert town through most of its history. When John Steinbeck came through more than 50 years ago while writing *The Log from the Sea of Cortez,* he found a town full of impoverished fishermen and a mission in ruins. In the late 1970s FONATUR identified Loreto as one of the country's top four locations in terms of tourism potential—along with San José del Cabo, Ixtapa, and Cancún. Although these other locations have since developed into major tourism centers loaded with major hotels and chain restaurants, Loreto remains a three-stoplight town—with only one that actually works. To be sure, there has been development in Loreto over the last 30 years. In fact, today tourism is Loreto's only industry. However, most of the local tourism development has been on a small scale with family-owned restaurants, eco-tourism entrepreneurs, and small, independent hotels. Loreto has no movie theater, no malls, and local height laws prevent any structure from being taller than the mission. Unlike in many tourist towns where visitors are hermetically sealed in their resorts while locals live miles away, visitors to Loreto coexist with its residents.

An increase of tourism in recent years has meant an increase in expendable income among Loreto's residents. Consequently, cars have become somewhat of a status symbol despite the fact that the town is ideal for walking and bike riding. On weekend nights, locals flood the streets, cruising up and down the *malecón* (seaside promenade) while laying on their horns well into the night. This makes Sunday mornings the ideal time for bike rides and strolls since most people sleep late. In fact, if you happen to be in Loreto on a Sunday, be aware that most businesses are either open until noon or closed altogether. The exceptions to this are the hotels, beer stores, and restaurants.

Although Loreto never developed into a tourist mecca like Los Cabos and Cancún, it is clear why FONATUR targeted it 30 years ago. The area is blessed with temperatures that average in the 80s year-round and rich marine life. In fact, Loreto is unique in that it offers world-class sport fishing, diving, and snorkeling in a serene atmosphere relatively untouched by annoying beach vendors, beggars, and time-share pitchmen. Loreto's charm lies in the fact that it is not just another Mexican resort conglomeration. Its 15,000 residents are laid-back and welcoming; its beaches, free of monstrous hotel complexes and rowdy bars. You'll find a range of accommodations, from quaint boutique hotels and bed & breakfasts to an all-inclusive resort in nearby Nopoló. For the traveler looking to get away from the crowds in Los Cabos and instead wants a less commercialized, quieter beach experience, you won't find many places better than Loreto.

2

TRANSPORTATION

How you get around during your trip to this region of Mexico will depend a lot on what kind of trip you would like to have. If you are looking for a relaxing vacation spent by the pool, transportation won't be much of an issue. Of course, a car provides the most freedom and you can rent a car in the airport or at most of the large resort hotels. However, taxis are plentiful around the airport and the hotels and the larger towns offer a variety of public transportation options to get you to and from hotspots and points of interest. If you are interested in visiting the towns along the Transpeninsular Highway, you may want to take advantage of the excellent bus system that exists here. These buses will take you to any point along the highway you want to go and at prices that are very reasonable even for the highest level of service. However you intend to get around, you will find this area rife with places to go, things to do, and good times all the way around.

CUSTOMS AND IMMIGRATION

Technically speaking, customs and immigration can be a real pain. You can mitigate some of this inconvenience by either driving in or crossing the border and flying out of Ciudad Juárez, Tijuana, or some other Mexican airport. Crossing the U.S.-Mexico border on foot or by car is much less of a hassle than making your way through airport security these days. Furthermore, while a passport is required to fly into the United States from Mexico, travelers ages 16 and older are required to present one of the documents below when entering the United States at land or sea ports of entry. Children under age 16 may present an original or copy of their birth certificate, a Consular Report of Birth Abroad, or a Naturalization Certificate. One of the following documents may be presented to prove both identity and citizenship:

- U.S. Passport
- U.S. Passport Card
- Trusted Traveler Cards (NEXUS, SENTRI, FAST)
- State-issued Enhanced Driver's License (when available this secure driver's license will denote identity and citizenship)
- Enhanced Tribal Cards (when available)
- U.S. Military identification with Military Travel Orders
- U.S. Merchant Marine document
- Form I-872 American Indian Card

OPPOSITE: *Balandra Beach in La Paz.*

For specific details of current passport rules, check out the Department of Homeland Security Web site (http://www.dhs.gov/xtrvlsec/crossingborders/whtibasics.shtm). The bottom line is that you should get a passport before you need it—as in *today*. There are ways to expedite a passport if you need one quickly. But getting one via a rush application can be expensive and stressful.

A tourist card is an official Mexican document declaring that you have stated that the purpose of your visit to Mexico is tourism and that your visit will last no more than 180 days. This document costs $20. Anyone staying in Mexico for more than 72 hours and traveling beyond the border zone (about 70 miles south) needs to have a tourist card. If you are driving into Mexico, you can get this document at the immigration station just across the border. If you are flying out of a Mexican airport, such as Tijuana, you will get this document as you pass into the boarding area of the airport. And if you are flying into Mexico from another country (such as Canada or the United States), the cost of this document is included in the price of your airfare and you will receive it, along with instructions on filling it out, while on the plane. Once you disembark, customs and immigration will stamp it, indicating that you are in the country legally.

DRIVING IN BAJA

Just a few decades ago, a description of driving to the southern regions of the Baja Peninsula would entail depicting rugged 4WD vehicles rumbling down rutted dirt roads and passing through dusty towns with few accommodations or provisions to arrive at deserted stretches of white sand with no tourists for miles. Although that Baja certainly had its allure, it is fading into history, greatly due to the paved and relatively well-kept Transpeninsular Highway that has made the southern regions of the Baja Peninsula accessible to minivans, SUVs, and hatchback sedans alike.

While Baja offers a variety of options for getting around, the spread-out nature of the region does not lend itself to public transportation. And though walking can be a great way to experience the cities such as Cabo San Lucas, La Paz, and Loreto, so much of what makes these places worth visiting is located outside the confines of the city that it really does make sense to have your own transportation. Rental cars are readily available at all of these locations (see the specific destinations for details). And for a little bit extra, you can even pick up the car in one city and drop it off in another. Furthermore, the beautiful destinations of southern Baja are located close enough to the United States that driving to them is a serious option for many travelers.

Driving in larger Mexican cities can be an intimidating undertaking, with other drivers prying their way into the smallest opening in traffic and putting the onus on you to avoid a collision—as well as treating stop signs and traffic lights as mere suggestions instead of requirements. With regards to driving in Baja California, these circumstances cease as soon as you get past Tijuana and get onto the open highway. Along the Transpeninsular Highway, the greatest danger is quite the opposite of intimidating traffic; here the biggest danger is complacency. The Transpeninsular Highway runs along the graceful Pacific Ocean and skirts the calm waters of the Sea of Cortés, providing dazzling vistas that are enchanting and are sure to make you forget your troubles. It's easy to forget that, despite its beautiful views and relative convenience, this road is also fraught with hazards. One of the most common is the livestock that commonly wander onto the road. This is generally not a

Traveling with Kids

This region of Mexico is an ideal setting to take a break from the kids. On the other hand, you will probably find yourself constantly thinking it would have been great to bring the kids. This is especially true if you happen to find yourself at one of the larger beach resorts that offer special services for children. If you do decide to take the kids along, there are extra hoops you will have to jump though. First, new passport requirements for U.S. citizens returning from abroad also apply to children. Getting a passport for a child under the age of 14 requires filling out additional documents as well as having both parents' consent. That said, it is no longer necessary for single parents or unaccompanied minors traveling in Mexico to have notarized documentation authorizing travel as long as each child has a valid passport and tourist card. Once that is taken care of, just remember to apply plenty of sunscreen.

Traveling with Pets

Bringing pets to Mexico is a common practice for those driving across the border. If you are flying in, airlines have their own rules about this, so you need to check with your specific air carrier for their specific rules and policies. When you get there, Mexico allows dogs and cats into the country as long as the owner has a notarized letter from a veterinarian stating that the animal is in good health and has the proper vaccinations. However, if you're driving, it's unlikely that this will even be an issue.

Keep in mind that there are certain risks to be considered before bringing an animal to Mexico. Very few hotels allow pets, and those that do generally charge extra. (Be sure to check ahead when making reservations.) Hot weather can also become an issue with some animals that are not used to it. However, the biggest danger with regard to pets is that Mexican towns—from giant Mexico City to tiny towns—have a problem with stray animals. There is always an outside chance that your animal could contract a disease from one of these animals or that some mishap may happen. Unless you are prepared to constantly look after your pets, it might be a better idea just to leave them at home.

Kids and pets have their own requirements for traveling in Mexico.

problem if you are minding your speed. However, you do *not* want to come careening through a mountain pass to find a herd of cattle sitting on the road ahead of you. Another, slightly related, problem is the lack of guardrails that exists on the road, even where it winds along steep cliffs. As you drive through such areas as these, it will become abundantly clear that the road was not engineered with the kind of safety standards that are common north of the border. Add to this the frequent potholes and steep or nonexistent shoulder, and you quickly come to a bit of advice that should be self-evident: Drive slowly.

There may be times when you will have the urge to throw this bit of advice out the window—say, you have found yourself trailing a slow-moving vehicle for miles before you have the opportunity to pass, and you feel the need to make up some lost time. Resist this temptation. I have seen some pretty horrible accidents involving tourists along the treacherous stretch of mountain highway just south of Loreto and north of La Paz.

Do not drive at night. The dangers presented by narrow roads, wandering animals, and unprotected cliffs are exacerbated at night. This especially true of animals, which congregate at the edge of the roadway where the grass grows greenest. One Baja traveler told me that he has successfully navigated Mexico 1 at night by sidling up behind trucks as a way of protection against loitering livestock. However, that seems like a lot of trust to put in the hands of the trucker in front of you. The best advice is to find a place to get some rest, and get going again in the morning when it's safe.

Interestingly, Baja drivers have developed signals to communicate safety to one another. For example, an extended forefinger and pinkie (similar to the "Hook 'em Horns" sign common at University of Texas football games) means that there are cattle on the road ahead. Another signal of danger ahead is flashing headlights. If you get this warning sign, slow down and proceed with caution. Except for a few brief stretches, the Transpeninsular Highway is a narrow two-lane highway that requires you to drive into the oncoming lane to pass slower-moving vehicles. Yet another indicator is a left-turn signal from a slower-moving vehicle in front of you, which indicates that it's safe to pass. Often the vehicle will move to the right slightly to make their intention even clearer. Be careful not to mistake this signal with a regular left-turn signal, which would generally be accompanied by brake lights. Also, keep in mind that regardless of what the driver in the vehicle ahead of you is signaling, what happens during the process of passing him or her is ultimately your responsibility. Do not pass along stretches with unbroken center lines (despite what you see locals doing), and make sure you have a good view of the road ahead as you proceed.

Speed limits are posted in kilometers. This can be a bit confusing if your speedometer does not include kilometers. However, because 60 miles per hour is roughly equal to 100 kilometers per hour, if you multiply the posted speed limit by 6 and drop the last decimal, that will give you a rough estimation of the allowed speed in miles per hour.

Tijuana has earned a reputation for being a place where tourists are singled out for traffic offenses, though the problem is not nearly as bad as it used to be. Cabo San Lucas is another place where tourists run the risk of being singled out if they drive expensive-looking rentals and act rowdy. It is true that in the past, some Mexican law enforcement officers supplemented their low incomes through *mordidas* (bribes), though this has happened less and less as Mexico has enforced anticorruption laws. The chances of this happening to you are slim, particularly if you drive safely and obey the traffic laws. After all, Baja California's economy depends on tourism, and it would not be in their interest to shake down every foreigner who passed through. If it does happen to you, you can either pay the officer and move on with your day, or accept the ticket. If you are ticketed, you have the right to ask to pay the ticket by mail. The most common practice, though, is to have you follow the officer to the nearest police station, where you will pay the fine. There have been incidents where tourists have refused to go and the officer has removed the license plates from the vehicle, obliging the driver to go down the station to pay the fine to get the plates back. Bottom line: Drive safely, and don't set yourself apart.

GETTING TO LOS CABOS

The best way to get to Los Cabos is to fly into the international airport located 13 miles north of San Jose del Cabo and 29 miles northeast of Cabo San Lucas. The airport is the busiest in Baja California Sur, with an average of more than 200 flights a week. Its two terminals service several major airlines, including Aeroméxico, Alaskan Airlines, American Airlines, America West, Continental, Delta, and Frontier. All ground transportation away from the airport is found outside the doors from the baggage-claim areas. The best option is one of the bright yellow minivans. They are reliable and charge a government-controlled rate of around $20, sparing you the annoying task of bartering down the $60 rate that is charged by the regular taxi companies. There is a much cheaper but inconvenient bus service that begins with a short $5 taxi ride and ends with a 20-minute walk.

The bus ride from Tijuana is about 1,000 miles and can take anywhere from 24 to 30 hours. Although it is a long and arduous ride, Mexican buses are generally comfortable and clean and usually play American movies with Spanish subtitles. The primary bus company operating in Baja California is Autotransportes de Baja California (ABC). Contact them at 664-683-5681; www.abc.com.mx. If you prefer to drive to Los Cabos yourself, Mexico Federal Highway 1 (the Transpeninsular Highway) is the only thoroughfare to get you there.

El Arco in Cabo San Lucas.

Traditional mariachis line up along the Marina.

You should not drive on this road at night because some areas that are pocked with pot-holes, cattle often wander across the road, and there are stretches that are rather treacherous to begin with.

If you are coming from mainland Mexico, you can catch a ferry to La Paz from Mazatlán or Topolobambo. Reservations are recommended. For more information, go to www.baja ferries.com and click on the American flag on the top right for English.

GETTING AROUND CABO SAN LUCAS

Downtown Cabo San Lucas is dense enough for walking. Even many of the outlying hotels are less than a 20-minute walk from the action. This option is made even more attractive by the fact that parking can be a problem here, particularly during spring break months when the streets become clogged with vehicles. Taxis are generally easy to get, though they do charge prices typical of tourist centers. Rides within the center of town usually cost around $5, whereas drives out to the Corridor will run you $20 and up. There are several car rental kiosks along Lázaro Cárdenas, but beware of their "specials." Some of them will try to bait-and-switch you with timeshare seminars in exchange for a "free" rental that turns out not to be free at all. Los Cabos does have a municipal bus system that runs within and between the two cities. You will see shaded bus stops, but you can flag down a bus from just about anywhere by waving your arms. When asked, most drivers have no problem with letting you off at specific beaches and hotels. The buses run approximately every 20 minutes along the main highway, and the fare is around $1.50 or less, depending on how far you are going.

Car Rental Companies

ALAMO
624-143-6060
Lázaro Cárdenas between Cicario and Mendoza
Open: Mon.–Sat. 7 AM–8 PM; Sun. 7 AM–7 PM

DOLLAR
624-143-1250
Lázaro Cárdenas at the corner of Narciso Mendoze
Open: Mon.–Fri. 7 AM–8 PM; Sat.–Sun. 7 AM–7 PM

HERTZ
624-105-1428
Lázaro Cárdenas #6
Open: Mon.–Fri. 8 AM–8 PM; Sat. 8 AM–7 PM; Sun. 8 AM–6 PM

NATIONAL
624-143-1414
Lázaro Cárdenas, Posada Cabo San Lucas
Open: Daily 7 AM–8 PM

THRIFTY
624-143-1666
Boulevard Marnia Local K-3
Open: Daily 7 AM–9 PM

GETTING AROUND SAN JOSÉ DEL CABO

The Los Cabos airport is actually much closer to San José del Cabo than Cabo San Lucas. There is bus transport from the airport into town, but taxis are also readily available and much more convenient. Once you arrive in town, San José provides plenty of pleasant vistas and window shopping for strolls. Since downtown San José is located several miles away from most of the town's hotels, taxis are the best way of getting back and forth from your hotel. Taxis are not metered, so be sure to agree on a price before getting in. This is a situation in which you can save yourself some money if you speak a little Spanish.

There is also no shortage of car rental agencies inside the main airport terminal and in San José. Because the Los Cabos area is full of beaches, restaurants, and other places you will want to visit, having your own car is much more convenient than buses, taxis, and even prearranged tours. Renting a car also makes daytrips to Todos Santos much easier. One tip: If you plan on renting a car while you're in Los Cabos, save yourself some money and book the car in advance.

Car Rental Companies

AVIS
624-143-2422
Los Cabos International Airport
Open: Daily 7 AM–8 PM

BUDGET
624-146-5333
Los Cabos International Airport
Open: Daily 8 AM–11 PM

DOLLAR
624-142-0100
Boulevard Mauricio Castro s/n
Open: Daily 7 AM–8 PM

HERTZ
624-142-5088
Los Cabos International Airport
Open: Daily 8 AM–10:30 PM

NATIONAL
624-146-5021
Los Cabos International Airport
Open: Daily 24 hours

THRIFTY
624-142-2380
San José Blvd. #2000A
Open: Daily 7 AM–9 PM

GETTING TO TODOS SANTOS

Todos Santos is roughly an hour's drive from both La Paz and Cabo San Lucas. The trip from either town is fairly straightforward, though, as always, driving the Carretera Transpeninsular at night is not recommended. Bus service from each city is also available and generally runs about every hour. If you are traveling to a hotel along the El Pescadoro, such as La Alianza, inform the bus driver, and he will let you out within walking distance of your destination. Taxis are another option for getting here and the fair can usually be bartered down to around $100. Because Todos Santos is generally noticeably cooler than either Los Cabos or La Paz during the summer and warmer during the winter, you may find it more pleasant than those places.

Within Todos Santos, the town is small enough that walking can get you pretty much anywhere you want to go except the beach. The buses that pass through town on their way to Cabo San Lucas can provide inexpensive transport to the more popular beaches. Just let the driver know where you want to get to, and he will let you out at the proper mile marker.

Taxis

Taxis are a fairly inexpensive option for getting around. As with most places in Mexico, in Baja taxis generally charge a flat rate for transportation within certain zones. However, they are not metered, so you will have to settle on a price with the taxi driver. If you are unsure what the rate should be, be sure to ask the front desk clerk at your hotel. Keep in mind that taxi drivers may charge you double the normal price if you call them to pick you up. This covers the trip to come and get you as well as the trip to drop you off at your destination. Also, fares typically rise between 10 PM and midnight.

Taxis are plentiful throughout the tourist centers and hotel zones, so you shouldn't have any trouble finding one to wave down. Remember to always ask the price of the ride before getting in the car—or better yet, know the going rate and state that price to the driver in the form of a question. Even the most experienced travelers have been known to have been hit by the "gringo tax" every now and then. If the driver quotes you a price that seems too high, don't be afraid to say, "*No, gracias*" and find another taxi. Also, in Cabo San Lucas you may encounter taxi drivers that approach you with offers to take you to a private beach and free meals and drinks. Don't accept these offers unless you want to spend your day listening to a hard-selling pitch man telling you the benefits of owning a timeshare.

Getting back, just wave down a bus heading toward town, and the driver will stop for you. There are also a few makeshift taxis in town that will take you out to the beach, and you can make arrangements to be picked up at a later time. Round-trip transport to Playa Cerritos runs around $40. Be sure to set all prices before you accept a ride, as there are no meters.

GETTING TO LA PAZ

La Paz is a unique blend of an authentic Mexican living and first-class recreation. Not only does it have a relatively close proximity to the United States, but it also has an infrastructure that few other Mexican cities enjoy. The city has an abundance of transportation services, including ferry, bus, and direct air service.

La Paz is 950 miles south of Tijuana and 140 miles north of Cabo San Lucas, making it highly accessible by way of the Transpeninsular Highway. You can drive to La Paz from Cabo in just a few hours and from Loreto in about four hours. The drive can be made from San Diego in about 24 hours if you drive straight through, though this is not recommended as it is dangerous to drive the Transpeninsular Highway at night.

The city's Manuel de Leon Airport is located about 7 miles south of the city off of the Transpeninsular Highway. Although it is a small airport, it has adequate facilities, such as two bars, car rental kiosks, an ATM machine, and a couple of gift shops. It is served by the Mexican airlines Aero California and Aeroméxico as well as major American carriers such as American Airlines, America West, Continental, and Delta. Connecting flights come from Los Angeles, Tucson, and Mexico City.

If you are in the market for a cheaper option, La Paz also lies directly on Baja California's bus routes that run from Los Cabos all the way north to Tijuana. One-way bus travel from the Tijuana bus terminal is about $90 on Baja's major bus line, Autotransportes de Baja California (ABC). This is not the overcrowded Mexican bus experience with rustic mariachis and roosters in the aisles as portrayed in Hollywood films. These buses have large reclining seats and TVs that generally play movies in English. However, even with

The Malecón in La Paz.

these comforts, the drive is quite long.

If you are traveling to or from mainland Mexico, La Paz is near the principal ferry port in Baja California. Located at Pichilingue, 10 miles north of town, ferries provide vehicle and passenger service between the mainland cities of Mazatlán or Topolobampo every day of the week. The ferry trip to Mazatlán takes about 18 hours, depending on wind, weather, and currents, and transit to Topolobampo takes about 10 hours. Third-class travel runs about $20, whereas a two-person cabin with a private bathroom has an additional cost of around $62. Transport for a small car runs about $225; larger vehicles cost about $290.

Getting Around La Paz

The *malecón* in La Paz provides a beautiful backdrop for an evening stroll, but to truly enjoy what La Paz has to offer, you will need some form of transportation. This is because only a couple of hotels in the city are located on the beach, and even the in-town beaches are difficult to reach by walking. The cheapest option is the bus station on Paseo Álvaro Obregón between Calle 5 de Mayo and Independencia. From here, buses run continuously to the beaches north of town as well as to the closer beaches. The trip out to Tecolote costs about $2 and takes around 45 minutes. You can also use this bus station to depart to other destinations from Cabo to Tijuana. Taxis are also readily available all along the *malecón*. It is a common practice here to rent a taxi to take you to the outlying beaches and make arrangements for the taxi to return at a set time to pick you up. If you would rather drive yourself, all the major car rental companies have offices somewhere along the *malecón*.

Car Rental Companies

ALAMO
612-122-3681
Avenida Álvaro Obregón 942-A
Open: Daily 7:30 AM–7 PM

AVIS
612-122-2651
Avenida Álvaro Obregón past Pineda
Open: Mon.–Sat. 8 AM–8 PM; Sun. 8 AM–4 PM

BAJA CALIFORNIA AUTO RENTAL
612-125-7662
Avenida Álvaro Obregón #826
Open: Daily 8 AM–7 PM

Taking the Ferry

Because the Baja Peninsula is cut off from the Mexican mainland by the Sea of Cortés, the southern region of the peninsula is the most isolated in the country. Most Mexicans view this state very similarly to the way most Americans view the state of Alaska.

La Paz is the touch point along the southern peninsula where ferries arrive from across the sea with supplies and passengers from the mainland. These ferries can be a great way to experience other parts of Mexico, particularly if you are driving through Baja. From La Paz, you can make your way to either Topolobampo or Mazatlán. There used to be ferry service between Cabo San Lucas and Puerto Vallarta, though that service is no longer available. You can book passage at the ferry terminal, though reservations are recommended. During peak seasons, you should try to book your ferry reservations between one week and one month in advance. Traveling with a pet is not recommended for ferry travel because your pet must remain in your vehicle for the duration of the trip—and since you are not allowed on the car deck, your dog, for example, can't be walked throughout the 10- to 18-hour voyage. But if you must take the voyage with a pet, you'll need a recent International Health Certificate, and have your vehicle prepared with water and newspaper and leave your windows slightly open.

The voyage between La Paz and Topolobampo takes 10 hours whereas the trip between La Paz and Mazatlán takes 18 hours. A variety of accommodations are offered, from a simple seat to a private cabin with a TV and private bath. These accommodations can be quite pricey though because passengers pay general seating first and the cost of the cabin is assessed on top of that. Also, you will have to wait in separate lines for vehicle tickets and passenger tickets. Arrive early and get your passenger ticket first (after having your vehicle weighed) because the good seats tend to sell out.

Be aware that Baja has a special trade-zone status in which drivers don't have to pass through customs. However, when you board the ferry, you will pass through customs, and you may have to pay duty fees. If you are transporting a vehicle, it will need to be weighed as you pass through customs. The fees for taking your vehicle into the interior of Mexico run around $16.90 plus a deposit of $400 to guarantee that you will leave the country with your vehicle.

BUDGET
612-123-1919, 612-124-6433
Avenida Álvaro Obregón 1775
Open: Daily 7 AM–11 PM

HERTZ
612-122-5300
Avenida Álvaro Obregón 2130-D
Open: Daily 8 AM–10:30 PM

THRIFTY
612-125-9696
Paseo Obregón at Lerdo de Tejada
Open: Daily 7 AM–11 PM

Insurance

Under Mexican law, motorists are required to have sufficient currency to cover damages or insurance from a Mexican company in the event of an accident. Non-Mexican insurance does not fulfill this responsibility. If you are involved in an automobile accident, you are basically considered guilty until proven innocent. You will be detained until the local authorities determine who is at fault, and you will be required to demonstrate financial responsibility. Financial responsibility is defined as being in possession of an inexpensive Mexican insurance policy or $5,000 and $10,000 in cash. Therefore, it is not a good idea to drive in Mexico without Mexican liability insurance. If you are renting a car, you will pay for this insurance through the rental company. However, if you are driving your own vehicle into Mexico, you'll need to purchase insurance on your own. This insurance is relatively inexpensive, and it comes with peace of mind. Plenty of companies offer this insurance at all major U.S.–Mexico border crossings and on the Internet. Here are a few just in case:

Adventure Mexican Insurance
800-485-4075 (U.S.)
www.mexadventure.com
P.O. Box 1469, Soquel, CA 95073

Baja Bound Insurance Services
888-552-2252
www.bajabound.com

Instant Mexico Auto Insurance
800-345-4701
www.instant-mex-auto-insur.com
223 Via de San Ysidro, San Ysidro, CA 92173

Loreto municipal building.

GETTING TO LORETO

With an international airport located just a few miles south of town, Loreto can be surprisingly easy to access. However, it's a small airport, which does present limitations. Direct flights to Loreto from the United States only originate out of Los Angeles and San Diego. Aeroméxico does offer service from Phoenix with a stop in Hermosillo in between.

Loreto also lies on Baja's Mexico Federal Highway 1 (Transpeninsular Highway), making it highly accessible by car as well. Loreto is 721 miles south of Tijuana and just 86 miles south of Mulegé. From San Diego, it takes about 17 to 20 hours of driving time. However, staying off the road at night is highly recommended. If you drive from the border, take time to make a reasonable itinerary and plan to stay at least one night in one of the many towns that dot the coast along the way. South of Mulegé, the road passes through some of the most scenic views in Baja as you skirt Bahía Concepción. The drive from the south is less scenic and at times much more treacherous. Loreto is 295 miles north of La Paz and begins with 50 miles of roads that wind intermittently through mountain passes. The road straightens as you drive through a desert of shrubbery and saguaro cactuses. This road takes you through Ciudad Constitución and on to Ciudad Inserjentes, where the road becomes winding and hazardous once again. Drive this road during the day only and take your time. If you have to stop for the night, Ciudad Constitución has many hotels to serve you. The fact that the locals drive this road at a much slower speed than the tourists should give you some clue as to how dangerous it can be.

If driving is not your thing, you will find hourly service to Loreto from La Paz for about $10. The bus station (613-135-1255) is on Salvatierra and Paseo Tamaral, about a 10-minute walk from the *malecón*. Its hours of operation are 7 AM–midnight. The buses are usually not too crowded except on holidays. You can also make arrangements for bus travel at the main office of **Autotransportes Baja California** (ABC bus line) located at the corner of Salvatierra and Boulevard Juárez. Call for the latest scheduling and prices 613-135-0767.

GETTING AROUND LORETO

With its narrow stone streets and manicured tree arches, Loreto is a town that lends itself to walking. Within the city itself, hotels, restaurants, shops, and other services are all within a few blocks of each other. However, the better beaches are all outside of town.

If you'd rather bike it, several of the town's ubiquitous tour companies also rent bicycles. Taxis are readily also available, though they are not metered, so you should agree to a price before getting in. Knowing a little Spanish in this situation is definitely an advantage. There is no municipal bus service in Loreto. And you can always rent a boat to take you to the offshore islands, where you will find some of the best beaches.

If you want to strike out on your own, several car rental companies operate out of the Loreto airport as well as in town.

Loreto's sculpted tree arches lead you to the sea.

Car Rental Companies

BUDGET
613-135-1090
Paseo Miguel Hidalgo s/n between López Mateos and Pípila
Open: Daily 8 AM–7 PM

EUROPCAR
613-135-2306
Salvatierra at the corner of Independencia
Open: Daily 8 AM–8 PM

HERTZ
613-135-0800
Calle Romanita between Hidalgo and Salvatierra
Open: Mon.–Fri. 8 AM–8 PM; Sat. 8 AM–7 PM; Sun. 8 AM–6 PM

GETTING TO MULEGÉ

Approaching the town from the south by car, you will cross the Rio Mulegé and make a right turn onto the town's main street, Avenida Gral Martínez, which turns into Calle Madero. Mulegé also sits on the bus route that travels up and down the peninsula via Mexico Federal Highway 1, (the Transpeninsular Highway). Arriving by bus, you will be dropped off in front of the Doney Taco Shop at the entrance to town. From here, the walk is downhill east into town. If you'd rather hire a taxi, rides anywhere in town cost between $2 and $5.

The nearest international airport is in Loreto, though a local airport with a 4,000-foot landing strip services regional and private charter planes. If you plan to arrive by plane, the airstrip's legal fight plan designation is El Gallito. Use frequency UNICOM 122.8. Be aware that fuel is generally not available here. For more information, call the Loreto Airport at 613-135-0565 daily between 7 AM and 7 PM.

GETTING AROUND MULEGÉ

There is no local bus service, though the town is small enough to explore on foot, and this is definitely the best way to take in the feel of the place. Taxis can usually be found near where the long-distance buses drop off passengers as well as around the main plaza. For taxi dispatch, call 615-153-0420.

There are plenty of small grocery stores and other shops to buy provisions here, as well as a few restaurants and several hotels. However, as mentioned previously, there is no bank or ATM in Mulegé and very few establishments accept plastic, so be sure to have your cash situation taken care of before you arrive. If you are desperate, the nearest ATM is 38 miles north in Santa Rosalia.

Road Signs
The first time you come upon some road signs in Mexico, it can be confusing and even disconcerting if you think you're missing out on something you should be aware of. If you

Military Stops

If you travel by road in Mexico, you will soon encounter being stopped at a military checkpoint. Along Baja California Sur, the main checkpoint is located northbound on the Transpeninsular Highway several miles north of Loreto.

For the average American who is not used to such things, this can be a jarring experience. After all, you just came down here to have a good time, right? Just keep in mind that everybody goes through this, and it isn't really a big deal. Despite what you may have heard about corrupt cops demanding payola, Mexico's economy—and especially the economy of Baja California Sur—depends on the influx of tourist dollars. It would not be in their interest to have the authorities shaking down every tourist who comes along. As long as you've done nothing wrong, you have nothing to worry about.

These stops are actually largely the result of Mexico attempting to satisfy their allies from north of the border that they are doing everything in their power to stop the flow of drugs northward. Keep in mind that these young soldiers are just doing their job. Many of them come from the poorer parts of Mexico, and they are occasionally even illiterate—meaning that your political opinions about unwarranted searches could hardly have less significance to them. Therefore, it is best just to cooperate so you can be on your way.

Generally, you will be stopped for only a few minutes. The soldiers will likely ask to see your identification and to look in your trunk. It is always a nice gesture to offer them a cold soda on a hot day. Assuming that you are not carrying any drugs, guns, or other illegal paraphernalia, you will soon be on your way.

In Case of Arrest

If you do get into trouble and are arrested, contact your nearest consulate immediately. Also, the State Tourist Assistance Office located in La Paz (612-122-5939) will assist you with legal help or if you wish to register a complaint during normal business hours.

CAUTION: Do not forget that guns are illegal in Mexico. There have been cases of Americans unwittingly crossing the border into Mexico while in possession of firearms that are perfectly legal in the United States only to find themselves locked up for months and even years in a Mexican prison. *Do not take firearms into Mexico with you.*

Stopping for Gas

Petroleos Mexicanos (PEMEX) is Mexico's state-owned nationalized petroleum company. Its midgrade gasoline, Magna Sin, is rated at 87 octane and should be fine for cars that run on unleaded regular in the United States. Mexican Premium is rated at 92 octane.

Although PEMEX stations are not as abundant as gas stations north of the border, you will find them in all major stops on your itinerary. They are generally open 24 hours a day, and they do not take credit cards; pesos only here. The upside to this is that PEMEX stations make a great place to break large bills, because the attendants carry a lot of cash. Speaking of the attendants, they will pump your gas and clean your windshield if you need it. It is customary to tip them about 10 pesos, or one dollar.

don't speak Spanish, you should try to acquaint yourself with these signs as much as possible before driving, since many of them have to do with safety.

Accesso a Playa	Beach Access
Alto	Stop
Ceda el Paso	Yield
Circulación	Direction of Traffic
Concida Cambio de Luces	Dim Your Lights
Conserve Su Derecha	Keep to the Right
Curva Peligrosa	Dangerous Curve
Despacio	Slow Down
Desviación	Detour
Doble Circulación	Two-Way Street
Inspección	Military Inspection Ahead
Maxima	Speed Limit (listed in kilometers per hour)
No Hay Paso	Road Closed
No Rebase	No Passing
No Tire Basura	No Littering
Peligro	Danger
Pendiente Peligrosa	Dangerous Downgrade
Precaución	Caution
Solo Izq.	Left Turn Only
Vado	Dip
Zona de Derrumbes	Falling Rock Zone

3

Cabo San Lucas

At the tip of the 1,000-mile Baja Peninsula along sun-drenched rocky cliffs and white sand beaches sits Cabo San Lucas, a once-tiny fishing village now transformed into a booming resort town. With its convenient location near the West Coast of the United States and its increasing reputation as a golf destination—not to mention its well-established reputation as a sport-fishing and party town—Cabo San Lucas has probably only begun to be a West Coast hotspot.

Located at the point where the Pacific Ocean meets the Sea of Cortés, Cabo is centered on a 300-slip marina that is usually filled with everything from small boats and luxury yachts. The boardwalk that runs along this marina is where you'll find the town's accumulation of tourist restaurants, disco bars, and shops pushing everything from hokey T-shirts to fine jewelry. While there are plenty of bargains to be had here, the vendors who line the streets harassing passersby can be rather annoying. At night this district comes alive with partying Americans taking advantage of the numerous drink specials offered up. It's not the height of Mexican culture, but you can have a good time here. Most visitors to Cabo confine themselves to their resort hotels and the waterfront; however, up in the hills is a surprisingly vibrant Mexican town where you can find good family-owned restaurants and cozy inns that cater to a slightly different crowd than you will find at the all-inclusive resorts.

Because Cabo is a tourist destination in the midst of a developmental boom, you will also find plenty of swindlers waiting to rip you off. Carrying your wallet in your front pocket or a money belt is never a bad idea, and be wary of people claiming that they can make you a special deal. If you are looking for a particular service—for instance, a car rental—and they offer you anything other than what you ask for, either insist on getting exactly what you want, or go somewhere else. This is particularly true when it comes to timeshare hucksters. If someone offers you a gift in exchange for "looking at a new hotel," be aware that what he or she is really offering is several hours in hard-sell hell. This is probably something that you want to avoid—especially since you came to Cabo to relax and enjoy yourself.

General Information

Emergency

POLICE

624-143-3977
Marina Blvd. at Plaza Bonita Mall (on the boardwalk), Cabo San Lucas

OPPOSITE: *Cabo San Lucas town square.*

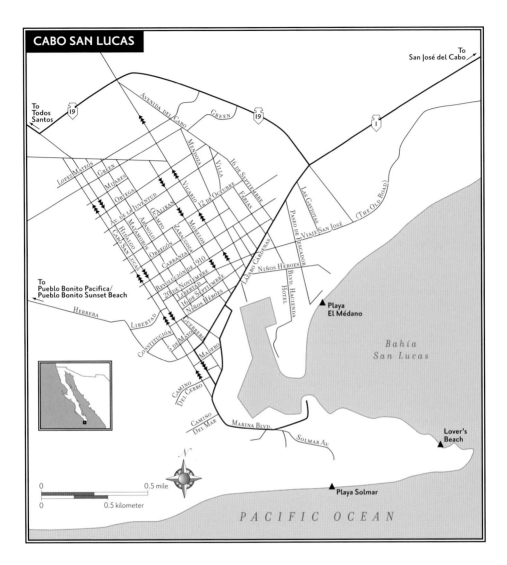

Medical Service
624-143-3434
López Mateos between Leona Vicario and Morelos Colonia Ejidal, Cabo San Lucas

FIRE DEPARTMENT
624-143-3577
Camino Real and Boulevard Marina behind McDonald's, Cabo San Lucas

AMERICAN EXPRESS OFFICE
624-142-1349
Plaza Misión and Boulevard Mijares, San José del Cabo

AMERICAN CONSULATE

624-143-3566

Boulevard Marina, Local C-4, Plaza Naútica, Cabo San Lucas

CANADIAN CONSULATE

624-142-4333

Plaza Jose Green #9, Boulevard Mijares, San José del Cabo

Courier Service

DHL WORLDWIDE EXPRESS

624-143-1430

Plaza Copán on Lázaro Cárdenas, Cabo San Lucas

MAIL BOXES ETC

624-143-3032

Plaza Bonita Mall, Cabo San Lucas

The Bungalows Breakfast Inn.

ACCOMMODATIONS

Cabo San Lucas is a tourist town, and as such, there is no shortage of hotel options here. Médano Beach is lined with resort hotels, and Solmar Beach has a good stretch of resorts, as well. For the most part, these resorts are designed to allow guests to fly into Cabo, never leave the hotel grounds during their stay, and fly out. They are glorious in scale and luxurious in atmosphere. However, the pampered experience provided at these large resorts can be not only expensive but overwhelming, as well. For travelers looking for a more down-to-earth vacation, Cabo San Lucas also has several boutique hotels where you can surround yourself with a more traditional sort of elegance. These hotels are generally on the smaller side and feature rooms with unique decors and are generally within walking distance to the many bars and restaurants that line Lázaro Cárdenas and Boulevard Marina. Whatever you choose, Cabo San Lucas has the facilities and service to meet your desires.

THE BUNGALOWS BED & BREAKFAST
624-143-0585 or 888-424-2226 (U.S.)
www.cabobungalows.com
Boulevard Miguel A. Herrera
Price: Moderate
Credit Cards: MC, V, AE
Special Features: Gourmet breakfast, heated pool

This charming hotel lies off the beaten path in the hills above Cabo San Lucas. While it may not be the best hotel for young partiers in town for spring break, it is perfect for couples and other travelers looking for a tranquil place to rest after a long day at the beach. The staff is friendly and accommodating and more than happy to help you plan excursions. The hotel's 16 air-conditioned rooms face an inner courtyard dominated by a heated pool and a lushly shaded garden. When you arrive in your room, you are welcomed with gourmet chocolates and freshly cut flowers. The rooms are decorated in a rustic Mexican style with thick wooden furniture and colorful fabrics. The grounds of the hotel are lush and meticulously manicured, and a trickling garden fountain sets a mood of quiet and privacy. Guests are invited to choose from the video library in the main house, where every morning a delicious gourmet breakfast is prepared. This meal is usually vegetarian, though special meals are available upon request. Breakfast is served on a *palapa*-roofed breakfast nook overlooking the pool, the perfect setting to plan an(other) adventurous day in Cabo. Rates: $95–155 for standard rooms ($75–95 during August and September). Honeymoon suites and bungalows are slightly more expensive.

CABO INN HOTEL
624-143-0819 or 619-819-2727 (U.S.)
www.caboinnhotel.com
20 de Noviembre and Mendoza
Price: Inexpensive
Credit Cards: MC, V (with reservations; walk-ins cash only)
Special Features: Community kitchen, spa, swimming pool, wireless Internet, convenient location

This charming budget hotel has 22 air-conditioned rooms constructed around a shaded courtyard that is perfect for getting to know fellow travelers. The entire hotel is decorated with colorful Mexican decorations, with *saltillo* tile floors, handmade furniture, and *palapa* roofs. The rooms are airy and clean, and are furnished with two double beds. They are also equipped with air conditioning. Wireless Internet is available throughout the hotel and the staff is friendly and knowledgeable about Cabo San Lucas. The hotel has a community kitchen, first-floor rooms have refrigerators, and a small pool is on the premises. There is an on-site spa that offers massages, waxing, manicures, and other services. However, the hotel's best feature may be its convenient location just a few blocks from downtown. Rates: $58–70 for a standard room, double occupancy, and $90–120 for *palapas.*

CABO VILLAS RESORT
624-143-9199 or 877-382-2932 (U.S.)
www.cabovillasbeachresort.com
Callejon del Pescador s/n Colonia El Médano
Price: Expensive
Credit Cards: MC, V
Special Features: Rooftop restaurant, two pools, on-site spa, beachfront bar, wireless Internet

This resort hotel is located on the northeast side of Médano Beach. The large property skirts the beach and has one small pool and another enormous one. Suites are attractively appointed in a modern style and equipped with two TVs, a full kitchen, and wireless Internet access for a small fee. Located atop the main building is a Mexican seafood restaurant called the Sunset Grill (143-9199 ext. 2026), where you can enjoy a gourmet meal with a fantastic view of the Sea of Cortés. It is open 7 PM to 10 PM and features live music on Monday and Friday nights. If you want to get closer to the action, visit the Baja Cantina (143-9773), a beachfront *palapa* bar with an all-day happy hour. Or if you'd rather be relaxing, visit the on-site Manos Massage & Treatment center for a rubdown and some aromatherapy. Rates: average $288.

CASA BELLA
624-143-6400 or 425-444-9104 (U.S.)
www.cabo-condo.com
Hidalgo #10, Colonia Centro
Price: Expensive
Credit Cards: MC, V
Special Features: Fitness center, satellite TV, wireless Internet, catering chef available

This colonial-style condominium with a lush garden courtyard features a beautiful patio pool and a convenient location. The terrace patio overlooks the Sea of Cortés and is a great place to relax in the evening. The house is spacious and gorgeously appointed, with handmade terra-cotta tile and original art throughout. Its three bedrooms can accommodate up to eight people. The master bedroom is furnished with a king-size bed and a spacious bathroom with a Jacuzzi tub. The first guest bedroom is furnished with a queen-size bed, while the second guest bedroom has two twin beds. The entire house is equipped with wireless Internet access and satellite TV, and continental breakfast is included in the price of your stay. Rates: $375–450 for a one-bedroom condominium. Two- and three-bedroom condominiums are more expensive.

CASA PABLITO BED & BREAKFAST HOTEL
624-143-1971
www.casapablitoloscabos.com
Miguel Hidalgo and Felix Ortega
Price: Inexpensive
Credit Cards: MC, V
Special Features: Jacuzzi, *palapa*-roof canteen

This 15-suite boutique bed & breakfast hotel located right in downtown Cabo San Lucas is built around an attractive central courtyard. In the center of this courtyard is a Jacuzzi *palapa*-roof canteen that borders a deep-blue pool. The hotel's interior and exterior are decorated in Mexican hacienda style, with salmon-colored stucco walls with blue and red accents, giving this hotel an authentic Mexican feel. Rooms are equipped with a queen or two twin beds as well as kitchenettes that include a small stove and refrigerator. Breakfast featuring fresh fruit and juices is served daily from 8 AM to 11 AM (9 AM to noon on Sundays) in a colorful canteen area. Rates: $90–110 between October 16 and April 30; $70–80 between May 1 and October 15.

CASA RAFAEL'S

624-143-0739
Calle Médano
Price: Moderate
Credit Cards: MC, V
Special Features: Fine-dining restaurant, piano bar, cigar room, wireless Internet

This boutique hotel is just a hundred yards from Médano Beach and a short walk from the marina. The tall aqua blue house is surrounded by desert landscaping and has a sun deck, swimming pool, and 10 large guest bedrooms that are uniquely decorated. Internet service, a fax machine, concierge service, as well as plain ol' translation service are all available at the front desk. The hotel also offers a fine-dining experience in their restaurant, complete with tropical birds and a piano bar. Here you will find an extensive wine list with more than 120 selections from around the world. Dine either in their attractive dining room, which is furnished with a tropical aquarium, or on their poolside patio. Room service from this excellent restaurant is also available to guests. Rates: $75–100 for double occupancy with an additional $25 per extra person.

CASTILLO BLARNEY INN

624-143-2160
www.blarneycastleinn.com
Calle Libertad, Colinia Lienzo Charro
Price: Moderate to Expensive
Credit Cards: MC, V
Special Features: Private accommodations, Internet access, Jacuzzi pool

This Irish-themed boutique hotel is located on a hill overlooking Cabo San Lucas and caters to travelers looking for something different than prepackaged all-inclusive resorts. It features nine private air-conditioned suites, each one with a view of the Sea of Cortés below. These suites vary in size from the 380-square-foot Studio Suite to the 2,900-square-foot Castle Suite and can accommodate anywhere from 3 to 10 people. Large, clean, and decorated in a modern style, each unit features a full kitchen—complete with cookware, dishes, and utensils—a private deck, and satellite TV as well as daily maid service. The property also has a swimming pool, Jacuzzi, and a communal barbecue grill. The hotel also offers a spectacular view of Cabo San Lucas from high above. Although this hotel is set off a bit from the action in town, it offers a great escape and is only a 5-minute drive away. Rates: average $185.

HOTEL FINISTERRA

624-143-3333 or 800-347-2252 (U.S.)
www.finisterra.com
Boulevard Marina
Price: Expensive
Credit Cards: MC, V, AE
Special Features: Beachfront location, three pools, two Jacuzzis, two restaurants

This resort hotel is located on Solmar Beach, south of the marina. This location on the wide Pacific beach gives the sense of being isolated while still being a short walk from the action in town. This hotel offers 287 terraced suites overlooking either the Pacific Ocean or the Sea of Cortés. Each room is furnished with two double beds or one king-size. The hotel is built into a cliff above the beach and faces a large area surrounded by palm trees. This area includes three swimming pools and two Jacuzzis. This hotel offers wedding and event services and features a 1,300-square-foot banquet hall for all types of special occasions. There is also an on-site fine-dining restaurant called the Blue Marlin (143-3333) that is open 6:30 AM to 11:30 AM for breakfast and again 6 PM to 10 PM for dinner. For more casual fare, check out La *Palapa* at Finisterra (143-3333 ext. 1948), a poolside *palapa* restaurant serving Mexican and American comfort food. Rates: average $140–229 for city-view rooms and $171–270 for ocean-view rooms. *Palapa* suites are more expensive.

HOTEL MAR DE CORTEZ

624-143-0032 or 800-347-8821 (U.S.)
www.mardecortez.com
Lázaro Cárdenas and Guerrero
Price: Inexpensive
Credit Cards: MC, V
Special Features: Garden pool, private parking, wireless Internet

Constructed in the late 1960s, this rather large hotel is located toward the south side of town near the marina. Built well before the tourist boom, the colonial-style hotel has a garden pool, private parking, and a restaurant on the premises. The 90 air-conditioned rooms come in a variety of options. First-level standard rooms are fairly good sized and offer a combination of queen-, double-, and twin-size beds or a single king-size. Second-level terrace rooms come with a queen-size and a twin bed as well as a terrace overlooking the courtyard. Garden-view rooms have two double beds and an extra-large shower and bathing area as well as a private patio or a balcony overlooking the pool. The hotel also offers free wireless Internet connection for their guests. Whichever kind of room you settle on, the rates are surprisingly reasonable. Rates: start at $50 for a standard room, double occupancy.

HOTEL QUINTA DEL SOL

624-144-4500; fax 624-144-4542
http://quintadelsol.com/
Lázaro Cárdenas and El Bordo
Price: Inexpensive
Credit Cards: MC, V
Special Features: Swimming pool, convenience store, private parking, security guard

This hotel, located in a small complex

slightly east of the main drag, is affiliated with the Best Western hotel franchise. Many Americans will find it very familiar because it's built like an American budget hotel: long two-story buildings, with exterior corridors leading to the parking lot. The 72 air-conditioned rooms are clean and comfortable and decorated like any other American budget hotel, with two double beds and a kitchenette. Rooms are available that are appropriate for disabled guests but they must be booked in advance over the phone. A small swimming pool is on the premises as well as a small convenience store and a 24-hour security guard who checks cars in and out. Rooms come with a continental breakfast. The hotel's biggest drawback is its location, which is a bit out of the way. Rates: $84–93 for a standard room, double occupancy.

HOTEL RIU PALACE CABO SAN LUCAS

624-146-7160 or 888-666-8816 (U.S.)
www.riu.com/palacecabosanlucas
Camino Viejo a San José
Price: Expensive
Credit Cards: MC, V, AE
Special Features: All-inclusive lavish vacationing

This all-inclusive resort resembles a giant southern Spanish palace built right on Médano Beach. It is one of the newer hotels in Los Cabos and puts an emphasis on lavish living. The hotel has 642 units of varying accommodations, including some rooms with their own Jacuzzis set on private patios overlooking the sea. All rooms feature balconies with attractive views. Rooms are spacious and nicely appointed in an extravagant modern style and have a fully stocked mini bar. Because of the all-inclusive rate, domestic and imported alcoholic beverages as well as juices, sodas, bottled water, and anything else you want is complimentary everywhere on the premises. The hotel features two separate pool areas—equipped with two swim-up bars—that open onto the beach, as well as a beauty salon and a fitness center. Rates: junior suites average $256.

HOTEL SANTA FÉ
624-143-4401 or 877-845-5247
www.hotelsantafeloscabos.com
Ignacio Zaragoza and Avenida Álvaro Obregón
Price: Inexpensive
Credit Cards: MC, V, AE
Special Features: Convenient location, satellite TV, laundry room, pool, private parking, gift shop

This 46-room budget hotel is about a 5-minute walk from downtown Cabo San Lucas. Rooms are arranged around a central courtyard and are appointed in a basic style and equipped with a queen-size bed and a sofa bed as well as a small, fully furnished kitchenette. A laundry room is on the premises, and the hotel also offers a laundry and dry-cleaning service. There is a small outdoor pool located in the hotel's central courtyard surrounded by chaise lounges and a few palm trees. Other amenities include a well-lit parking area, a small restaurant, and a gift shop. The hotel also provides guests with satellite TV as well as a currency exchange service. Rates: average $75.

HOTEL SOLMAR SUITES
624-146-7700 or 800-344-3349 (U.S.)
www.solmar.com
Avenida Solmar #1 Colonia Centro
Price: Expensive
Credit Cards: MC, V, AE
Special Features: Saturday-night fiesta, satellite TV, Jacuzzi, heated pools, on-site activity center

This hotel is located on Solmar Beach and sheltered from the city by granite cliffs. However, despite its secluded location, the main strip of Cabo San Lucas is only a 10-minute walk away. With 190 units, the hotel offers guests a variety of accommodations.

Each room is furnished with either a king-size or two double beds and a living-room area that varies depending on your room choice. All rooms are also equipped with satellite TV and a mini bar. The property features two heated pools, a Jacuzzi, and tennis courts, and an activity center offers everything from scuba diving and snorkeling to horseback riding and ATVs. After working up an appetite, visit the Fiesta Mexicana Restaurant (146-7700 ext. 5360) for oceanfront Mexican cuisine. It's open daily 6 AM to 10 PM. On Saturday nights from 7 to 10, catch live mariachi music and an all-you-can-eat buffet. Rates: average $155 for Gardenview suites with double occupancy. There is an additional charge of $25 for each additional person and Junior, Studio, and Deluxe suites are more expensive.

LAS MARGARITAS INN
624-143-6770
Lázaro Cárdenas and Zaragosa
Price: Inexpensive
Credit Cards: MC, V, AE
Special Features: Convenient location, private parking

Located in the heart of downtown Cabo San Lucas, this hotel provides a convenient location and roomy accommodations. The 16 one- and two-bedroom air-conditioned units are decorated in basic-budget hotel whites, blues, and pastels. The bedrooms have a king- or queen-size bed, and the living rooms are equipped with sleeper sofas and fully furnished kitchenettes. Provisions won't be a problem, as the hotel is located across the street from a large grocery store and bakery. There is also plenty of on-site parking, which can be a big plus during the busy season when the streets fill up with tourists. Rates: $70–90 for a standard room, double occupancy.

LOS MILAGROS
624-143-4566
www.losmilagros.com.mx

Matamoros 116
Price: Inexpensive
Credit Cards: None
Special Features: Internet access, laundry
service

Los milagros means "the miracles," and
though it is no miracle what makes this
little hotel so tranquil, it is certainly a
surprising find in the heart of bustling
downtown Cabo San Lucas. The two-level
white adobe-style building, with 12
attractive rooms, a private roof terrace,
and a small pool in a shaded courtyard, is
less than two blocks from Cabo Wabo.
Despite its proximity to the action, the
emphasis at this hotel is tranquility.
Double rooms are furnished with two
full-size beds while single rooms have a
queen-size bed, and each has a large
bathroom. They are tastefully decorated
in a classical Mexican style with *saltillo*
tile floors, thick wooden dressers, and
wrought-iron headboards. Suites also
have kitchenettes. The hotel provides
cable TV and high-speed Internet
hookups in every room as well as laundry
service for a nominal fee. Rates: $70–85
for a standard room, double occupancy.

MARINA CABO PLAZA
624-143-1833 or 619-954-8000 (U.S.)
www.marinacaboplaza.com
Boulevard Marina 39
Price: Inexpensive
Credit Cards: None
Special Features: Convenient location,
security guard

This condominium hotel is located right on
the marina and near Médano Beach. The
rentals are appointed in a spare, modern
style with tile floors, lots of wooden furniture, and monotone fabrics. They come
equipped with wet bars, air conditioning,
and kitchenettes. They also have private
patios or balconies that overlook the
marina, where you can lounge on patio furniture and watch the fishing boats leave in
the morning or return in the evening. A
security guard is on duty at all times, and
guests will have no problem finding plenty
of dining choices and other services within
short walking distance. Rates: average
$100.

MARINA FIESTA RESORT & HOTEL
624-143-1220 or 877-243-4880 (U.S.)
www.marinafiestaresort.com
Marina Cabo Lote 37 and 38
Price: Expensive
Credit Cards: MC, V, AE
Special Features: Two swimming pools,
swim-up bar, two restaurants, massage
room, gym

This large resort hotel has 155 suites built
around a large swimming pool area that
opens right onto the marina. Its location
puts the resort within walking distance of
the city's bars and restaurants, but with all
the featured amenities, you don't even have
to leave the hotel grounds if you so choose.
The hotel offers a variety of accommodation
options ranging from a relatively cramped
junior suite on up to the 1,800-square-foot
Presidential Suite or the 2,000-square-foot

Cabo San Lucas marina.

penthouse. All rooms are decorated in a colorful Mediterranean style and furnished with either double- or queen-size beds. The on-site spa offers guests the opportunity to pamper themselves with a massage or a facial. The hotel's casual poolside *Palapa* Restaurant offers snacks and light entrées from 7 AM to 7 PM, and a lobby bar is open daily until 10 PM. For other dining options, several restaurants along the marina are a short walk away. Rates: $260–360 double occupancy.

MELIÁ SAN LUCAS

624-145-7800 or 800-336-3542 (U.S.)
www.me-cabo.com
Playa El Médano s/n
Price: Expensive
Credit Cards: MC, V, AE
Special Features: Fitness center, concierge service, baby-sitting service

Located on Médano Beach, this resort offers guests a fashionable and lavish retreat. The 150 units are done up in a modern décor, including numerous paintings and sculptures by renowned Mexican artist Yuri Zatarain. Rooms are furnished with a king-size or two double beds and are appointed in an attractive modern style that speaks to the opulence of this hotel. These rooms face a gorgeous pool area surrounded by shaded white beds for lounging and a swim-up *palapa* bar in the center. Just beyond is the beach. When you get hungry, you can check out Nikki Beach (145-7800, ext.789), a stylish fusion restaurant open 9 AM to 11 PM. To accommodate many types of travelers, amenities include 24-hour room service, a children's pool, and a tennis court. Rates: $275–700 per night plus 10% service charge.

PLAYA GRANDE RESORT

624-145-7575 or 800-344-3349
www.playagranderesort.com
Avenida Playa Grande #1

Price: Expensive
Credit Cards: MC, V, AE
Special Features: Multiple pools, Jacuzzi, satellite TV, fitness center, on-site sport fishing and diving, tennis courts

Located on an isolated stretch of Solmar Beach south of Cabo San Lucas, this elegant hotel is a collection of colorful buildings that together resemble a Mediterranean villa. These buildings are set around an enormous beachfront pool area boasting waterfalls, children's areas, two swim-up bars, and a Jacuzzi overlooking the ocean. The 259 units all feature private balconies facing the Pacific Ocean. These rooms feature satellite TV, king-size beds, and full-sized baths. The hotel also offers fine cuisine from its Brigantine Restaurant (145-7575, ext. 3305), a Mexican restaurant open daily 6 AM to 10 PM. For a more relaxed atmosphere, check out the poolside Calima Restaurant (145-7575), with a party atmosphere and Mexican fare, which is open daily 6:30 AM to 10 PM. The hotel also offers spa services in open-air *palapa* tents on the beach. Rates: $273–310 for a junior suite, double occupancy.

PUEBLO BONITO LOS CABOS

624-142-9797 or 800-990-8250
www.pueblobonito-loscabos.com
Médano Beach
Price: Expensive
Credit Cards: MC, V, AE
Special Features: Concierge service, gym, dry cleaning/laundry, childcare facilities

This resort is located right on Médano Beach and has 148 suites, all with private balconies that open to a view of Land's End. Junior suites, which are quite large and can accommodate up to four people, are equipped with a living room area, two double beds, and a kitchenette. Not that you will be doing much cooking with two restaurants and a casual dining pool bar on site. Cilantro's (142-9797, ext. 642), a fine-dining seafood restaurant with an ocean view, is open 11 AM to 11 PM. Las Palomas (142-9797) is the hotel's Mexican restaurant, where you can dine from 7 AM to noon in an air-conditioned dining hall or on a large terrace. The hotel is decorated in the style of a Mediterranean villa, with white stucco and blue trim. The hotel towers over a large palm-tree-lined pool area that opens onto the beach. Rates: start at $215.

PUEBLO BONITO ROSÉ

624-142-9898 or 800-990-8250 (U.S.)
www.pueblobonito-rose.com
Médano Beach
Price: Expensive
Credit Cards: MC, V, AE
Special Features: On-site spa and workout facilities, laundry/dry cleaning, baby-sitting

This massive 260-suite resort located on Médano Beach is the sister hotel of the Pueblo Bonito Los Cabos. Like that hotel, this one has a Mediterranean theme, with long white-stucco buildings built around a central square dominated by an expansive pool area and palm gardens. Large junior suites are furnished with two double beds in a bedroom separated from a living room that has a sofa, chairs, and a kitchenette. All rooms have a private terrace or balcony. An on-site spa has a gym and treatment facilities where you can get a massage or a facial. The resort also has two fine-dining restaurants. Mare Nostrum (142-9898, ext. 8310; open 7 AM to 10:30 PM) is a seafood restaurant with international specialties; L'Orangerie (142-9898, ext. 8300; open 6 PM to 10:30 PM) is a French restaurant with oceanfront dining. For more casual dining, lounge at the pool bar with some chips and guacamole. Rates: $207–343 for a junior suite, double occupancy.

SEVEN CROWN HOTEL

624-143-7787
www.sevencrownhotels.com

Lázaro Cárdenas and 16 de Septiembre
Price: Inexpensive
Credit Cards: MC, V, AE
Special Features: Outdoor swimming pool, convenient location

This hotel offers 40 air-conditioned rooms furnished with either one king-size or two double beds. These rooms are somewhat blandly decorated with bare walls and carpeted flooring. However, they are clean and actually somewhat spacious. Plus the location is close to bars and restaurants as well as the marina. Rooms are all equipped with cable TV and a mini fridge, though you should be careful about running up extra charges with the fridge. There is also a small outdoor pool in the courtyard is perfect for touching up your tan before heading to the beach. Rates: $75–85 for a standard room, double occupancy.

SIESTA SUITES HOTEL

624-143-2773 or 866-271-0952 (U.S.)
www.cabosiestasuites.com
Zapata between Guerrero and Hidalgo
Price: Inexpensive
Credit Cards: MC, V
Special Features: Swimming pool, convenient location

This hotel is a great option for those travelers who are looking for simple, inexpensive accommodations that are centrally located but also have the comforts of home. This hotel has 20 air-conditioned units equipped with separate bedrooms, cable TV, and good-size, fully furnished kitchens. One-bedroom suites are furnished with a double bed and a sofa and dinette set in the living room. They also have a few hotel-style rooms that are furnished with two queen-size beds and a sofa. There is a small swimming pool located in a shaded central courtyard, surrounded by several tables and chaise longues for relaxing and talking about the day's adventures. Rates: start at $64 for a standard room, double occupancy, and $76 for a penthouse suite. There is also an outdoor barbecue and a sundeck for guests of the hotel. Weekly and monthly rates are also available.

TESORO LOS CABOS

624-143-1220
www.tesororesorts.com
Boulevard Marina, Lot 9
Price: Moderate to Expensive
Credit Cards: MC, V, AE
Special Features: Swimming pool, satellite TV, convenient location, on-site spa

This large 286-room hotel is located on the marina and is walking distance to the restaurants and bars of Cabo San Lucas. The property has a large pool, where activities are planned daily as well as an on-site spa that offers everything from manicures to body treatments. Standard rooms come furnished with two twin-size beds or a single king-size. They also have sofas, satellite TV, and a terrace or balcony facing either the city or the marina. The mini fridge is stocked with beer and soda, but you will thank yourself later and save some money by purchasing refreshments elsewhere. If you're hungry, the on-site La Vista Restaurant (143-1220), open daily 7 AM to 11 PM, serves a buffet breakfast with a view of the marina. For lighter fare, check out Café Canela Bistro & Bar (143-3435), located on the marina, which is open daily 7 AM to 6 PM. Another fun option is the Caborey Dinner Cruiser (143-8260), a 144-foot catamaran that departs from Tesoro Los Cabos. Rates: $132–187 for a standard room, double occupancy (January–April 15) and $99–110 (April 16–December).

VILLA DEL PALMAR RESORT & SPA

624-145-7200 or 877-845-5247 (U.S.)
www.villadelpalmarloscabos.com
Camino Viejo at San José
Price: Expensive
Credit Cards: MC, V, AE
Special Features: Fitness center, on-site

medical clinic, cybercafé, kids' playroom

This enormous 459-unit resort is located on Médano Beach. Guests arrive at a stunning vaulted lobby area that leads to the back of the property, where one finds a hotel built around a graduated patio—with two pools—that opens up to the beach with Land's End visible in the distance. Attendants roam the property catering to lounging guests. Find a variety of room options here, from junior suites to three-bedroom suites. All rooms are spacious and attractively appointed in a modern style. The rooms here are also furnished with patio furniture situated on private balconies with a view of the sea. For dinner, try the Bella California Restaurant (145-7000, ext. 512; open 7 AM to 10:30 PM) for fine Italian and Californian cuisine. Rates: start at $176. The hotel also offers an optional all-inclusive rate that covers food and beverages as well.

VILLA LA PALOMA

624-143-3461
www.hotelvillalapaloma.com
Lázaro Cárdenas and El Bordo
Price: Inexpensive
Credit Cards: MC, V, AE
Special Features: Concierge service, wireless Internet

This 32-suite condominium hotel is located within a gated community of four-story buildings set around a central swimming pool and *palapa* bar and restaurant. The concierge at the front desk will arrange golf, sport fishing, or any other activities or tours that are on your itinerary. Each air-conditioned unit has a furnished living room, with cable TV and wireless Internet, as well as a full kitchen. Bedrooms are furnished with queen-size beds with wooden headboards and vanity tables. The pool is rather small with only a few chaise longues for relaxing but the hotel is conveniently located just a 10-minute walk from the beach. It is also close enough to walk to all of the action in downtown Cabo but still far enough away so that you can get some peace and quiet when you want it. Rates: average $80.

VIVA CABO HOTEL

624-143-5810
Plaza de la Danza, Boulevard Marina
Price: Inexpensive to Moderate
Credit Cards: MC, V, AE
Special Features: Restaurant/bar, satellite TV, laundry facilities

This quiet and quaint hotel may be small on the outside, but it has plenty to offer. It features eight large air-conditioned studio suites that are furnished with either a king-size bed or two twin-size. Rooms are decorated in whites and pastels that seem to evoke old Americana and come equipped with kitchenettes and satellite TV. Guests of the hotel have access to the pool and fitness center next door at the Plaza Nautica. This hotel also enjoys a great location—walking distance from the bars and restaurants of Cabo San Lucas. It specializes in catering to small groups, particularly fishermen since it is located just one block from the marina. Rates: average $95.

RV Parks

EL ARCO TRAILER PARK

624-143-1686
Carretera Transpeninsular (Mexico Federal Highway 1)

This park is located just over 3 miles east of Cabo San Lucas on the north side of the Transpeninsular Highway. It features 40 RV spaces and 24 campsites. Facilities have hot showers, flush toilets, and a laundry room. The property is also equipped with a pool and a restaurant/bar. Rates: around $15 per night for RVs with full hookups and $8 for tents. Reservations are accepted.

EL FARO VIEJO TRAILER PARK

624-143-0561
Antonio Mijares at Matamoros

Located 12 blocks north of downtown Cabo San Lucas—two blocks off a paved road—this facility features 28 large spaces with full hookups. There is also a restaurant/bar and a gift shop on the property. Rates: $15 per night for two people plus $3 for each additional person.

VAGABUNDOS DEL MAR RV PARK

624-143-0209
Carretera Transpeninsular

This property is located on a 3-acre site a couple of miles out of town on the south side of the Transpeninsular Highway. It features 85 spaces with full hookups, flush toilets, coin laundry, and hot showers. The property also has a large heated pool, restaurant/bar, boat washing facilities, and a 24-hour security guard. Rates: $24 per night.

RESTAURANTS

Cabo San Lucas has plenty of great places to eat. That's all you need to know. You will not have a tough time finding somewhere to eat in this town. In fact, some restaurants along the main strip of Lázaro Cárdenas and Boulevard Marina will come looking for you, encouraging you to come in and enjoy their specials. This can get annoying. Farther away from this area, the atmosphere becomes more relaxed, and you can find some real gems off the beaten path.

LOS AJOS

624-143-7706
Lázaro Cárdenas between Vicario and Mendoza
Open: Daily 8 AM–9 PM
Price: Inexpensive
Cuisine: Mexican
Serving: B, L, D

Lunchtime along the boardwalk in Cabo San Lucas.

This all-you-can-eat buffet-style Mexican restaurant is located on Cabo's main strip near the Puerto Paraiso Mall. The buffet features more than 20 different Mexican dishes as well as a salad bar. There is also nightly karaoke here just in case you need a place to break into song. You can either dine in or order to go. Although it's not fancy, this place is very popular among locals, particularly for breakfast. In fact, there is a daily all-you-can-eat breakfast buffet for around 50¢. The lunch buffet is around 75¢.

ALEXANDER RESTAURANT
624-143-2092
On the marina at Plaza Bonita
Open: Mon.–Sat. 8 AM–11 PM; Sun. 5 PM–11 PM
Price: Expensive
Cuisine: Steak and Seafood
Serving: L, D

This marina fine-dining restaurant is located among the many hotspots of Plaza Bonita. The diverse menu mixes the influence from the owner's Swiss origin with Mediterranean and tropical flavors, and seafood lovers in particular will have plenty to choose from. The chef specializes in fondue, with cheese, beef, and seafood fondue on the menu. Several interesting seafood, steak, and chicken dishes are offered as well. The restaurant also features an extensive wine list. If you're traveling as a family and looking for a nice place to enjoy a meal, there is also a small children's menu.

ARTS & SUSHI
624-144-4554
Plaza Bonita
Open: Daily 11 AM–11 PM
Price: Moderate
Cuisine: Japanese
Serving: L, D

This unique restaurant, located behind Olé-Olé on the east side of Plaza Bonita, features a combination of sushi and Japanese food with a gallery of Latin American art. The restaurant offers patio seating for those who want to enjoy Cabo's prime people watching, or enjoy people watching of a different kind by sitting inside at the sushi bar, where the chefs put on a show of acrobatic cutlery. For refreshments, enjoy a Japanese beer or one of a variety of sakes offered here.

BAJA CANTINA DOCKSIDE
624-143-1591
Marina at Tesoro Los Cabos Hotel
Open: Daily 7 AM–1 AM
Price: Moderate to Expensive
Cuisine: International Mexican
Serving: B, L, D

This casual-dining restaurant has a relaxed atmosphere quite different from the pushy experience offered at some of the tourist restaurants along the main strip. They offer a few traditional Mexican specialties and plenty of good ol' American favorites. They also have an extensive breakfast menu. For families looking for a fun place to have a meal, there are a few kids' meals on the menu, as well. Baja Cantina Dockside is located in a waterfront *palapa*-roofed building at Tesoro Los Cabos at the marina. A second location, Baja Cantina Beach at Cabo Villas Resort, Médano Beach, offers beachside dining daily from 8 AM to midnight.

BILLYGAN'S ISLAND RESTAURANT
624-143-4830
Médano Beach and Paseo del Pescador
Open: Daily 8 AM–10 PM
Price: Moderate
Cuisine: Seafood
Serving: B, L, D

There's nothing quite like having breakfast in your bathing suit just steps away from the sand. At this Médano Beach restaurant, you can enjoy that experience and come back for lunch or dinner to find that the party is still going strong. That party atmosphere includes daily bikini contests, two-for-one drink specials beginning at 8 AM, and spicy couples dance contests that would barely be legal in some states. Oh, yeah, and they have food, too—seafood as well as burgers and sandwiches. Needless to say, this restaurant attracts a younger crowd, but it's a great place for people watching.

BRASIL STEAK HOUSE
624-143-8343
Zapata between Guerrero and Hidalgo
Open: Daily 5 PM–11 PM
Price: Expensive
Cuisine: Brazilian steak
Serving: D

Located a block off Lázaro Cárdenas, this traditional Brazilian steakhouse will make you thank heaven that you're not a vegetarian. There are no menus here. Instead, *garzóns* come to your table periodically, starting you off with an array of appetizers, then moving to a variety of pasta and vegetable salads, and finally a selection of 12 cuts of meat that are sliced directly onto your plate. These cuts include New York steak, rib eye, lamb, ribs, chicken, and turkey. The tropical atmosphere and Brazilian music complete the experience. Dine either on their covered patio or in their two-story dining area.

CABO WABO CANTINA
624-143-1188
Vincente Guerrero at Lázaro Cárdenas
Open: Daily 11 AM–11 PM
Price: Moderate to Expensive
Cuisine: International
Serving: L, D

Inspired by the 1988 Van Halen song of the same name, this cantina is probably the

World-famous Cabo Wabo Cantina.

most famous restaurant in town. Located right in the heart of Cabo's main strip, this bar/restaurant serves up a variety of steak and seafood dishes at reasonable prices. Dine on their open-air patio, and then stick around for the party as live music is played at the Cabo Wabo nightclub every night during the winter. Occasionally, the Red Rocker himself, owner Sammy Hagar, shows up to perform. The club is open 7 PM to 2 AM.

CAPO SAN GIOVANNI

624-143-0593
Vincente Guerrero near Cabo Wabo
Open: Tue.–Sun. 5 PM–11 PM
Price: Moderate
Cuisine: Italian
Serving: D

This Italian restaurant, located right in the middle of the action in Cabo San Lucas, has a friendly atmosphere and plenty of good food. The dining room is cozy to the point of being slightly cramped, but the patio is comfortable and romantically lit. In any case, the crowds are an indication of how good the food is here. Chef Gianfranco Zappala likes to mingle with his guests to make sure that they are enjoying themselves. His menu is filled with southern Italian specialties that feature plenty of seafood and pasta as well as an extensive wine list. Reservations are highly recommended during the high season.

LA CASA DEL DORADO

624-143-2017
Narciso Mendoza and Álvaro Obregón
Open: Mon.–Sat. 8 AM–10 PM
Price: Expensive
Cuisine: Mexican
Serving: B, L, D

Located four blocks north of Lázaro Cárdenas, this seafood restaurant is a bit off the beaten path but well worth the effort. It has a relaxed, family atmosphere. The menu includes many traditional Mexican seafood dishes prepared with the freshest ingredients, including the day's catch right out of the sea. If you cannot decide what to eat, try the sampler plate, which features small portions of about half a dozen items off the menu. The food is attractively prepared and served on an open-air patio that provides beautiful views of the sea to complement your meal.

CASABLANCA

624-143-0447
Médano Beach
Open: Daily 10 AM–10 PM
Price: Moderate
Cuisine: Steak and seafood
Serving: L, D

This is one of the nicer restaurants located on Médano Beach. It offers an eclectic fusion of international, Mexican, and Moroccan flavors. The menu here features a wide variety of seafood specialties, as well as several steak and chicken dishes. Sit down to a nice meal with a great view of the beach and enjoy everything from a chicken quesadilla to filet mignon. Or relax and enjoy shrimp cooked in a variety of ways. This restaurant also serves fresh sushi served daily from 1 PM to 10 PM. Whatever flavors you decide on, you will have a prime spot for people watching or just enjoying the beautiful view of the sea.

LA CASA DEL POZO
624-143-6569
Avenida el Pescador and Niños Héroes
Open: Mon.–Sat. 1 PM–9:30 PM
Price: Expensive
Cuisine: Mexican
Serving: L, D

If you are tired of the tourist traps, La Casa Del Pozo provides a nice alternative for experiencing some authentic Mexican cooking. This steak-and-seafood restaurant has an extensive menu that includes several traditional Mexican dishes such as *chiles rellenos* (cheese-stuffed chiles), which accompany all steak meals. Chase your meal down with a tequila off the restaurant's extensive list. Handmade tortillas and homemade breads are also featured. Meals are served on an open-air patio.

EL CORAL
624-143-0150
Boulevard Marina and Hidalgo
Open: Daily 10 AM–11 PM
Price: Inexpensive
Cuisine: Mexican and International
Serving: L, D

The sign out front says it all: TEQUILA SHOTS FREE!! (AFTER DINNER ONLY) ALL YOU CAN DRINK 6 PM TO 10 PM. Okay, so maybe this isn't five-star dining, but you can get a steak-and-seafood dinner here for about what you'd pay for a hamburger in the United States. Located right on the main strip, this restaurant has an open-air dining area dominated by a large bar. The tables are handmade and hand painted, sporting colorful Mexican tablecloths, and faded portraits of Pancho Villa adorn the wall. After dinner, stick around and enjoy some drinks from their well-stocked bar. This restaurant's convenient location makes it a good option for dining either right after the beach or just before you head out to the clubs along Cabo's main strip.

THE CRAZY LOBSTER
624-143-6535
Hidalgo and Zapata
Open: Daily 8 AM–10 PM
Price: Inexpensive to Moderate
Cuisine: Seafood
Serving: B, L, D

With happy hour running from 10 AM to 6 PM, there is no doubt that the atmosphere at the Crazy Lobster is to party. This is the Cabo that many travelers come looking for: lobster, beer, and fun. In fact, you can go surf and turf with lobster and a New York steak (the most expensive item on the menu) for well under $20, or pace yourself with fish tacos for less than $2. Located near the center of town, this restaurant is hard to miss with a giant lobster adorned with a sombrero out front.

LA DOLCE ITALIAN RESTAURANT
624-143-4122
Hidalgo and Zapata
Open: Daily 6 PM–11 PM
Price: Moderate
Cuisine: Italian
Serving: D

Located a block off Boulevard Marina, this quaint restaurant is just slightly off of the beaten path, though it is located near the town square. This casual-dining establishment offers traditional Italian dishes with plenty of pasta choices and antipasti salads as well as some great wood-fired pizza. If you're in the mood for something a bit more substantial, they also have several seafood dishes prepared with the day's freshest catch. Be sure to save room for one of the delicious desserts.

EDITH'S
624-143-7580
Médano Beach
Open: Daily 5 PM–11 PM
Price: Moderate to Expensive
Cuisine: Steak and seafood
Serving: D

This beachside steak-and-seafood restaurant is a stylish outdoor restaurant featuring palapa-roofed dining areas. Edith's offers the best of Baja cuisine, with prime cuts of beef and freshly caught lobsters as well as classic Caesar salads (a Baja innovation in itself) to fresh sea bass and rack of lamb. The dining area looks out at the sea and the mood is enhanced with brightly colored tablecloths and candle light. Tropical plants surround this area giving the restaurant an elegant and intimate feeling. All of this adds up to an elegant dining experience right on the main beach of Cabo San Lucas. Reservations are recommended, particularly for groups.

FELIX RESTAURANT
624-143-4290
Hidalgo between Madero and Zapata
Open: Daily 4 PM–10 PM
Price: Inexpensive to Moderate
Cuisine: Mexican
Serving: D

This restaurant is located a block and a half from the marina in the heart of Cabo's old town. It offers very traditional Mexican dishes such as pozole (a soup with meat and hominy) as well as interesting dishes that are not so traditional, such as puerco con piña (pork with pineapple). Additionally, this restaurant features a wide array of seafood, such as Coconut Mango Shrimp, Baby Bay Scallops, and Veracruz-style fish of the day, served in a mild tomato and garlic sauce. You can dine either in the indoor dining room decorated in traditional Mexican style, or on their outdoor patio.

LA FONDA RESTAURANT
624-143-6926
Avenida Hidalgo and 12 de Octubre
Open: Daily 1 PM–10 PM
Price: Moderate
Cuisine: Mexican

Although this restaurant is a fair distance off the beaten track, the authentic Mexican flavors found here make it worth the trip. The dining room has colonial décor, and the servers are attired in traditional garb. The attentive, friendly service and elegant atmosphere stand in contrast to the gaudy, over-the-top experience offered by many of the restaurants on the main strip. This restaurant has been designed to accommodate couples as well as larger groups with two separated dining rooms—one smoking and the other nonsmoking. There is also a full bar that serves all manner of delicious mixed drinks and Mexican beers.

GIGGLING MARLIN BAR & GRILL
624-143-1182
Boulevard Marina and Matamoros
Open: 8AM–1 AM
Price: Inexpensive to Moderate
Cuisine: Seafood
Serving: B, L, D

The specialty at this restaurant/bar located right at the center of Cabo's main strip is the laid-back atmosphere, where travelers can meet up with old friends and make new ones. Any place that offers stiff drinks and more than 15 appetizers is somewhere to kick back and enjoy yourself. However, if you're looking for a full meal instead, you can get anything from hamburgers to filet mignon. At night, the party picks up with people taking body shots, upside-down tequila shooters, and a live show that includes audience members. This restaurant also televises all major sporting events.

LA GOLONDRINA TRADING POST
624-143-0542
Paseo del Pescador
Open: Daily 5 PM—10:30 PM
Price: Expensive
Cuisine: Steak and seafood
Serving: D

This restaurant is named after a trading post that was established in Cabo San Lucas 1896. Today, this old trading post is now one of the oldest buildings in Cabo. The dining area of this restaurant is a large open courtyard with dozens of lanterns hanging from the trees. Here you will find an extensive menu with all sorts of steak and seafood as well as traditional Mexican specialties, including lobster, coconut shrimp, and filet mignon. There is also a good list of wines and spirits as well. Dinners are large and reasonably priced.

HACIENDA DEL CUERVO
624-105-1615
Plaza Náutica at Boulevard Marina
Open: Daily 8 AM—MIDNIGHT
Price: Moderate to Expensive
Cuisine: Mexican
Serving: B, L, D

Located in a plaza near the marina, this restaurant offers traditional Mexican cuisine as well as several dishes with a modern twist. Dine in their large indoor dining room complete with a rustic wood cantina or on an open patio with a fountain in the center, and be entertained by strolling mariachis. The chef, who hails from Mexico City, prepares such mainland favorites as chicken mole with sheer authenticity and

also offers coastal specialties such as fresh fish served Veracruz style. Or try a Mexican innovation such as lobster in vanilla sauce and coconut rice.

LAN'S CABO
624-143-8828
Plaza Bonita
Open: Daily 1 PM—10 PM
Price: Moderate
Cuisine: Chinese
Serving: L, D

This Pan-Asian restaurant is located in the Plaza Bonita mall, the heart of the action in Cabo San Lucas. If you are in the mood for Chinese, Lan's does it up right with plenty of great selections, including soups and specialty dishes that will make your mouth water. Try such Asian specialties as Peking duck, and Osaka curried chicken, as well as Japanese Kobe beef. There are also plenty of seafood choices such as Hong Kong basil shrimp, sea bass *kara yaki,* and tuna *tataki.* Here you will also find a nice wine list and an excellent list of martinis.

MANGO DECK BAR & GRILL
624-143-0901
Médano Beach and Paseo Pescadores
Open: Daily 8 AM—11 PM
Price: Moderate
Cuisine: International
Serving: B, L, D

Located right on Médano Beach, this place attracts a younger crowd with an extensive menu and a two-for-one happy hour that runs from 8 AM to 6 PM. Come here to dip your feet in the sand while you throw back a few cold beers and enjoy some good Mexican seafood or international specialties. The fajitas here are very good, but the menu also features steaks, lobster, and even fettuccine. Be sure to enjoy a margarita while you take in the beautiful view and the ocean breeze.

MARGARITAVILLA
624-143-3630
Plaza Bonita on the marina
Open: Daily 8 AM–11 PM
Price: Expensive
Cuisine: International
Serving: B, L, D

This restaurant is hard to miss since it is on the corner of Plaza Bonita, right on the marina. This two-story restaurant has two bars and terrace seating overlooking the marina yachts. Sit on the terrace and enjoy beautiful views of the marina as well as prime people watching while you dine. The menu is extensive, offering many kinds of fare from salads to steaks and seafood to pasta and Mexican dishes. They also show all major sporting events on TVs mounted throughout the restaurant.

MI CASA
624-143-1933
Avenida Cabo San Lucas
Open: Daily noon–10:30 PM

Price: Moderate
Cuisine: Mexican
Serving: L, D

Mi Casa is located on the west side of the town square, a couple of blocks north of Boulevard Marina. It is a huge restaurant located on two levels and can seat up to 500 people. The open-air dining areas are cool and inviting in the evening and provide a wonder atmosphere for discussing the day's adventures. Besides being painted in bright pastel colors, this restaurant looks like an old Mexican cantina. There is no doubt that the food here is authentic with dishes like *chiles en nogada* and *mole poblano*.

NICKSAN JAPANESE RESTAURANT
624-143-4484
Plaza del la Danza on Boulevard Marina
Open: Daily 11:30 PM–10:30 PM
Price: Expensive
Cuisine: Japanese
Serving: L, D

Mariachis croon along the marina.

This restaurant is located near the point where the Sea of Cortés meets the Pacific Ocean and thus provides beautiful views for dining and watching the sun go down. With a very extensive menu, this Japanese restaurant and sushi bar offers a fine dining experience not to be forgotten. The cuisine here is made with the finest ingredients and the freshest fish. The restaurant also features a full bar with many types of sake. Its long hardwood bar and soft lighting creates a wonderful atmosphere that is perfect for that special night out.

THE OFFICE RESTAURANT
624-143-3464
Médano Beach at Paseo del Pescador
Open: Daily 7 AM—10 PM
Price: Moderate to Expensive
Cuisine: Mexican
Serving: B, L, D

This beachside restaurant provides a surprisingly elegant atmosphere. Visitors dine at rows of tables lined up directly on the sand at Médano Beach. This allows for plenty of room because there are no walls to confine you. Kick off your flip-flops, dig your feet into the sand, and enjoy. The extensive menu is packed with seafood and steaks prepared with Mexican flair. Pair this traditional Mexican cuisine with one of their 16-ounce margaritas and you have the makings of a very enjoyable meal. They put on a fiesta every Thursday night at 6:30, with piñatas and candy for the kiddies and tequila shooters and dancing for the older "kids."

OLÉ-OLÉ TAPAS RESTAURANT & BAR
624-143-0633
Plaza Bonita
Open: Daily 7 AM—11 PM
Price: Expensive
Cuisine: Spanish
Serving: B, L, D

Located in Plaza Bonita on the marina, this Spanish restaurant has a surprisingly diverse menu with plenty of steak and seafood dishes to choose from as well as items like barbecued ribs and several Mexican dishes. The menu also offers some nice dessert choices plus espresso drinks for after dinner. The restaurant also has an extensive wine list as well as many types of mixed drinks. The location on the marina makes this a great place to enjoy people watching as well as views of the docks.

PANCHO'S RESTAURANT AND TEQUILA BAR
624-143-0973
Hidalgo and Zapata
Open: Daily 7 AM—11 PM
Price: Moderate
Cuisine: Mexican
Serving: B, L, D

With chefs from all over Mexico, this restaurant specializes in very traditional Mexican cuisine. It has an atmosphere that is nothing if not festive. The restaurant is decorated in traditional Mexican style with a hardwood bar and handmade furniture. Pancho's offers an extensive menu of national favorites, particularly seafood dishes that take advantage of the fresh seafood to be had here. These dishes include seafood burritos, fried coconut shrimp, and grilled red snapper. The restaurant also offers a long list of tequilas. Located one block off Boulevard Marina.

LA PARRILLADA MEXICAN STEAK & BBQ
624-143-7424
Hidalgo near Boulevard Marina
Open: Hours vary by season
Price: Moderate to Expensive
Cuisine: Barbecue
Serving: L, D

This casual restaurant features live music every night in the style of Jimmy Buffet, James Taylor, and the Beatles. Here at this Mexican steakhouse—located a block off

Boulevard Marina—you will enjoy baby back ribs as well as chicken and seafood with a baked potato and steamed vegetables. And plenty of free chips and salsa. This is a fun restaurant with a casual atmosphere, including live music every evening. Reservations are recommended during the busy tourist season.

LA TRATTORIA RISTORANTE
624-143-0068
Plaza Bonita
Open: Daily 11 AM–midnight
Price: Moderate
Cuisine: Italian
Serving: B, L, D

This Italian restaurant is centrally located at the Plaza Bonita mall and features a wood-burning oven, an inviting outdoor patio, and authentic Italian cuisine. Despite the fact that it is across the street from the El Squid nightclub, it provides an intimate and romantic dining experience with low lighting. The friendly staff serves all of your favorite Italian dishes, including lasagne, seafood fettuccine, antipasti salads, and pizza baked in a wood-fired oven. There is also an extensive wine list.

BARS AND NIGHTLIFE

Partying is serious business in Cabo, and people come here to party morning, noon, and night. By day, most of the action is found at Médano Beach. At night, the restaurants fill up early, whereas the clubs and discos get going around 11 PM or midnight, and many continue until 3 or 4 AM. In Baja California, not even Tijuana's Avenida Revolución can match Cabo's propensity for drinking, dancing, and letting it all hang out.

AGAIN & AGAIN
624-143-6323
Lázaro Cárdenas across from the Puerto Paraiso Mall

If you're bar hopping, you'll probably end up here at some point. The music at Again & Again varies from disco to Spanish rock to Norteño. They often have theme nights with contests.

BAROMETRO
624-143-1466
Marina Boardwalk next to Puerto Paraiso Mall

This lounge, conveniently located in the center of Cabo's nightlife, is a great place to kick back with a martini and enjoy some live music. They also offer a menu with Italian specialties and wood-fired pizza. Open daily 11 AM to 2 AM.

CALIENTE RACE, SPORTS, & BOOK
624-143-2866
Boulevard Marina at Plaza Náutica

This Mexican mainstay is a great place to check out your favorite sporting event and maybe place a bet or two. Plenty of drinks, good food, and off-track betting are offered at this bar. They show all major sporting events, and with TVs tattooing almost every inch of wall space, you won't miss a moment of the action. Open 10 AM to midnight during the week and 9 AM to midnight Saturday and Sunday.

CASINO REAL SPORTS BAR
624-143-1934
Boulevard Marina at Plaza Náutica

This bar offers a full menu and every sporting event imaginable on more than 40 TVs. There is also a game room with pool tables, video games, and dartboards. Open 10 AM to midnight during the week and 9 AM to midnight Saturday and Sunday.

EL AGAVE BAR
624-143-5460
Lázaro Cárdenas near Squid Roe

This tequila bar, conveniently located near

all the action, offers more than 150 kinds of tequila. They also have some nice appetizers to keep your energy up while you people-watch.

EL SQUID ROE BAR & GRILL
624-143-0655
Boulevard Marina near Plaza Bonita

This club is located in a building that somewhat resembles a giant chicken coop from the outside. Inside, its three levels of pure pulsating partying, making it one of the most famous and popular clubs on the Cabo scene.

JUNGLE BAR
624-143-7401
Plaza de los Mariachis, Boulevard Marina

This bar, located between Cabo Wabo and the Giggling Marlin, offers food drinks, and dancing. Don't forget to add your signature to the thousands that cover the walls and furniture. Nightly specials. Open 10 AM to 4 AM.

LOVE SHACK
624-144-3253
Morelos and Niños Héroes

This sports bar has a small pub atmosphere combined with loud music. It is located just north of Lázaro Cárdenas and offers pool, burgers, and drinks until 3 AM.

THE NOWHERE BAR
624-143-4493
Plaza Bonita on the Marina

Located right on the marina at Plaza Bonita, this bar has the perfect location to sit back with a drink and enjoy the view. It opens at 10 AM—happy hour runs from 5 PM to 9 PM—and the party continues until 3 AM. It features dancing with a DJ and a Tuesday ladies' night.

VOS
624-143-6700
Lázaro Cárdenas and Boulevard Marina
This upstairs lounge in the middle of Cabo's nightlife scene offers a small menu of interesting cuisine and plenty of mixed drinks and cocktails. It also has a great view of the downtown area. Closed Tuesday.

ZOO BAR
624-143-5500
Boulevard Marina across from Plaza Bonita

Don't be afraid to party like an animal at this centrally located dance club. Local and guest DJs mix rock, hip-hop, and techno music. Every Thursday is ladies' night. Open 9 PM to 4 AM.

Squid Roe is famous for late-night fun.

WEATHER

Cabo San Lucas certainly has a unique location that gives it one of the most pleasant cli-
mates you'll find anywhere. The city is located below the Tropic of Cancer and at the meeting point of the cool Pacific Ocean and warm Sea of Cortés, factors that act to moderate the
weather. Consequently, the climate in Cabo San Lucas is slightly cooler than La Paz and
even San José del Cabo. During the summer, the heat can be a bit uncomfortable, with
highs reaching into the mid-90s in August and September. These months are also the
height of the hurricane season. Landfall for hurricanes is relatively uncommon in Los
Cabos, though Hurricane John, a Category 3 storm, did cause havoc when it made landfall
near San José del Cabo in early September 2006. Usually, though, these occasional storms
only manage to cause heavy rains. The average annual rainfall is around 10 to 12 inches,
and September is the wettest month, during which Cabo usually sees about three or four
days with rain that adds up to about 4 inches. Rain is uncommon from February through
July, during which period temperatures range from the 70s to the upper 80s. At night temperatures can drop to the low 60s during the winter but remain in the upper 70s during
summer months. However, given that Los Cabos sits at the juncture of the Pacific Ocean
and the Sea of Cortés, the weather has quite a different effect on the surrounding areas,
with the Pacific side of Los Cabos generally about 10 degrees cooler than the eastern side
that borders the Sea of Cortés.

BEACHES

Despite the fact that Cabo San Lucas is located right on the water, the choices of beaches
within the town of is a bit spare. Médano Beach, though clean and great for a swim, can get

Panga *rides are the easiest way to get to Lover's Beach.*

Lover's Beach.

crowded and is not always the best place to relax if you're traveling with children. Lover's Beach is a must, but the area that is appropriate for swimming can get crowded, and access to this beach is limited. Solmar Beach is gorgeous but not appropriate for swimming. If you are looking for more tranquil beaches for snorkeling or just playing in the water, your best bet is to take a trip out to the Corridor in the morning, before the crowds show up.

Lover's Beach (Playa del Amor)

No trip to Cabo San Lucas is complete without a jaunt over to Lover's Beach. Located adjacent to the famous arch, this beautiful white-sand beach is a wonderful place to play in the water. The most common way to get to this beach is by water taxi or glass-bottomed boat. This 10-minute trip comes complete with a tour of the arch as well as Land's End, a rock sticking out of the water that represents the very tip of the Baja Peninsula. Before depositing you on Lover's Beach, tour guides will also take you around to the beach's treacherously choppy Pacific side, commonly referred to as Divorce Beach. When you disembark, keep in mind that the men who run up offering to help you off the boat and carry your cooler onto the beach are not doing it out of the kindness of their heart. They will expect a tip for this service. Shoo them away if you don't want to pay them. Being the attraction that it is, Lover's Beach can be a bit crowded, but generally there's plenty of room to wade out and play in the waves that lap onto the shore. It's probably a good idea to stay out of the water on Divorce Beach because the waves strike hard against the shore, and the rip currents are strong. Be sure to bring plenty of good sunscreen; shade is scarce here and the Cabo sun is strong. There are also no bathrooms on this beach, and the only service provided is by a few vendors walking around selling bottles of water at a significantly inflated price. Tours to the beach begin running around 9 am. You make arrangements with your guide when you want to be picked up; the last boat departs from the beach at around 3 PM.

Las Playitas

A series of small beaches lie along the inner harbor from the cannery out to Lover's Beach. Often under water during high tide, these beaches are often overlooked by tourists. However, when the tide goes out, they become a favorite picnic spot for locals and a great place for snorkeling.

Médano Beach

Médano Beach is the main beach in Cabo San Lucas. Located east of Lázaro Cárdenas and the Puerto Paraiso Mall, this is where you will find all the beachfront action. You can get to the beach through any of the hotels that line it, or take a water taxi from the marina for about $3 per person. The beach lies along several miles of arc-shaped bay and is lined with resorts and restaurants. The sand is clean and combed, and the water is calm and safe for swimming.

In the morning you should have no problem finding a *palapa* or umbrella to sit under. However, the beach fills up as the afternoon wears on. The beachside restaurants allow you to use the shaded chairs as well as their restaurants as long as you continue to order drinks and snacks. This is not a bad tradeoff for a shady place to people-watch and escape the hot sun.

Médano is also filled with vendors selling goods ranging from jewelry and beach coverups to linens and home decorations. Feel free to bargain if you find something you like. Many times you can get a good deal over a nice margarita. If you are not interested, a simple "*No, gracias*" will let them know, and they will be on their way.

For entertainment you can parasail, banana-boat, kayak, or rent Jet Skis at this beach.

Las Playitas are popular among locals.

Solmar Beach.

Jet Skis usually run around $50 for a half an hour, but here, too, you can bargain down for a cheaper price or extended time. If you're in the mood to stay on the beach, there's always a party going on, with all-day happy hours and various beach contests. Médano is by no means a tranquil beach, but you can have a good time here.

Solmar Beach

Solmar Beach, located on the Pacific Ocean south of Cabo San Lucas, is kind of the polar opposite of Médano. This wide, peaceful beach is free of vendors and great for long walks but not safe for swimming or playing in the water. The beach runs from south of the marina east to the rocks of Land's End. At the east end of the beach, you'll often find guides who will lead you over the rocks to Lover's Beach for a nominal fee. This climb requires minimal footwear, such as a pair of Teva sandals, and is a bit strenuous. As with most of the area beaches along the Pacific side, Solmar has dangerous rip currents and undertows. The sound of the ocean crashing against the sand may make for an appealing atmosphere. But you're much better playing in the lapping waters of the Sea of Cortés. Get to this beach through the resorts that are facing it, located on Avenida Solmar at the south end of Boulevard Marina.

RECREATION

Cabo San Lucas is a playground, and numerous types of diversions are available just minutes away from wherever you're staying. Almost any hotel can sell you tickets or make arrangements for these activities, but you might consider making your own to ensure that you go with a company that you're comfortable with. This is particularly true if you're staying in a larger, less personal hotel and are going on more expensive excursions such as fishing or diving trips. For outings like these, you definitely want to make sure that you're hiring a quality company.

Diving and Snorkeling

Cabo San Lucas's unique location at the convergence of two major bodies of water makes it a prime spot for diving and snorkeling. In fact, famed French oceanographer Jacques Cousteau called the Sea of Cortés the world's richest sea. Two major ocean currents meet in the waters off Cabo San Lucas: the California Current, which moves south along the West Coast of the United States, and the Northern Equatorial Counter Current, which brings warm tropical water north up the coast of Mexico. This convergence mixes nutrient-rich water, creating eddies and gyres that concentrate baitfish in this area, resulting in the waters off Cabo having some of the most diverse marine life found anywhere on the planet. The best dive sites in Cabo San Lucas are found around the sea side of El Arco and Lover's Beach. Here, divers plunge into a world that contains a myriad of sea life.

LAND'S END

This dive site is located at the southernmost rock of Baja that pokes out of the water just south of Lover's Beach and El Arco. Depths begin at around 25 feet and drop to around 70 feet. Because this is where the Sea of Cortés meets the Pacific Ocean, there are typically strong surges and currents. Therefore, this dive is best suited for experienced divers. Several sea lions hang out here and there are opportunities to get up close and personal with them. Farther down, you will encounter rock walls covered with anemone and other sea organisms, as well as angelfish, parrotfish, tuna, barberfish, lobsters, and giant hawkfish, among others. Lucky divers may even encounter giant whale sharks.

Land's End near Lover's Beach and El Arco.

NEPTUNE'S FINGER

This dive site is located in Cabo Bay between El Arco and Lover's Beach and is marked by a huge slab of rock that juts out of the ocean. Here you will drop down to a depth of about 25 feet to a pile of huge boulders covered with seafans. This area is rich in other gorgonias, as well, plus sea sponges and plenty of tropical fish.

PELICAN ROCK

This is a clam-protected dive site. With depths beginning at about 20 feet and bottoming out at around 60 feet, Pelican Rock is appropriate for all skill levels. Sea fans cover the slopes of this rock along with schools of Mexican goatfish, angelfish, par-

Neptune's Finger.

rotfish, and lobsters. It is also not unusual to spot eels, rays, and whitetip reef sharks hanging out here.

SAND FALLS

East of Neptune's Finger and Pelican Rock, away from the rocky cliffs and Lover's Beach, is an underwater canyon that sinks 120 feet into a blue abyss. This site—appropriate for advanced divers only—is where you will find the famous Sand Falls first discovered by Jacques Cousteau. These are sand formations that resemble huge cascades. These vertical canyon walls are covered with sea fans and other gorgonias, and all around is such sea life as octopuses, sea horses, and frogfish, among others.

Fishing

Within 40 miles of the Cabo marina is some of the best sport fishing to be found anywhere. In fact, Cabo San Lucas is known as the marlin capital of the world, having earned this moniker with year-round opportunities for nabbing the game fish. Striped marlin migrate into the area in late winter and stay plentiful until midsummer. This is a smaller species of marlin, though it is not unheard-of to hook 600-pound striped marlin in the cape area. The larger species of blue and black marlin populate the waters in the summer and fall.

But Cabo is not just for marlin. Over 50,000 sailfish are caught in the waters off Cabo every year. Other fish commonly caught here include dorado, yellowtail, wahoo, and roosterfish. Your experience will depend significantly on the time of year you come and how

Deep-sea fishermen return to Cabo San Lucas Bay.

much you want to spend. The more than 350 charter boats operating out of the marina include everything from 21-foot *pangas* to 100-plus-foot luxury yachts. When making arrangements for your fishing trip, ask plenty of questions, and be sure that you are comfortable with the company you choose. A day of fishing on an average-size boat with a capacity of four to eight passengers can run $500 to $1,000, so you want everything to be just right. Make sure you know exactly what is included and what their refund policy is just in case you get to the dock to find a floating jalopy waiting for you. Most trips come with a lunch, but you should be prepared to bring your own *cerveza.* Also, you will generally have to buy your own baitfish, which runs about $2 per fish down at the docks. Your skipper should arrange for that to be available for you. Keep in mind that only one billfish is allowed per boat, though there is no limit of catch and releases. During the busy season, running from May through October, it's best to book your boat as far in advance as possible. This is particularly true during October, when the fishing tournaments are taking place.

Kayaking

Cabo San Lucas offers exciting excursions for kayakers of all skill levels. The calm waters of Cabo San Lucas Bay are great for testing your skills, whether paddling around Médano Beach or heading out to Lover's Beach and El Arco. (For more advanced kayakers, multiday trips up the coast are also available.) Kayaks also provide an ideal method of eco-tourism. Kayaking tour companies offer this service as a way to get up close and personal with gray whales, whale sharks, and other sea creatures as they pass through the Sea of Cortés.

A glass-bottomed boat offers a good view of local sea life.

Off-Roading

Most people come to Cabo San Lucas to jump in the water. However, Cabo's dusty back roads offer plenty of adventure, as well. Several tour companies in town offer dirt bikes, quads, and dune buggies. Some have their own facilities and some offer multiday adventures in the Baja desert, trekking along isolated beaches and dunes or down roads used in the Baja 1000.

Whale Watching

If your trip to Cabo San Lucas takes place between January and March, you will no doubt see whales breaching the water as they complete their 6,000-mile journey from their summer homes in Alaska and Siberia or begin their journey in the opposite direction. The most common whale is the gray whale, which calves its young in shallow lagoons midway up the Baja Peninsula. (Although these lagoons are hundreds of miles from Cabo San Lucas, they are wonderful settings for viewing these majestic creatures.) Several tour companies in town offer trips right off the coast in small boats or kayaks to get you close up and even eye-to-eye with the grays and other whales passing through the region. There are also more in depth trips available to Magdelena Bay, the closest calving lagoon to Cabo San Lucas, where you can witness these beautiful creatures frolic with their newborn offspring.

Other Diversions

Information booths are set up all around Cabo San Lucas where tourists frequent and where you can ask about activities going on around town. This is a place where you can do many things in a day that you don't otherwise have the opportunity to do *ever*. For example, in a single afternoon, you can swim with dolphins at Cabo Dolphins (173-9500) then head down to Médano Beach where several tour companies offer parasailing, in which you rise hundreds of feet in the air while being pulled behind a motorboat. Trips last about 15 minutes and cost around $40. Another great way to spend an afternoon in paradise is to ride horseback along a deserted beach. You will also have no trouble finding tour companies that offer Jet Ski tours of the cape or relaxation on a sailboat that takes you out into the deep blue waters of the Sea of Cortés. Don't forget your Dramamine.

For a more mundane afternoon, the **Cinema Paraíso** (143-3838) at the Puerto Paraíso mall shows Hollywood's latest releases. Or you can head over to **Caliente** (143-2866) or **Casino Real** (143-1934) at Plaza Náutica and try your luck with off-track betting or place a bet on your favorite team, and then kick back and enjoy the action. Whatever your taste for adventure, you'll find some way to satisfy it in Cabo.

Street stylists braid hair near the marina.

SHOPPING

Although San José del Cabo and nearby Todos Santos are known for shopping much more than Cabo San Lucas, Baja's party-central town is also well equipped with shops offering everything from marginally offensive T-shirts to Mexican handicrafts and fine jewelry. A walk down Cabo's main strip in the middle of the afternoon will repeatedly be met with the calls of merchants soliciting your business, so you don't have to look too hard to find these shops. The stores listed here represent a sampling of what you'll find.

Tour Companies

Aereo Calafia Eco-Adventure Flights
624-143-4302
www.aereocalafia.com.mx
Boulevard Marina, Local A-4, Hotel Plaza las Glorias

This company operates a fleet of light planes and offers tours throughout Baja California Sur. Check their Web site for flights, fares, and packages.

Amigos del Mar
624-143-0505 or 513-898-0547 (U.S.)
www.amigosdelmar.com
Boulevard Marina

This is a PADI-, SSI-, NAUI-, and NASDS-certified diving facility. They offer guided tours as well as diving instruction and certification. They also provide natural history sunset cruises and whale-watching excursions.

Andromeda Tours
624-143-2765 or 624-147-7136 (cell)
www.scubadivecabo.com
Médano Beach between Paseo del Pescador and Paseo de la Marina

This PADI-certified diving company offers dives from 40 to 120 feet, depending on skill level. They also rent jet skis, wave runners, and kayaks and offer parasailing as well as glass-bottomed boat trips to Lover's Beach.

Baja Outback Hummer Expeditions
624-142-9215 or 624-145-2105 (cell)
www.bajaoutback.com
Boulevard Marina

This company offers day tours as well as four-day tours of the cape in H2 Hummers. Day tours last from five to seven hours and can handle groups of up to 45.

Baja's Activities
624-143-2050
www.bajasactivities.com
Located in front of the Tesoro Hotel

This company arranges a variety of land and water activities. In the Cabo San Lucas area, they offer ATV tours of secluded Pacific beaches as well as Jet Ski tours. On the East Cape, they give ATV tours of the coast near Punta Gorda as well as horseback riding and snorkeling tours. They also rent scooters for getting around town. Open 8 AM to 5 PM.

Cabo Dolphins
624-173-9500 or 888-303-2653 (U.S.)
www.cabodolphins.com
Boulevard Marina, Lote 7

These facilities are home to a family of Pacific bottlenose dolphins. For $165 you can swim with the dolphins for an hour. Children must be at least 5 years old and those under 10 must be accompanied by an adult. For $299 you can be "trainer for a day" and swim with the dolphins for more than four hours. Participants must be at least 12 years old and in good physical condition. Open Monday through Friday 10 AM to 2:30 PM.

Cabo Expeditions
624-143-2700
www.caboexpeditions.com.mx
Plaza Las Glorias Resort, Local C-7

This company offers action-filled excursions on the water. These include parasailing ($35 for single and $70 tandem), scuba diving, and snorkeling adventures as well as Wave Runner tours and whale-watching adventures.

Cabo Magic Sportfishing
624-105-0403 or 888-475-5337 (U.S./Canada)
www.cabomagic.com
Lázaro Cárdenas

This company operates a small fleet of boats and specializes in sport-fishing expeditions, but they also offer quad ATV tours. They operate 10 fishing yachts ranging in size from 35 to 78 feet as well as several smaller boats in the 31- to 34-foot range, and rent about a half dozen 23-foot *pangas*.

Charter Los Cabos
624-143-4050 or 624-355-3106 (cell)
www.chartercabos.com
Plaza Bonita Mall

This company operates a fleet of eight luxury vessels, including three sailboats and two yachts.

Fly Hooker Sportfishing
624-143-8271 or 624-147-5614
www.flyhooker.com
Lázaro Cárdenas

Fly Hooker offers sport-fishing excursions aboard their 31-foot Bertram Flybridge Sportfisher.

Land's End Divers
624-143-2200, 624-157-0582 (cell), or 408-785-6318 (U.S./Canada)
Boulevard Marina at the Tesoro Los Cabos Hotel

Land's End Divers operates three customized boats that can accommodate six to eight divers per boat. They take divers to the popular diving spots in the bay, as well as great spots farther afield such as Cabo Pulmo and Gordo Banks. Open daily 8:30 AM to 7 PM.

Oceanus
624-143-3929
www.oceanusloscabos.com.mx
Boulevard Marina Across from the marina

This company takes divers and snorkelers out on their 70-foot, two-deck party boat. Snorkeling trips run $45, and you will be dropped at Cabo's famous arch and nearby spots to enjoy the sea life. For $85, you can also dive in a personal mini sub, an odd-looking air tank that fits around your head like a fish bowl and that you ride like a bicycle.

Ocean Riders Adventure Tours
624-144-4129 or 624-129-8222 (cell)
www.oceanriders.com.mx
Plaza Bonita

Adventurers go out on speedboats for a fun and bumpy tour of Los Cabos. You'll definitely want some Dramamine for this.

Pisces Fleet Sportfishing
624-143-1288 or 619-819-7983 (U.S.)
www.piscessportfishing.com
Cabo Maritime Center Marina 8-6, Suite D-1

This fleet has been operating out of Cabo for more than a quarter of a century. They have several fishing charter boats of around 30 feet as well as many yacht charters ranging from 32 feet all the way up to a 111-foot-deep sea vessel.

Silverados Sportfishing
624-144-4903
www.silveradosportfishing.com
Hidalgo and Madero

This company operates a fleet of ten vessels ranging from 26 feet to 43 feet (most are around 33 feet).

Sun Rider Adventure
624-143-2252
www.sunridertours.com
Marina Dock #4

This company provides boat tours of Los Cabos as well as snorkeling and whale-watching tours. A restaurant right aboard the boat can accommodate up to 150 people, with covered and open-air seating.

Tio Sports Ocean & Desert
624-142-4599 or 624-147-7310 (cell)
www.tiosports.com
Médano Beach in front of Hotel Meliá

This sports-adventure company offers a variety of excursions, including Wave Runners, kayaking, ATVs, and scuba diving at Cabo San Lucas and the East Cape.

Tropicat
624-143-3739
www.tropicatcabo.com
Camino del Cerro 215 El Pedregal

This company offers sailing tours and private charter aboard a 65-foot-long, 30-foot-wide Hobie Cat that can accommodate up to 90 passengers.

Underwater Diversions
624-143-4004 or 949-226-8987 (U.S.)
www.divecabo.com

This PADI-certified dive center takes guests to dive sites all around Los Cabos. They can accommodate up to 16 divers.

Ursula's Sportfishing
624-143-6964 or 624-147-7104 (cell)
www.ursulasfishing.com
Boulevard Marina and Hidalgo

This company operates three sport-fishing vessels that range between 28 and 35 feet.

Wide Open Adventures
624-143-4170 or 949-635-2292 (U.S.)
www.wideopencabo.com
Plaza Naúdica, Marina Blvd Local B1

This off-roading tour company offers a four-day adventure that runs from Cabo San Lucas to La Paz. They also operate a test track on a 1,500-acre ranch located north of the city.

Yael Classic Sail Boat
624-148-6977
www.cabosail.com
Marina Dock G

This company offers three- to five-hour snorkeling tours aboard the *Yael*, a 44-foot classic sailboat.

Arts and Crafts

Artesanías Diana II (624-143-6989; Boulevard Marina and Hidalgo) This shop offers Talavera (artistic pottery) as well as Taxco silver jewelry and arts and crafts from around Mexico. Open daily 9 AM to 9 PM.

Casa María (624-143-8861; Lázaro Cárdenas and Matamoros) Find a nice selection of arts and crafts, including hand-blown glass, Mexican pottery, and metalwork here. Open Monday through Saturday 9 AM to 9 PM and Sunday 9 AM to 2 PM.

Lombok (624-105-0142; Plaza del Sol, Boulevard Marina #3) This shop carries interesting beachwear, handmade furniture, plus a wide variety of Mexican *artesenía* and handmade jewelry. Open daily 10 AM to 7 PM.

Mexican Pottery (624-105-0046; Madero between Hidalgo and Guerrero) This store sells Puebla Talavera of all sorts. Open Monday through Friday 10 AM to 9 PM and Saturday 10 AM to 4 PM.

Clothing and Swimwear

Cabostyle (624-143-8595; Plaza Bonita) Here you'll find a wide range of beachwear and beach accessories for the whole family. Open daily 9 AM to 10 PM.

Chicas Sin Limites (624-143-1500; Hidalgo at Plaza Amelia Wilkes) Beachwear, evening wear, and lingerie are offered at this boutique. Open Monday through Saturday 9 AM to 1 PM and 2 PM to 6 PM. Cash only.

H2O (624-143-1219; Guerrero and Madero) This boutique sells swimwear as well as evening dresses and women's sportswear. Open Monday through Saturday 9 AM to 8 PM and Sunday 11 AM to 5 PM.

No Worry's (624-143-8575; Boulevard Marina) Come here for a wide variety of casual resort clothing and beachwear. Open daily 9 AM to 10 PM.

Home Furnishings

Diaz de Luna (624-144-4976; Plaza San Basilio, Local #9) This shop features desert-style art, furniture, and accessories. Open Monday through Friday 9 AM to 7:30 PM and Saturday 9 AM to 4 PM.

El Callejón (624-143-3188; Hidalgo #3914) Here you'll find a nice selection of home furnishings such as lamps and fabrics as well as Mexican furniture. Open Monday through Saturday 9:30 AM to 7 PM.

Jewelry

Cabo Silverado (624-143-6454; Boulevard Marina, Local #4) This shop offers a large selection of silver jewelry. Open daily 8:30 AM to 10 PM.

Diamonds International (624-105-0810; Lazaro Cárdenas between Guerrero and Madero) A diverse array of designs and watches can be found in this branch of the international jewelry concern. Open daily 9 AM to 9 PM.

La Mina de Taxco (624-144-4531; Hidalgo between Boulevard Marina and Zapata) This silver shop specializes in silver jewelry and gifts from Taxco. Open daily 9 AM to 9 PM.

EVENTS

JANUARY

RUN CABO HALF MARATHON

The run starts on Cabo's main strip, Lázaro Cárdenas, and takes runners into the desert and along the coast on the Transpeninsular Highway before returning them to downtown Cabo. Entry fee is $44 for the half marathon and $22 for the 5K. For more information: www.runcabo.com/data/caboruninfo.html.

FEBRUARY

CANDLEMAS

This is a traditional event that marks the end of winter. A day in early February when the holiday season officially ends, it is celebrated across Mexico and blends European and indigenous traditions. Call (866) LOS-CABOS for more information.

JULY

SURF 'N PANGA ROOSTERFISH KLASSIC

This annual Roosterfish tournament is held in early July. It features daily prizes for the largest fish, with various species categories.

OCTOBER

LOS CABOS BILLFISH TOURNAMENT

This three-day team event is held around mid-October. The entry fee of $4,000 covers up to six anglers, and a percentage of the total pot goes to the top three winners of the tournament. Daily cash prizes are also given out for the largest fish in a number of species categories. For further information: www.loscabosbillfishtournament.com.

NOVEMBER

TUNA JACKPOT

This four-day tuna tournament is held in early November. Participants earn daily cash prizes and a percentage of the entry fees goes to the overall winner. The 2006 tournament champion brought home the prize with a 318-pound yellowfin tuna. For more information: www.loscabostunajackpot.com.

4

San José del Cabo and the Corridor

Twenty miles northeast of the bustling streets of Cabo San Lucas—and a world away—lies the quiet colonial village of San José del Cabo. There are roughly two parts to this quaint place: the hotel zone where you will find hotels along a series of beautiful beaches and the downtown area with its clean, tree-lined streets and interesting shops and restaurants. The two areas are connected by Boulevard Antonio Mijares. Located just off the airport road from Cabo San Lucas, San José experienced somewhat of a boom of its own when Cabo San Lucas exploded in the 1980s. Despite this growth, the town has managed to retain its provincial charm and even build on it with an influx of cafés and galleries. Its main square, located on the site of an old mission, is larger and more attractive than Cabo's, with a well-preserved gazebo in the center and a cathedral just beyond it.

Given its serene charms, San José is not the ideal location for those travelers looking for a rowdy beach clubs or late-night parties. This is a relaxing place with a slower pace than you'll find in Cabo San Lucas. In the hotel zone, you will find a tranquil estuary where the silence is broken only by the sounds of the many birds that call it home and the occasional ATV that rumbles through. This is a wonderful place to have an early-evening walk.

The stretch of coast that runs between San José del Cabo and Cabo San Lucas is referred to commonly as the Tourist Corridor or just simply, the Corridor. Here, along the southernmost stretch of the Transpeninsular Highway you will find sprawling beach resorts, golf courses, and breathtaking views of the ocean. This 20-mile stretch and San José are perfect places to relax or jump off and explore the natural beauty of the East Cape, the pristine stretch of coastline to the northeast.

General Information

POLICE
624-142-0361
Emergency dial 066

FEDERAL HIGHWAY POLICE
624-146-0573

OPPOSITE: *The main square in San José del Cabo.*

83

THE CORRIDOR & SAN JOSÉ DEL CABO

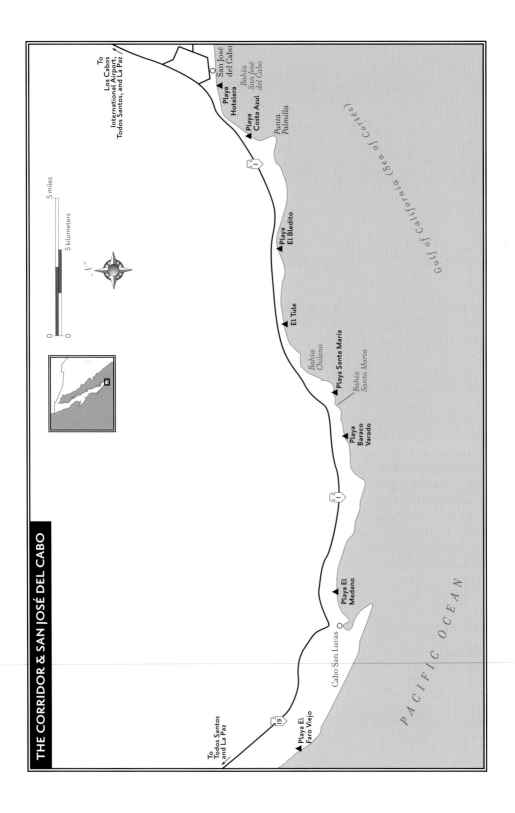

5 miles

5 kilometers

To
Los Cabos
International Airport,
Todos Santos, and La Paz

San José
del Cabo

Playa
Hotelera

Bahía
San José
del Cabo

Playa
Costa Azul

Punta
Palmilla

Gulf of California (Sea of Cortés)

Playa
El Bledito

El Tule

Bahía
Chileno

Playa Santa María

Bahía
Santa María

Playa
Baraco
Varado

Playa El
Medano

Cabo San Lucas

To
Todos Santos
and La Paz

19

Playa El
Faro Viejo

PACIFIC OCEAN

AMBULANCE
624-142-2770

MEDICAL SERVICE
624-142-0056

Taxi Service
CABO SHUTTLE
624-142-3939

ACCOMMODATIONS

In contrast to Cabo San Lucas, accommodations in San José del Cabo are geared toward an older crowd, and room rates and hotel ambience reflect this. You'll find very few truly inexpensive hotels here and even fewer that cater to young party types. There are several boutique hotels in town and a few others in the hotel zone, though most hotels here are large resorts. With a few exceptions, the hotels along the Corridor are sprawling resorts built to minimize their guests' need to leave the hotel grounds. Even the smaller hotels here have more than 50 units. Notable exceptions are the Cabo Surf Hotel, Los Nidos Hotel, and Vista Azul Suites, but even these hotels are generally expensive. However, these accommodations do offer a unique combination of seclusion and easy access to the golf courses that have become such big business here.

CABO SURF HOTEL
624-142-2666 or 858-964-5117 (U.S.)
www.cabosurfhotel.com
Playa Acapulquito, Carretera
Transpeninsular Km 28, Tourist Corridor
Price: Expensive
Credit Cards: MC, V, AE
Special Features: Surfing beach, Internet access, satellite TV

Located right on Playa Acapulquita, this hotel features 19 air-conditioned rooms with two double or one king-size bed. Each room also has Internet access and satellite TV. The hotel is aptly named as the beach it sits on is great for surfers of all skill levels, and the world-famous Costa Azul break is also nearby. Those guests not raring to get out in the waves can enjoy a pool and Jacuzzi in a garden courtyard facing the beach. This area also provides for stunning photo opportunities. Also on site is the 7 Seas Restaurant (142-2666), a fine-dining restaurant that features seafood dishes and a view of the beach. Rates: $250–595 per night plus $7 per night service charge.

CASA DEL MAR GOLF RESORT & SPA
624-145-7700 or 888-227-9621
Carretera Transpeninsular Km 19.5, Tourist Corridor
Price: Expensive
Credit Cards: MC, V, AE
Special Features: On-site spa, Jacuzzis

This golf resort and luxury spa hotel features 56 colonial-style units overlooking the Sea of Cortés. The hotel is conveniently located near the best golf courses in Los Cabos, and guests receive preferred tee times and course discounts. The on-site spa offers many services to help you rejuvenate after playing a round of golf. The hotel grounds are beautifully fashioned like a hacienda, with a stone fountain at the center of a garden courtyard and an arched pathway opening onto the sea. Rooms feature marble tile bathrooms and in-room

Jacuzzis. The on-site El Tapanco Restaurant (144-0030) offers gourmet Mexican cuisine on a terrace overlooking the pool area and in an air-conditioned dining room. Rates: average $434 for double occupancy.

CASA NATALIA

624-142-5100
www.casanatalia.com
Boulevard Antonio Mijares #4
Price: Expensive
Credit Cards MC, V, AE
Special Features: Beach club, pool service, concierge service

Located in the heart of San José, this boutique hotel features 18 luxury European-style suites. Its tranquil setting of waterfalls, tropical flowers, and dozens of palm trees seemingly slows down time. Rooms are individually decorated with unique local artwork and equipped with a private terrace and a personal hammock. Every morning guests receive a full breakfast on these terraces. The hotel also has a full-service gourmet restaurant on site that provides unique dishes. Exclusive beach club shuttle transportation and in-room spa service are also available. Children under 13 are not allowed. Rates: begin at $295 for double occupancy.

CROWNE PLAZA LOS CABOS

624-142-9292 or 866-365-6932 (U.S.)
www.crowneplaza.com
Paseo San José
Price: Expensive
Credit Cards: MC, V, AE
Special Features: High-speed Internet, workout room, five pools, concierge service

This 333-room resort hotel located in the hotel zone is one of the newest on the cape and certainly one of the most beautiful in San José del Cabo. The rooms are spacious—each has a view of the Sea of Cortés—and some have easy wheelchair access. The high-ceilinged lobby has bright and colorful furnishings and opens into the main pool area, where you will find poolside service and an aqua bar. All-inclusive rates are available. The hotel tries to offer something for everybody, including several large meeting rooms for business and a baby-sitting service for parents looking to get away for a while. Also available: a workout room, high-speed Internet access, and five pools, including a children's pool and one set aside for adults only. The one thing this hotel is short on is nightlife (which is common in San José del Cabo). There is live music three times a week, but those shows are usually sparsely attended. If you are looking for nightlife, see the concierge to arrange transportation to Cabo San Lucas. Several on-site restaurants provide a variety of cuisines from Italian to a sushi bar. The hotel is located across the street from the San José Golf Course. See the golf concierge to make arrangements. Snorkeling, deep-sea fishing, and whale-watching tours are also located conveniently nearby. The waters directly in front of the hotel can be treacherous, so be sure to look out for red flags warning you to stay out. Rates: $216–329 for double occupancy.

EL DELFIN BLANCO

624-142-1212
www.eldelfinblanco.net
Pueblo La Playa, San José del Cabo
Price: Inexpensive
Credit Cards: MC, V (for reservations)
Special Features: On-site activities

This hotel is a collection of five thatched-roof bungalows set right along the beach in a seaside village. Each bungalow features two double beds, a small refrigerator, and a ceiling fan. These rooms are simply appointed with plenty of natural light. Two of the bungalows have private bathrooms, while three bungalows feature shared baths. Amenities are very few here but the rooms are clean, comfortable, and fairly spacious. In all, the hotel can accommodate a group of up to 15 people. The property is dispersed with palm trees and other tropical plants and there are several areas for lounging. There is also a full kitchen on the property and several restaurants are within walking distance. Rates begin at $52 a night.

DREAMS LOS CABOS ALL SUITES RESORT

624-145-7600
www.dreamslocabos.com
Carretera Transpeninsular Km 18.5, Tourist Corridor
Price: Expensive
Credit Cards: MC, V, AE
Special Features: Spa, fitness center, three pools, five restaurants

This luxurious 194-suite hotel is constructed around a large oasis-style pool area that is lined with palm trees among three swimming pools and two swim-up bars. The property also features a full-service spa and a fitness center. Five on-site restaurants offer a variety of cuisines. Portofino offers Italian specialties; Himitsu serves Pan Asian; the Seaside Grill near the pool offers casual dining; Oceana has international seafood specialties; and El Patio is a patio restaurant that is open for breakfast, lunch, and dinner. Twenty-four-hour room service is also available, as are all-inclusive rates. Rooms are luxuriously furnished in a European décor. Junior suites are furnished with one king-size or two double beds with a sitting room and a balcony overlooking the sea. They are also equipped with a fully appointed kitchenette. Rates: begin at $265 for double occupancy.

EL ENCANTO INN

624-142-0388
www.elencantoinn.com
Morelos #133, San José del Cabo
Price: Moderate
Credit Cards: MC, V

Special Features: On-site spa service, Internet access

This small hacienda-style hotel features 26 intimate rooms set around a garden courtyard. Guests may choose either the garden wing of the hotel or the pool wing. Rooms are decorated in various styles, each with attention to detail and a modern Mexican feel. The pool is heated for year-round use, and the pool area is equipped with wireless Internet access. The hotel also offers two-hour in-room body treatments and Swedish massages. Several nearby restaurants offer room service with various cuisines, including Italian, Thai, and even haute. Rates range from $99 to for standard rooms to $200 for deluxe suites.

FIESTA AMERICANA GRAND LOS CABOS

624-145-6200 or 800-343-7821
www.fiestaamericana.com
Cabo del Sol, Carretera Transpeninsular Km 10.3, Tourist Corridor
Price: Expensive
Credit Cards: MC, V, AE
Special Features: Spa, kids' club, five pools, two tennis courts, fitness center, laundry service, money exchange

Luxury accommodations for all types of travelers are offered at this 255-room resort. Air-conditioned rooms are spacious and equipped with private balconies facing the pool area. The hotel itself is constructed in an arc shape around an oasis pool area consisting of five swimming pools and a beach club. This area gives way to a wide beach on the Sea of Cortés. Additionally, the hotel has three restaurants, a full-service spa, a kids' club, and two lit tennis courts. Guests also receive discounted golf rates. The on-site Viña Del Mar Restaurant (145-6200, ext. 8234) has an international menu and a Mexican buffet on Tuesdays. Rates: $270–350 for double occupancy.

HACIENDA DEL MAR RESORT & SPA

624-145-8000
www.sheratonhaciendadelmar.com
Carretera Transpeninsular Km 10, Tourist
Corridor
Price: Expensive
Credit Cards: MC, V, AE
Special Features: Two championship golf
courses, full-service spa, kids' club, high-
speed Internet, Jacuzzis

This 270-room resort is housed in a huge
hacienda-style building on 28 acres overlooking the Sea of Cortés. Rooms, which feature a warm Mexican décor, have a private
balcony and come equipped with high-speed
Internet access and a Jacuzzi tub. The hotel
offers guests four restaurants with a choice
of buffet meals, casual poolside service, or
gourmet dining. Twenty-four-hour room
service is also available. The hacienda buildings tower over a pool area that opens onto
the beach, while the property is surrounded
by the Cabo del Sol golf courses. The on-site
Cactus Spa provides European-style treatments to help you relax after a tough day on
the greens. Rates: begin at $329–399 from
December through March and $239–279
from April through November.

HILTON LOS CABOS RESORT

624-145-6500
www.hiltonloscabos.com
Carretera Transpeninsular Km 19.5, Tourist
Corridor
Price: Expensive
Credit Cards: MC, V, AE
Special Features: Jacuzzis, fitness center,
spa, two tennis courts, kids' club

Situated on a bend on the west side of El
Bledito Beach, this Mediterranean-style
resort has 375 rooms with balconies overlooking the Sea of Cortés. Junior suites are
nicely appointed with king-size beds and
separate dressing areas, and bathrooms are
equipped with deep Jacuzzi tubs. Guests
have several dining options, including 24-

hour room service. The Fenicia Restaurant
offers Mediterranean cuisine and live
music, La Hacienda serves Mexican and
American dishes in an informal atmosphere, while the Sun Fun Hut swim-up bar
serves fresh sushi at noon. The hotel is
conveniently located near several of the
best golf courses in Los Cabos. The resort
also has a large spa, two lit tennis courts,
and a kids' club. Rates: $214–330 for dou-
ble occupancy.

HOTEL LOS NIDOS INN

624-144-0588 or 877-417-9658
(U.S./Canada)
www.losnidos.com
Carretera Transpeninsular Km 18, Tourist
Corridor
Price: Inexpensive to Moderate
Credit Cards: MC, V, AE
Special Features: Personal accommoda-
tions, large suites

This small bed-and-breakfast inn may
seem out of place among the huge resorts of
the Corridor, but it has a relaxing atmosphere and places an emphasis on privacy
and quiet luxury. It features six individually
appointed suites organized around a swimming pool patio. There is a *palapa* bar next
to the pool, and the whole patio is surrounded by manicured gardens. Suites are
furnished with a king- or queen-size bed or
a queen-size and a twin bed. Rates:
$95–149 for double occupancy.

HOTEL TWIN DOLPHIN

624-145-8191
www.twindolphin.com
Carretera Transpeninsular Km 12, Tourist
Corridor
Price: Expensive
Credit Cards: MC, V, AE
Special Features: Wireless Internet, tennis
courts, fitness center, spa

The 50 rooms of this hotel—relatively spacious and nicely appointed in a desert

décor—are spread throughout a secluded 160-acre property in front of Santa Maria Beach. There is wireless Internet access throughout the property. The pool area features a Jacuzzi and a swim-up *palapa* bar. The on-site La Tortuga Restaurant (145-8190) serves Mexican seafood. On Saturdays they offer a Mexican buffet. Rates: begin at $385 for double occupancy.

INTER-CONTINENTAL PRESIDENTE LOS CABOS RESORT

624-142-9229
www.loscabos.interconti.com
Paseo San José
Price: Expensive
Credit Cards: AE, MC, V
Special Features: Offers an all-inclusive rate, three pools, concierge service

One of the hotel zone's older resorts. Its layout is spread out over a large area, so it does not have tall, grand stature of the newer resorts. The rooms are also a bit smaller, though manageable. Not every room has a view of the water, so be sure to make that request when making reservations. Upgrading to a room with a terrace and hammock is also well worth the extra cost. The hotel has three pools, each with a different "personality." A "quiet pool" is for adults only and is ideal for relaxing and reading. The "family pool" is perfect if you are traveling with children. And the "activities pool" is where you will find loud music and the activities director leading games such as bingo and water volleyball. Six restaurants are on site. Breakfast is served buffet style, with all-you-can-eat waffles, omelets, and pastries. Be sure to try the watermelon *agua fresca,* a traditional Mexican refreshment. For night owls, the lobby bar closes at midnight. For nightlife later than that, you will have to take a taxi into Cabo San Lucas. The hotel offers an 8 PM shuttle that costs $15 per person and returns at 1 AM. Rates: average $474 for double occupancy.

MARBELLA SUITES

624-143-6268 or 866-654-6160 (U.S.)
www.marbellasuites.com
Lot 20, El Tezal, Carretera Transpeninsular Km 3, Tourist Corridor
Price: Expensive
Credit Cards: MC, V, AE
Special Features: Free phone service to U.S., fitness center, Internet service

This hacienda-style hotel offers spacious suites situated along a cliff overlooking the Sea of Cortés. Rooms are equipped with balconies, kitchens, and Internet service. Not all rooms have a view of the sea, so be sure to request this when making reservations. Rooms are built around a central pool patio area where you will find a poolside bar. The Marbella Beach Club Restaurant (144-1057) is an open-air *palapa* restaurant with nice views of the sea, and serves breakfast, lunch, and dinner. Rates: $150–300 for double occupancy.

MARISOL PETIT HOTEL

624-142-4040
www.marisol.com.mx
Plaza Garuffi, Paseo San José
Price: Inexpensive
Credit Cards: MC, V
Special Features: Satellite TV, ocean view, wireless Internet, beauty salon, convenience store

This pretty little boutique hotel is located in the hotel zone near the beach in San José. It has eight rooms decorated in Mexican art and pale white and cream colors. Rooms feature satellite TV, two double beds, vaulted ceilings, and a balcony with an ocean view. The rooms are basic but clean and comfortable. The property also has a beauty salon and a convenience store and is located near the beach. Room rates include a continental breakfast Monday through Saturday. Rates: $55 to $75.

MELIÁ CABO REAL

624-144-2222 or 800-336-3542
www.meliacaboreal.com
Carretera Transpeninsular Km 19.5, Tourist
Corridor
Price: Expensive
Credit Cards: MC, V, AE
Special Features: All-inclusive rates,
Jacuzzi, two tennis courts, fitness center,
spa, kids' club, swim-up bar

This 349-unit mammoth hotel has a great
location at the edge of El Bledito Beach.
Nearly all rooms have an ocean view and are
furnished with either two double beds or
one king-size. Guests are offered an all-
inclusive experience, which includes an
all-day unlimited buffet and à la carte dining in four restaurants plus unlimited
drinks and cocktails in three bars. The
property also features a lagoon-style swimming pool with an oceanfront Jacuzzi. For
further diversion, the hotel has two tennis
courts, a fitness center, and a health spa.
Rates: begin at $272 for double occupancy.

ONE & ONLY PALMILLA

624-146-7000
www.oneandonlyresorts.com
Carretera Transpeninsular Km 27.5, Tourist
Corridor
Price: Expensive
Credit Cards: MC, V, AE
Special Features: Golf course, spa, satellite
TV, pet friendly

Located right on Palmilla Beach, this hotel
has 172 balconied units that enjoy ocean
views plus flat-screen satellite TVs.
Amenities include butler service and twice-
daily maid service. Located near the point
where the Sea of Cortés meets the Pacific
Ocean, this hotel has played host to
celebrities from Earnest Hemingway to
John Travolta on his fiftieth birthday party.
The hotel features an executive conference
center and a full-service spa. It also offers a
kid's club as well as accommodations for

pets. The hotel grounds are also home to
the Palmilla Golf Club. Rates: begin at $475
per night for double occupancy.

LOS PATIOS

624-145-6070
www.lospatioshotel.com
Carretera Transpeninsular Km 4, Tourist
Corridor
Price: Inexpensive
Credit Cards: MC, V, AE
Special Features: Beach club, poolside serv-
ice, conference center

Here, 76 air-conditioned units are sited
around a spacious pool area. Rooms are
colorfully appointed in an ocean décor.
Junior suites are furnished with either a
king-size or two queen-size beds; all have a
private terrace, patio, or balcony with a
relaxing hammock. The on-site El Tabachin
Restaurant serves international specialties
either on an outdoor patio or in an air-conditioned dining room, with a Sunday
breakfast buffet. Rates: $70–85 for double
occupancy.

POSADA REAL LOS CABOS

624-142-0155
Paseo San José
Price: Expensive
Credit Cards: MC, V
Special Features: All-inclusive rate, tennis
courts, putting green, Jacuzzi, satellite TV

Located in the hotel zone, this all-inclusive
beachfront resort is affiliated with the Best
Western hotel chain. It has 148 rooms overlooking the beach. These rooms are furnished with a private balcony and either a
king-size bed or two double beds. Suites
also have a sofa bed. They are appointed in
a modern style that is not interesting but is
comfortable. The all-inclusive rate covers
all meals, snacks, and unlimited domestic
drinks and cocktails. The property has a
swimming pool and a Jacuzzi as well as an
on-site professional putting green, tennis

courts, two bars, two restaurants, and beach volleyball. Rates: start at $140 for double occupancy.

ROYAL SOLARIS LOS CABOS
624-145-6800 or 800-557-7684 (U.S.)
www.clubsolaris.com
Paseo San José
Price: Expensive
Credit Cards: MC, V, AE
Special Features: Gym, tennis court, spa, juniors club, theater, satellite TV

This mammoth all-inclusive hotel-zone resort has 400 air-conditioned rooms. All rooms are furnished with one double and one king-size bed, satellite TV, and a balcony. Rooms are relatively roomy and appointed in a colorful modern style. Not all rooms have an ocean view, so be sure to request one that does when making reservations. The property is equipped with a slew of amenities. Some of them are common, such as swimming pools, a game room, a spa, tennis courts, and four restaurants with bars. Others are rather uncommon, such as a mini water park and a theater offering live shows. Rates: $163–276 for a standard room, double occupancy.

SUITES LAS PALMAS
624-142-2131
www.suiteslaspalmas.com
Carretera Transpeninsular Km 31
Price: Expensive
Credit Cards: MC, V, AE
Special Features: Satellite TV, wireless Internet, heated pool

Guests of this 69-unit resort hotel are offered a variety of accommodation options. Standard rooms are furnished with a king-size or two queen-size beds. Standard one-bedroom suites are equipped with a queen-size bed and a sofa bed as well as a kitchenette. They are appointed in a Mediterranean style with *saltillo* tile floors

and muted solid colors. All rooms have a balcony and satellite TV. Wireless Internet access is also available for a small fee. The hotel's Casita Cabeña Restaurant offers traditional Mexican cuisine in a casual dining experience. The property also features a modest swimming pool. Rates: $94–130 for double occupancy.

SUITES TERRAZAS DE POSITANO
624-143-9383
Plaza Positano, Carretera Transpeninsular Km 3.7, Tourist Corridor
Price: Inexpensive
Credit Cards: MC, V
Special Features: Boutique hotel, private terraces, spa services, ocean view

This boutique hotel is among the smallest and most affordable hotels along the Corridor. It has eight air-conditioned suites, each with a private terrace overlooking the ocean. These rooms are appointed in a colorful Mediterranean style with tile floors, bright fabrics, and wrought-iron furniture. Rooms are furnished with one king-size or two twin beds. Suites also have fully equipped kitchens and breakfast nooks. An on-site deli restaurant offers Mexican coffee and plenty of healthy choices. You can also schedule a full body massage or a facial at the front desk. These services are performed in the privacy of your own room. Rates: $77–85 for double occupancy.

TROPICANA INN
624-142-2311
www.hoteltropicana.com/tropicana_los_cabos
Boulevard Antonio Mijares #30, San José del Cabo
Price: Moderate
Credit Cards: MC, V, AE
Special Features: Swim-up bar

Comfortable and quaint, this hotel has 40 Colonial-style air-conditioned rooms. The rooms in this hotel have *saltillo* tile floors and arched doorways for a particularly Mexican feel. Most are furnished with two double beds. The rooms are built around a tiled courtyard with a large Romanesque pool that has a swim-up bar in the middle. This area is surrounded by lush gardens. The property also features a beautifully appointed *palapa* guest house—perfect for a romantic getaway. Rates: $108–168 from May through October and $127–187 from November through April.

LAS VENTANAS AL PARAÍSO

624-144-2800
www.lasventanas.com
Carretera Transpeninsular Km 19.5, Tourist Corridor
Price: Expensive
Credit Cards: MC, V, AE
Special Features: Spa, fitness center, satellite TV

This 61-unit hotel offers large suites on a secluded and spacious property next to the Cabo Real golf course. Guests arrive to complimentary tequila and are given free access to a spa and fitness center. Rooms are quite large and nicely appointed with a variety of amenities, depending on your room choice. They are decorated in an attractive Mediterranean style with dark woods and muted colors. The on-site Restaurant at Las Ventanas (144-2800, ext. 8201) offers Mediterranean and Mexican specialties along with a long wine list and live music nightly. The Seagrill Restaurant (144-2800, ext. 8205) serves Mexican seafood specialties in an elegant setting. Reservations are required. Rates: begin at around $600 per night for double occupancy plus and 15% service charge.

A couple enjoys the serenity of the estuary.

VISTAZUL SUITES & SPA

624-144-4727
www.vistazulsuites.com
Carretera Transpeninsular Km 3.5, Tourist
Corridor
Price: Moderate
Credit Cards: MC, V, AE
Special Features: Spa, satellite TV

This boutique spa hotel, located just off the highway east of Cabo San Lucas, offers 20 suites and 8 studios arrayed in front of an attractive desert courtyard. Standard rooms feature a queen-size bed and a balcony overlooking the courtyard. One- and two-bedroom suites are also available. All of the accommodation options feature rooms that are large and comfortable. There is also a good-size pool set in the patio overlooking the ocean with several chaise longue chairs perfect for relaxing the time away. The on-site spa provides a variety of services, including Swedish massage, shiatsu, hot stone massage, deep-tissue massage, and Temazcal, an ancient Mexican purification ritual. Rates: average $160 for double occupancy.

WESTIN LOS CABOS BEACH & GOLF RESORT

624-142-9000 or 800-937-8461
www.westin.com/loscabos
Carretera Transpeninsular Km 22.5, Tourist
Corridor
Price: Expensive
Credit Cards: MC, V, AE
Special Features: Private balcony, tennis courts, spa, satellite TV, kids' club

In a tribute to Cabo's most famous landmark, this interesting arch-shaped hotel rises out of the desert and towers over a wildly shaped swimming pool area that seems to teeter on a cliff above the Sea of Cortés. Rooms are furnished with one king-size bed or two double and have a private balcony with an ocean or partial ocean view.

The hotel features a kids' club for children 4 to 12 years old. For adults, there are tennis courts, business activities center, and a full-service spa. The hotel's Arrecifes Restaurant (142-9000 ext. 8319) offers fine cuisine with Asian, Mexican, and French influences as well as a full bar and live music daily. La Cascada Restaurant—open for breakfast, lunch, and dinner—offers fresh seafood and traditional Mexican recipes. The La Playa poolside restaurant serves more casual fare. Rates: $415–579 for a standard room, double occupancy.

RV Parks

BRISA DEL MAR RV RESORT

624-142-2935
Transpeninsular Highway Km 28, Tourist
Corridor

This RV park is the only one in the Los Cabos area that is located right on the beach. They offer 120 sites with full hookups as well as clean bathrooms with flush toilets, a swimming pool, and boat-storage facilities. A convenience store is located on the property, and they also have bike and water sports equipment rentals. Rates: $28–38 per night for RV sites with full hookups and $11 per night for tents. There are also cabanas with kitchenettes available for $60 per night.

VILLA SERENA RV PARK

624-143-0290
Transpeninsular Highway Km 7.5, Tourist
Corridor

Situated on a hill overlooking Cabo San Lucas Bay, this property features 54 spaces with full hookups. It also has a pool and Jacuzzi as well as a laundry room and bathrooms. Extended and permanent stays can be arranged with the management. Rates: $21 per night.

RESTAURANTS

For being such a small town, San José del Cabo offers a good many fashionable restaurants and good, reasonably priced eateries. For the most part, you will find them along Boulevard Antonio Mijares and Calle Zaragoza, near the town's main plaza. Perhaps it's due to the fact that San José proudly retains its traditional feel, or maybe it's because San José caters to a different crowd, but you won't find any of the overbearing peddlers drumming up business in front of these restaurants such as are present in Cabo San Lucas. The quiet culture that distinguishes San José carries over to its restaurants. Most restaurants in

Relaxing in a Hammock

There's nothing quite like relaxing in a beachside hammock with a cool beer in your hand, listening to the waves lap against the shore. However, for the inexperienced hammock sitter, you're likely to wonder what the big deal is all about if you don't know what you're doing. After straddling the hammock in the center and then lifting up your legs, with your head up on one end and your butt in the middle, pressing almost all the way to the ground, you will probably be there only a minute or two before realizing that it's actually not all that comfortable. But it's easy to fix this back-wrenching posture. By lying in the hammock diagonally, with your head as far to one side as you can get it, the center of your body going across the center of the hammock, and your feet either at the edge or hanging off the other side, you will find that your weight is spread out across the hammock webbing instead of its being concentrated at the butt. Suddenly you will find yourself comfortably lost in contemplation, drifting away into a hang-loose haze.

the Tourist Corridor are affiliated with the large resorts, but visitors to the area should try to check out a few independent places before they leave, including Zipper's Bar & Grill, Mama Mia, Lattitude 22+ Steakhouse, and Sunset Da Mona Lisa to watch the sun go down.

BAAN THAI

624-142-3344
Morelos s/n Comonfort
Open: Daily noon–10:30 PM
Price: Moderate
Cuisine: Asian
Serving: L, D

This Pan-Asian restaurant has an extensive menu of soups, wok dishes, and curries. The smell of its Far Eastern spices alone is enough to lure you to the table. Here you will dine on cuisine that evokes such exotic cultures as Thailand, Laos, and China—a meal that you won't soon forget. They have a very good wine list, as well. Although it is not far off the main square, this restaurant is notoriously hard to find, so you may have to ask directions. If you are taking a cab, your driver can certainly point you in the right direction. Reservations are recommended.

CENTRAL GOURMET

624-104-3274
Plaza La Europea, Carretera
Transpeninsular Km 6.7, Tourist Corridor
Open: Tue.–Sun. 8 AM–10:30 PM
Price: Inexpensive to Moderate
Cuisine: International
Serving: B, L, D

For a nice change of pace, this sophisticated Corridor café offers a large menu of sandwiches and gourmet pizza, not to mention sushi. It combines menu items from Society Signature Coffee, Mangiamo Pizza, and Nicksan Japanese Restaurant and provides full bar service as well. Cap things off with a darn good cup of coffee. This restaurant has indoor and patio seating with an ocean view, as well as a small lounge area with leather sofas and a HDTV. Delivery is available.

EL CHILAR RESTAURANT

624-142-2544
Benito Juárez #1490, San José del Cabo
Open: Mon.–Sat. 3 PM–10 PM
Price: Moderate
Cuisine: Mexican
Serving: L, D

Because you're in Mexico, you'll want to enjoy some authentic Mexican cuisine. In this rustic and cozy restaurant, chef Armando Montano does his best to make you feel at home in his country. Murals of the Virgin of Guadalupe adorn the walls, and the open kitchen adds a casual atmosphere. Although the chef's dishes are a little less than traditional, the creativity of his menu more than makes up for it. He changes the menu every month, but you're sure to find several imaginative offerings such as grilled flank steak with chipotle-based pumpkin-seed sauce and baby squash or duck enchiladas with a sweet and creamy white-mole sauce. The restaurant has a wide selection of wines and tequilas, with suggested pairing to your meal. At night the tables are lit by candles—just the right touch for travelers on a romantic vacation.

EL COMAL

624-142-5508
Plaza La Casa de Don Rodrigo
Open: Daily 11 AM–3 PM; 6 PM–10 PM
Price: Moderate
Cuisine: Mexican
Serving: L, D

This attractive Mexican restaurant—tucked off San José's main street behind several *artesenía* shops—offers up wonderful takes on traditional Mexican cuisine. The menu is filled with interesting dishes from all over Mexico, such as *carne asada a la*

Tampiqueña (marinated steak topped with poblano peppers); *tamales bandera* (chicken tamales in a tomatillo sauce); and *sabana de pollo poblana* (pan-fried chicken in two sauces, topped with cheese). These succulent dishes are carefully prepared and presented in an attractive Mexican style. The restaurant is housed in a historic building from the 1800s. However, meals are served on a gorgeous outdoor patio, with handmade chairs and fragrant trees providing shade and atmosphere.

DAMIANA RESTAURANT BAR & PATIO
624-142-0499
Boulevard Antonio Mijares #8
Open: Daily 10:30 AM–10:30 PM
Price: Moderate
Cuisine: Mexican
Serving: L, D

Located in a mid-18th-century hacienda, this restaurant retains the feeling of long ago with a high wooden-beam ceiling and Mexican folk art on the walls. Inside the restaurant there are two small salons with only a few tables, and the patio in back is dominated by a huge bougainvillea. At night, the tree is lit, giving the patio a romantic radiance. The menu features international and Mexican cuisine, with seafood specialties such as imperial shrimp and bay scallops ceviche. You won't find a more perfect restaurant for a romantic night out. This restaurant is popular with the locals, so if you plan on eating here from November to May, be sure to make a reservation.

DELIGHT CAFÉ GOURMET
624-144-6043
Las Tiendas de Palmilla Local A-101,
Carretera Transpeninsular Km 27.5, Tourist Corridor
Open: Daily 7 AM–9 PM
Price: Inexpensive
Cuisine: Coffee and Pastries
Serving: B, L, D

Located within a shopping center in the Corridor, this European-style coffee house features gourmet coffee, espresso drinks, and freshly baked pastries. Here you will find a good selection of espresso drinks, including frappé coffees, as well as teas, fruit drinks, and sodas.

FRENCH RIVIERA RESTAURANT
624-104-3125
Plaza Del Rey, Carretera Transpeninsular Km 6.5, Tourist Corridor
Open: Daily noon–4 PM; 5 PM–10:30 PM
Price: Expensive
Cuisine: French
Serving: L, D

Despite the inauspicious name, this stylish French restaurant, located in the Tourist Corridor, offers some of the most elegant cuisine in Los Cabos. French master chef Jacques Chrétien combines fresh seafood, organically grown produce, and a French sensibility to create dishes such as braised red snapper with potatoes au gratin and steamed seafood with onion flan and mushrooms with fried calamari. This is a great choice if you happen to be a foodie in the mood for a fine meal or a good wine. A bakery spinoff of this restaurant, located on the corner of Miguel Hidalgo and Doblado in San José, is called the French Riviera Restaurant & Bakery (142-3350). It's open daily 7:30 AM to 10:30 PM.

HABANERO'S
624-142-2626
Plaza Misión, Boulevard Antonio Mijares
Open: Daily 11 AM–10 PM
Price: Moderate
Cuisine: International
Serving: L, D

Chef Tadd Chapman offers varied dishes of Mexican fusion cuisine at this local hotspot. The menu includes tacos, burritos, and organic salads for lunch and steak and seafood with signature sauces for dinner.

Dishes include such eclectic choices as tempura tuna in honey sauce, *fettuccine pomodora* with garlic bread, and filet mignon. The restaurant offers a good wine list as well. Despite the exquisiteness of the menu, Habanero's is decidedly casual. The first thing you see upon entering the restaurant is a table loaded with famous tequila labels. Call ahead for reservations, or expect to wait.

JAZMIN'S RESTAURANT
624-142-1760
Morelos between Zaragoza and Obrogón
Open: Daily 8 AM–11 PM
Price: Moderate to Expensive
Cuisine: Mexican
Serving: B, L, D

Located near the historic cathedral of San José, this colorfully decorated Mexican restaurant offers an interesting menu of vegetarian and seafood specialties as well as several traditional Mexican dishes. The menu also features drinks from the restaurant's full bar in addition to a nice kid's menu. This restaurant is done up in a rustic décor with a brightly colored Mexican ambience. The walls are decorated with Pancho Villa memorabilia and the establishment is furnished with authentic, handmade wooden furniture. Outdoor patio seating is available.

LATTITUDE 22+ ROADHOUSE
624-143-1516
Carretera Transpeninsular Km 4.5, Tourist Corridor
Open: Wed.–Mon. 8 AM–11 PM
Price: Inexpensive to Moderate
Cuisine: Steak
Serving: B, L, D

Show up at this popular Corridor steakhouse ready for a casual meal and a good time. The walls are covered with old fishing memorabilia and other tchotchkes, providing the perfect atmosphere for hanging out

and having a good meal. And you'll be doing plenty of that with food this good and so reasonably priced. Entrées include Mexican-style steaks and seafood as well as American-style steaks, barbecue ribs, and hot wings. Live music is featured Thursday through Saturday nights. The kitchen closes at 10 PM.

LOCAL EIGHT
624-142-6655
Plaza Misión, Boulevard Antonio Mijares
Open: Mon.–Fri.11 AM–10:30 PM; Sat.–Sun. 6 PM–10:30 PM
Price: Expensive
Cuisine: International
Serving: L, D

This fine-dining restaurant serves international cuisine with an emphasis on seafood. Dishes such as Cajun blackened snapper and Tagarashi tuna demonstrate how far flung the influences run here. If you are a seafood lover, you are sure to find some interesting selections here. Menu items such as macadamia sea bass and stuffed dorado are not only delicious but attractively presented as well. They also have a generous wine list, mostly populated with selections from California, Baja California, and Chile. Dinner is served on an intimately lit patio.

MAMA MIA
624-142-3939
Carretera Transpeninsular Km 29.5, Tourist Corridor
Open: Daily 8 AM–10 PM
Price: Moderate
Cuisine: International
Serving: B, L, D

With a menu that offers plenty of Mexican fare, Italian food, and international cuisine, this restaurant is hard to define. There is a different theme each night of the week, with everything from rumba on Wednesdays to a Saturday night reggae barbecue.

Reservations are recommended on Tuesday nights, when the restaurant features a Mexican fiesta complete with folkloric dancing, fireworks, and a piñata. The menu is as eclectic as the atmosphere, with everything from traditional Mexican favorites to wood-fired pizza to pasta. It is located in a large thatched-roof *palapa* on the beach and offers live music every night. The atmosphere here is definitely one of revelry.

LA PANGA ANTIGUA

624-142-4041
Zaragoza #20
Open: Daily 11:30 AM–10:30 PM
Price: Expensive
Cuisine: Steak and Seafood
Serving: L, D

The menu at this elegant steak and seafood restaurant is based largely on the freshest locally seafood available. The fine menu items are prepared by an award-winning chef and served on an intimate patio courtyard. The restaurant's atmosphere is stylishly rustic and reminiscent of a 19th-century hacienda. Despite this, the cuisine is decidedly contemporary, with menu items such as seared sea scallops with dry chili oil–saffron risotto, asparagus tips, and bell peppers; ahi tuna lacquered with honey, rosemary, and guajillo pepper over squash blossom and corn kernel rice; and whole red snapper with roasted green tomatillo salsa and black beans. There is also an extensive wine list.

PASSAPAROLA

624-146-3825
Plaza José Green, Boulevard Antonio Mijares
Open: Daily 1:30 PM–10 PM
Price: Inexpensive to Moderate
Cuisine: Italian
Serving: L, D

This Italian bistro is located in downtown San José, upstairs from Banamex. They prepare every meal from scratch with the freshest of ingredients. The menu features pizzas in the thin-crusted southern Italian style. These pizzas are prepared in the restaurant's open-air pizza kitchen, which showcases this craft of pizza-making. The restaurant serves several salads that are prepared with organic greens and topped with shrimp, chicken, salmon, or tuna. There is a large pasta menu that features spaghetti, penne, ravioli, and lasagne plates. Fresh tuna and salmon dishes are also extremely popular.

SUNSET DA MONA LISA

624-145-8160
Carretera Transpeninsular Km 5.5, Tourist Corridor
Open: Daily 8 AM–11 PM
Price: Expensive
Cuisine: Italian
Serving: B, L, D

Not many restaurants are so stunningly beautiful that they host wedding ceremonies. This fine-dining Italian restaurant is one of the exceptions. It is located in the Corridor in a building with multilevel glass-enclosed terraces specially designed for enjoying the sunset. It features three separate dining rooms, each with a spectacular view of the famous arch of Cabo San Lucas in the distance, providing the perfect setting for a romantic Italian dinner. These dishes are prepared with such care that they actually compete with the view in terms of beauty. Their pasta is hand-made and the focaccia bread is baked each evening in their wood-fired oven. There is also a nice wine list.

THE TULIP TREE

624-146-9900
Plaza José Green, Boulevard Antonio Mijares, San José del Cabo
Open: Daily 5 PM–10 PM
Price: Moderate

Cuisine: Steak and Seafood
Serving: D

This steak and seafood restaurant specializes in generous portions of traditional fare at reasonable prices. Their menu is eclectic and you can get anything from blackened ahi tuna with papaya and pineapple salsa to Oriental shrimp stir-fry. Besides the surf-and-turf, they offer pastas, soups, salads, and a full bar. Meals are served in a pleasant courtyard setting. They also have a modest wine list and several types of martinis.

VILLA SERENA RESTAURANT & BAR
624-145-8244
Carretera Transpeninsular Km 7.5, Tourist Corridor
Open: Daily 7 AM–10 PM
Price: Moderate
Cuisine: Mexican
Serving: B, L, D

This Mexican seafood restaurant is located in the Corridor 5 miles east of Cabo San Lucas. The *palapa* dining area provides nice views of the sea as you dine on traditional and down-to-earth Mexican fare. The service is welcoming, and the drinks are very good. Additionally, the restaurant offers sweeping views of the sea to enjoy while you kick back and enjoy your meal, and even has a dipping pool just in case the heat gets to be too much for you. Perfect for couples and families alike.

ZIPPER'S BAR & GRILL
624-172-6162
Carretera Transpeninsular Km 28.5, Tourist Corridor
Open: Daily 11 AM–10:30 PM
Price: Inexpensive to Moderate
Cuisine: Mexican and American
Serving: L, D

This well-known Corridor bar and grill serves Mexican and American fare on a patio overlooking the Sea of Cortés. Come here after you have had your fill of Mexican food and enjoy one of their charcoal-grilled Angus beef hamburgers with French fries, just to remind you of home. They also feature live music every Friday night and satellite TV for all major sporting events. The atmosphere is decidedly casual, as you can dine right on the beach. So kick off your flip-flops, dig your toes into the sand, and grab a beer.

BARS AND NIGHTLIFE

Okay, San José doesn't have anywhere near the nightlife that you'll find down the road in Cabo San Lucas. However, the bars and lounges that the town does have generally cater to an older crowd. Most people beyond their mid-20s who are looking for nightlife should be able to find a spot that suits them in San José. If you are staying in the Tourist Corridor and would like to remain there for nighttime diversions, your options are generally limited to resort lounges and a number of restaurants that keep their bars open late.

CACTUS JACK'S
624-142-5601
Boulevard Antonio Mijares at Juárez
Open: Wed.–Mon. 9 AM–4 AM

This fun-loving bar and grill is a popular hangout that stays open late on the weekends and features karaoke on some nights.

ESCALA KARAOKE SPORTS BAR
624-142-5155
Boulevard Antonio Mijares
Open: Daily 10 AM–4 AM

How often do you get to have a combination of karaoke and sports? This bar has eight TVs for all major sporting events, as well as DJ music along with live music and dancing on Saturday nights.

LA SANTA WINE BAR
624-142-5601
Miguel Hidalgo and Álvaro Obregón
Open: Mon.–Sat. 6 PM–2 AM

Located in an old building with a wooden-beam ceiling and quarry stone walls, this stylish lounge carries more than 130 wines from around the world. They also offer a nice menu of tapas.

SHOOTERS SPORT BAR
624-146-9900
Manuel Doblado and Boulevard Antonio Mijares
Open: Mon.–Fri. noon–midnight, Sat.-Sun. noon–2 AM

This sports bar is located upstairs at the Tulip Tree Restaurant. They have pool tables and satellite TV to go along with "cheap drinks and good eats."

BEACHES

San José and the Corridor have no equivalent to Médano Beach, the party beach in Cabo San Lucas. The long beach that fronts the resorts of San José's hotel zone is wide and beautiful, but because of its rough surf and strong undertow, it is unsuitable for swimming and thus pretty deserted. The Corridor, though, has several beaches that are located in protected coves and provide great swimming and snorkeling. Although a few of them have some services located nearby, they are for the most part pretty secluded, especially when compared to Médano Beach. This is not to say that these Corridor beaches are empty. Buses and tour groups usually begin bringing crowds in late morning, so early morning generally provides the best snorkeling and swimming.

Playa Hotelera
This single expansive stretch of sand runs west from the estuary past all of hotels on the hotel zone until it reaches the Mayan Resorts Golf Course and the beach of Costa Azul. But unlike Médano Beach in Cabo San Lucas, Playa Hotelera is not commonly regarded as a swimming beach because it has a fairly brutal shore break. Furthermore, because nearby tour companies lead horseback-riding tours along this beach—particularly the eastern end near the estuary—the sand is sometimes littered with horse droppings. For these reasons you won't find many people along this beach, and vendors are pretty much nonexistent here. Visitors to the resorts that line this beach generally appreciate it solely for its view and rely on hotel pools for swimming.

Costa Azul
A bend in the coast marks the end of Playa Hotelera and the beginning of Playa Costa Azul. This half-mile stretch of beach is world famous for its surf break, which carries the same name. To reach this beach, exit the Transpeninsular Highway at Km 28.5 and turn right at the bridge. The beach is just a few meters beyond. For nonsurfers, perhaps the only reason to come here is to eat at Zippers (624-172-6162), a *palapa* restaurant overlooking the ocean at the southwest end of this beach. They serve American-style food daily from 11 AM to 10 PM. Farther west, just past the rocky bluffs, you'll find Playa Acapulquito, also known as "Old Man's Beach," which is a good beach for inexperienced surfers. However, because this is an easy access beach with plenty of parking, it does tend to get crowded, particularly on weekends.

Get to Playa Chileno early to beat the crowds.

Playa Palmilla

Located off the Km 27 exit of the Transpeninsular Highway, this beautiful white-sand beach is quite different than either Costa Azul and Playa Acapulquito that lie just to the east. Here a protrusion of rocks creates a protected cove that makes this beach safe for swimming. For this reason, this beach attracts families and snorkelers. The beach itself stretches for about a mile, with plenty of *palapas* to provide shade. If you're interested in snorkeling or scuba diving, a dive shop is located just off the east side of the beach, along with a restaurant that offers snacks and cold drinks and a restroom for patrons.

Playa Bledito

This somewhat secluded beach is located in front of the Meliá Cabo Real and the Hilton Los Cabos beach resorts off Km 19.5 of the Transpeninsular Highway. You can access the beach by going through the resorts. The wide, crescent-shaped stretch of sand has a man-made breakwater that diminishes waves and undertow, making it a great place for families looking to get away from the crowds of their resort pools. But you should still use caution, particularly during the late summer and early fall storm season. Just to the east of this beach is Playa La Concha, which has a tide pool, restaurant, showers, and equipment rental.

Playa El Tule

With its waves and secluded location, this beach is often overlooked by tourists. This is a good surfing beach with a right reef break that has its biggest swells during the wintertime.

However, watch out for the boulders that are scattered about in the surf. This beach has easy access, and camping is allowed here—an option best achieved with a four-wheel-drive vehicle. To get here, look for the EL TULE sign at around km. 16.2 of the Transpeninsular Highway.

Playa Chileno

This beach—located at km. 14 of the Transpeninsular Highway, just west of the Hotel Cabo San Lucas—is an excellent place for diving and snorkeling. Chileno is also one of the most popular beaches among locals, so it can get crowded on weekends. On the beach's western end, you'll find a reef that is abundant with tropical fish, and on the eastern end there are tide pools that are great for kids. There are restrooms with showers and some palm trees set back from the beach, but it's a good idea to bring a beach umbrella if you have one. Get here in the morning before the tour buses arrive, and you'll find the beach empty—for a few hours, at least, you can have it to yourself. However, toward the afternoon, it does tend to fill up.

Playa Santa Maria

The beautiful horseshoe-shaped cove known as Playa Santa Maria is a protected marine sanctuary and offers some of the best snorkeling in Los Cabos. To get here from the highway, look for the beach access sign around km. 13, near the Twin Dolphin Hotel, and follow the dirt road to the parking area. Once again, arrive early to beat the crowds and for the best snorkeling. Tour operators often bring clients here around 10 am. There are no services here and very little shade, so come prepared.

Snorkelers at Playa Chileno.

Playa Las Viudas

If Playa Santa Maria is too crowded for
your taste, scramble over the rocks on
the west end of the beach and to reach
Playa Las Viudas, also known as
"Widow's Beach" or "Twin Dolphin
Beach." Or locate this picturesque beach
from km. 12 of the Transpeninsular
Highway. After you exit onto the beach
access road, head down a rough dirt
stretch for almost a half mile before
reaching the beach. This is a lesser-
known beach, free of crowds and vendors, making it a great place to come for
a secluded picnic and soaking up the
sun. Dogs are also allowed here, though
here again there are no facilities and
almost no shade, so bring your own
gear.

Playa Barco Varado

A Japanese freighter once crashed into
the rocks at this site. The rusting wreck-
age of the freighter remains on the
rocks, providing an interesting backdrop to the ocean view near Cabo Del
Sol Hotel and the finishing hole of the

Playa Santa Maria.

resort's golf course designed by Jack Nicklaus. If you decide to explore the waters near the
wreck, use caution. There is a strong undertow here. Access this beach through the Cabo
Del Sol Hotel entrance off km.11 of the Transpeninsular Highway.

RECREATION

San José del Cabo and the Tourist Corridor is a playground that straddles the desert and the
sea, providing activities that feature the best of both worlds. The area is world famous for
both its sport fishing and golfing. Since the late 1980s, the Tourist Corridor has become
tattooed with courses designed by the biggest names in golf, including Jack Nicklaus and
Robert Trent Jones. These courses are generally well kept and provide spectacular vistas of
the ocean and desert. Not a golfer? All along the coast you will find wonderful opportunities for snorkeling and diving as well as surfing. Inland, the desert roads and mountains
provide a great setting for hiking, horseback riding, and piloting ATVs. Unlike its sister
city Cabo San Lucas, San José del Cabo does not have great nightlife. A few bars stay open
late, but for the most part you'll need to head to Cabo for late-night partying.

Jet Skiing along the Corridor.

Diving and Snorkeling

The waters all along the coast of Los Cabos offer excellent diving and snorkeling opportunities, many accessed easily and just minutes from the hotels along the Corridor. The relatively calm waters of Playa Chileno and Playa Santa Maria offer dives that are spectacular yet close by and appropriate for inexperienced divers. For more experienced divers, the farther-out Gorda Banks provides a deep-water experience that includes the large sport fish that have made Los Cabos famous. And for an amazing day trip appropriate for divers of all skill levels, Cabo Pulmo along the East Cape will give you a unique diving experience.

CHILENO BAY

This dive spot is located in front of Playa Chileno. Here, a web of finger-shaped reefs covered in tree coral awaits. This reef formation begins right at the shore of the beach and extends out into the bay for about a half mile. The reef is home to a wide assortment of tropical sea life such as starfish, sea fans, sponges, and sea urchins. The reef also attracts large numbers of schooling tropical fish and occasionally sea turtles and nurse sharks. This dive spot is appropriate for snorkelers and divers of all skill levels, beginning with a drop to about 30 feet, then gradually plunging to around 80 feet.

SANTA MARIA REEF

This dive spot in front of Playa Santa Maria is ideal for underwater photographers. Located within Santa Maria's sheltered cove, this site is home to colorful gorgonians, including sea fans that line the cove's rock walls, as well as hard and soft corals, octopuses, and eels. Tropical reef fish are in abundance here, plus the occasional bat ray, sea bass, and sea turtle. Appropriate for intermediate divers, this dive drops to around 40 feet.

WHALES HEAD POINT

This point at the west end of Playa Barco Varado is formed by a large cliff that juts out of the bay. The cliff drops 20 to 30 feet into the water, depending on tidal conditions. It features dazzling rock formations that are the habitation of nurse sharks, sea turtles, octopuses, and the occasional guitarfish. This dive, which drops to depths from 30 to 60 feet, is appropriate for intermediate to advanced divers.

THE BLOWHOLE

This dive spot—located near Playa Chileno—features a rock formation with a hole about 25 feet below the surface that, as the current surges through, shoots water out an opening at the top. When this happens, as the name suggests, it resembles a whale spouting from its blowhole. The underwater site itself is a labyrinth of rocks and canyons. The rock walls are covered in gorgonians and large coral heads. The area is inhabited by small nurse sharks and guita fish along with a variety of rays. This is an intermediate dive, with depths of 40 to about 100 feet.

GORDA BANKS

Many wonderful dive sites can be found farther afield along the East Cape, and most of the diving guides of Los Cabos offer trips to these places. One of these dive sites is known as Gorda Banks, a seamount some 50 miles south of the cape that necessitates a 2-hour boat ride to reach it. The tip of this seamount lies at a depth of about 110 to 120 feet. It is covered with bushes of black coral. Marine life commonly seen on this deepwater dive includes dorado, tuna, wahoo, marlin, and even hammerhead and giant whale sharks. This dive is for advanced divers only because of the depths and currents that are involved.

Snorkelers at Playa Chileno.

CABO PULMO NATIONAL MARINE SANCTUARY

This East Cape diving location features the only live coral reef in the Sea of Cortés and more than 350 species of marine life. Getting to this remote location usually takes a 2-hour drive from Los Cabos. There are nearly 20 prime dive sites that are appropriate for beginning to advanced divers.

Fishing

San José del Cabo and the East Cape offer plenty of great sport fishing opportunities. Here you can find reef *panga* fishing close to the shore as well as excellent offshore fishing. You also have your choice between Pacific waters and great spots in the Sea of Cortés. Discovered in the 1950s, the Gorda

Fishermen have long flocked to Baja California Sur.
Jason MacBeth

Banks in particular offer great opportunities to catch marlin, wahoo, and tuna. The inshore fishing seasons for cooler-water fish, such as yellowtail, peaks between March and June. The season for roosterfish, cabrilla, and various species of snapper peaks between April and July. The chances of catching wahoo and snook are the best during the warmer months of July through October. A catch-and-release policy is encouraged by most fishing charters.

Golfing the day away in the Corridor.

Golf

Over the last decade, Los Cabos has become one of North America's premier golf destinations. This is due in large part to a California developer named Don Koll who, in 1990, commissioned Hall of Fame golfer Jack Nicklaus to design 27 holes of golf at the Palmilla resort in San José del Cabo. Since then, Nicklaus has gone on to design two other golf courses in the area (El Dorado Golf Club at Cabo Real and Cabo del Sol), and other well-known golfers have also designed courses here. Los Cabos has been the site of the PGA Senior Slam Tournament since 1995, and golfing has grown to be the number two attraction in Los Cabos, with panoramic ocean views lending themselves to create an incredible golfing experience. Most of the courses are fairly new and in very good condition. All these courses are located in the Corridor, fewer than 20 minutes from just about any hotel in the area.

CABO DEL SOL

624-145-8200; U.S. Tee Time Reservations: 877-944-2226
Km 7.5 Carretera Transpeninsular

This is actually comprised of two golf courses, which are closer to Cabo San Lucas than San José del Cabo. The 18-hole Ocean Course was designed by Jack Nicklaus and was the location of the 1998 Senior Slam. The front nine is 3,597 yards, the back nine is 3,440 yards, and the course has a par-72 rating. The Desert Course, designed by Tome Weiskopf, is farther inland but ocean views are guaranteed from every hole. Carts are available. Green fees for the Ocean Course are $350 from October through June and $250 from July through September. Green fees for the Desert Course are $185–220 from October through September and $165 from July through September. Twilight rates are also available at the Desert Course as well.

CABO REAL

624-144-0040; U.S. Tee Time Reservations: 877-944-2226
Km 19.5 Carretera Transpeninsular

This 18-hole Robert Trent Jones–designed course is located about halfway between Cabo San Lucas and San José del Cabo. Offering very nice ocean views, the course has a front nine of 3,943 yards, a back nine of 3,452 yards, and a par-72 rating. Greens fees are regularly $176 and $115 during the summer. Carts are available.

CABO SAN LUCAS COUNTRY CLUB

624-143-4653; U.S. Tee Time Reservations: 877-461-3667
Lázaro Cárdenas

This 18-hole course is located just outside downtown Cabo San Lucas on the north side of the Transpeninsular Highway. It was designed by Roy Dye with a front nine of 3,651 yards, a back nine of 3,596 yards, and a par-72 rating. This course features seven lakes, with natural desert and mountain terrain. Greens fees are $182 before 2 PM and $125 after 2 PM. Fees include a cart.

EL DORADO COUNTRY CLUB

624-144-5451 or 800-393-0400 (U.S.)
Km 19.5 Carretera Transpeninsular

This is the latest Jack Nicklaus-designed course in Los Cabos. The front nine is 3,440 yards, the back nine is 3,610 yards, and the course has a par-72 rating. The 18-hole course has four lakes and five holes overlooking the Sea of Cortés. Greens fees are $246 for daytime hours and $168 for twilight hours.

PALMILLA GOLF CLUB

624-144-5524; U.S. Tee Time Reservations: 800-637-2226
Km 27.5 Carretera Transpeninsular, Los Cabos

This 18-hole course was the first designed by Jack Nicklaus in Mexico. It was also the site of the 1997 Senior PGA Senior Slam. Totaling 6,900 yards, it has a par-72 rating. Greens fees are regularly $185 and $90 during the summer.

Hiking

Several locations near San José del Cabo are great for hiking. The estuary is an obvious first choice for a nice, relaxing day hike. For a more demanding jaunt, the Sierra de la Laguna Mountains to the north of San José will provide you with a challenging adventure. The trails to these mountain passes are easily accessible, though they narrow out and become more difficult to follow as you climb in elevation and the terrain becomes rockier. Along the way, the vegetation quickly changes from desert to forest. Guided day hikes and eco-tours include hot springs and waterfalls near Santiago, a small village an hour to the north. These pools provide a great location for relaxing and having a picnic. Other hiking tours feature fossil fields and old mining ghost towns. Make sure you have good footwear and plenty of water. Because the dry temperatures can get so hot during the day and fall so precipitously at night, you should have at least 2 liters per person per day as well as warm clothing for the evening. Also be aware that from July through October, rains can cause flash floods and wash out hiking trails. Hiking is best in the winter, with comfortable temperatures in the 70s.

Off-Roading

ATV tours with seaside vistas or in the mountains have become a popular way to spend a day in Los Cabos. In the San José area, the local mountains and dirt roads north of town offer a particularly good setting for off-roading. Tour operators are available throughout San José and the East Cape who will guide you through desert arroyos, sand dunes, and even through the heart of town. Other off-road options include dirt-bike rentals and guided tours, horseback riding, and extended multiday Hummer tours. An abundance of relatively flat terrain around San José is great for dirt bikes, particularly along the unpaved roads of the East Cape.

A tour guide rolls his quad through San José del Cabo.

Surfing

The Corridor provides several surfing spots that are appropriate for all skill levels. This area picks up southerly and southwesterly swells, though westerly swells are blocked by the tip of Cabo San Lucas. When there is a swell, the most famous break along the Corridor is Costa Azul at km. 28.5 on the Transpeninsular Highway. A surf shop here rents boards and gives advice. However, fame has also brought crowds, and chances are, you'll be fighting for position if you surf here. Less experienced surfers should head just to the west to Playa Acapulquito, where a right-breaking swell offers good surfing for beginners. At El Tule—at km. 16.2, roughly the center of the Corridor—expert surfers will find a fast break that goes both ways. Closer to Cabo San Lucas just in front of the Misiones del Cabo Hotel, a left-point break provides decent-size waves. This also should be left to more experienced surfers.

Whale Watching

From January to March, visitors to Los Cabos are treated to the sight of gray whales spouting offshore as they make their 6,000-mile journey to their winter homes in the warm waters of the Sea of Cortés. These bottom-feeding animals are gentle travelers that tend to stay close to shore. They once traveled the coasts of Europe and Asia but are now confined to the North Pacific from Alaska to Mexico. These whales seek shelter in the protected, shallow lagoons of San Ignacio, Ojo de Liebre, and Magdalena Bay, where they birth their calves. In the lagoons the calves learn survival skills as they prepare to make the summer journey back to Alaska. Although several other species frequent this area, grays are the most common. The visible tip of the whale breaking the surface of the water as it exhales is usually the first sign of whale activity. Lucky whale watchers may catch sight of these giant mammals breaching as they propel themselves almost completely out of the water.

Other Diversions

Unlike most places in on the east coast of Baja California Sur, San José del Cabo is not great for kayaking. Ocean waves slam along its shores, making San José beaches a dangerous place to set off from. The exception to this is the estuary, where you will find a calm lagoon rich with wildlife, making it an excellent kayaking destination.

The deserts and mountains around San José provide a great setting for mountain biking. Bikes can be rented in town for about $5 an hour or $20 a day. However, you should not head out to Los Cabos's remote back roads alone, and you should always have a detailed map and plenty of supplies.

Another activity that has been growing in popularity in Los Cabos in recent years is rock climbing. Several local outdoor tour groups offer guided climbing tours of the area.

Does hanging onto a cable suspended over a river gorge appeal to you? If so, for a quick thrill, head out to the Costa Azul Canyon just north of the Transpeninsular Highway from Playa Costa Azul for a zip-line ride over the river canyon.

OTHER ATTRACTIONS

SAN JOSÉ ESTUARY

Estero San José, the San José Estuary, is the largest body of fresh water in southern Baja, and its 2,000-plus acres of marshland provides a home to 150 species of birds. In addition

Tour Companies

Baja Ride

624-120-5335; cell 624-122-0203

www.bajaride.com

Km 28 Carretera Transpeninsular, San José del Cabo

This tour company specializes in off-road motorcycle and quad adventures. Half-day tours run around $150, and full day tours are $225. Groups are guided through desert valleys and mountain terrain as well as trails along the Pacific Ocean and the Sea of Cortés. Three- and four-day tours are also available from October through June. Or if you just want to ride around town, scooters available for rental.

Baja Wild

624-172-6300

www.bajawild.com

Km 28 Carretera Transpeninsular, San José del Cabo

This company operates a wide variety of outdoor tours. On water, they offer full- and half-day kayak snorkeling combination tours on the East Cape as well as half-day trips in Cabo San Lucas Bay. They also provide surfing lessons along the Corridor and whale-watching expeditions. Inland, they offer hiking adventures that take you to the desert canyons and waterfalls north of San José, as well as ATV and repelling adventures.

Baja Xplorer Expeditions

624-142-4082

www.bajaxplorer.com

Retorno #8 s/n Col. Magisterial, San José del Cabo

This company offers Wave Runner tours of the Cabo coast. From January through March, they also provide whale-watching expeditions in which you can view whales from the close-up view of your own Wave Runner. They also book tours to Todos Santos and dolphin-swimming adventures.

Canopy Costa Azul

624-105-9311

www.canopycostaazul.com

Cañon Costa Azul, San José del Cabo

This facility is located just north of the Transpeninsular Highway from Playa Costa Azul. The company operates more than 3 miles of zip line suspended over the Costa Azul river canyon. Zip-line tours include ecological information. You should wear comfortable clothing, and a small backpack is allowed. Tours are not physically demanding, but the company advises that people with severe back or neck problems, heart concerns, or other disabilities should carefully evaluate if the ride is suitable for their particular condition. Riders must be at least seven years old and weigh less than 250 pounds.

Gray Line Los Cabos

624-146-9410 or 206-331-3812 (U.S.)

www.graylineloscabos.com

Plaza San José Suite 1, San José del Cabo

This is a full activities-management company that books everything from scuba diving adventures and eco-tours to cultural events and bar-hopping tours. They can also arrange transportation, from a transport van to limousine service.

Mike Doyle Surf School
624-172-6188 or 858-964-5117 (U.S.)
www.cabosurfshop.com
Km 28 Playa Acapulquito, San José del Cabo

Perched above Playa Acapulquito, this surf school is open daily 8 AM to 8 PM. One hour of personal instruction runs about $65. A surf shop here rents surf boards, boogie boards, and snorkel gear.

Panchito Tours
624-143-8532
www.panchitotours.com
Col. Cerro de los Venados #19, Cabo San Lucas

This company offers city van tours of Los Cabos. The four-hour tour takes you to historical missions, beaches, golf courses, and other notable locations. Panchito also offers snorkeling, kayaking, and whale-watching adventures.

Transcabo Group
624-146-0888 or 866-403-5987 (U.S./Canada)
www.transcabo.com
Km 43 Carretera Transpeninsular, San José del Cabo

This is a private transportation company that can provide you with high-class transportation around southern Baja. They can also book adventure tours of all types.

to birds, this large lagoon is a sanctuary for insects, aquatic mammals, turtles, many species of fish, and more than 300 types of flora. You can observe this abundance of life while kayaking or just wandering down the path. You can also explore this area by horseback, mountain bike, or even ATV. Open daily from dawn until dusk.

CACTI MUNDO
624-146-9191
Boulevard Antonio Mijares

This unique botanical garden features an incredible variety of cacti and other rare plants. For more than 15 years, the nurseries of Cacti Mundo have successfully reproduced and conserved these rare species. Today the circular-shaped garden contains about 5,000 plants representing 850 different species.

SHOPPING

San José del Cabo is known for its shopping, and here you'll find *artesenía* and interior-design products of good quality in the shops along Calle Zaragoza and Boulevard Antonio Mijares. However, this good quality is often accompanied by high prices. Along the Tourist Corridor, shopping is mostly segregated to resort gift shops. But a few malls offer good shopping, in particular Las Tiendas de Palmilla at Km 27.5 on the Carretera Transpeninsular (Transpeninsular Highway).

Plenty of fine artesenía *can be found in San José del Cabo.*

Arts and Crafts

Forja Casa y Jardin (624-143-9383; Carretera Transpeninsular Km 4, Tourist Corridor) Although quarters are cramped, you'll find a nice variety of traditional Mexican pottery and ironwork at competitive prices. Open daily 10 AM to 6 PM.

Copal (624-142-3070; Plaza Mijares 10, San José del Cabo) A selection of traditional *artesenía*, such as colorful carved animals from Oaxaca and masks from Guerrero Negro. Although the prices are much higher than they would be in those places, they are not unreasonable. Open daily 9 AM to 10:30 PM.

Curios Carmela (624-142-1117; Boulevard Antonio Mijares 43, San José del Cabo) A large assortment of Mexican handicrafts, such as glassware, pottery, and woven hammocks, at very reasonable prices. Open daily 10 AM to 7 PM.

Clothing and Swimwear

Big Tony (624-142-0744; Zaragoza, San José del Cabo) This surf shop sells casual beach wear and swimsuits at reasonable prices. Open daily 9 AM to 9:30 PM.

Casa Vieja (624-144-6161; Las Tiendas de Palmilla, Local B-204, Km 27.5 Carretera Transpeninsular, San José del Cabo) A unique collection of styles for men and women by Mexican designers. Accessories include handbags, scarves, and shoes. Open Monday through Saturday 10:30 AM to 9 PM.

Tropica Calipso Swimwear (624-144-6158; Las Tiendas de Palmilla, Local A-125, Carretera Transpeninsular Km 27.5, San José del Cabo) This swimwear shop has an extensive selection of swimwear in a variety of styles, colors, and print designs as well as accessories. Open daily 9 AM to 9 PM.

Home Furnishings

Adobe Design (624-142-4281; Plaza San José, Carretera Transpeninsular Km 32, Tourist Corridor) A first-rate collection of antique and modern Mexican-style furniture. You will also find a variety of Adobe-style decorations such as iron work, pottery, and Mexican tile. Open Monday through Friday 9 AM to 8 PM.

Antigua de Mexico (624-144-6121; Las Tiendas de Palmilla, Local A-107, Carretera Transpeninsular Km 27.5, Tourist Corridor) This store has plenty of knickknacks along with contemporary and Mexican colonial-style furniture from Jalisco. Open Monday through Saturday 9 AM to 6 PM.

Casa Maya Los Cabos (624-142-6611; Carretera Transpeninsular Km 32.5, Tourist Corridor) Custom-made antique-wood and forged-iron furniture along with a selection of tapestries and window treatments. However, not all pieces are flawless. Open Monday through Friday 9 AM to 7 PM and Saturday 9 AM to 5 PM.

Jewelry

La Mina (624-142-3747; Boulevard Antonio Mijares #33, San José del Cabo) Here you will find silver and gold jewelry designs embedded with diamonds and other precious stones. Open daily 9 AM to 9 PM.

Legacy Jewelers (624-144-6038; Las Tiendas de Palmilla, Local 202-B, Carretera Transpeninsular Km 27.5, Tourist Corridor) This fine-jewelry shop sells gold jewelry designs embedded with precious gemstones. Open daily 10:30 AM to 6 PM.

Silver Toños Taxco (624-142-6470; Boulevard Antonio Mijares, San José del Cabo) A wide variety of jewelry and silver knickknacks from Taxco. Open daily 9 AM to 9 PM.

5

SIDE TRIPS ON THE CAPE

Most visitors to Baja's cape region never make it outside the Tourist Corridor of Los Cabos, and some don't even leave their hotel's grounds. These travelers likely have a very well-defined set of expectations for their visit to the region, which the facilities found in Los Cabos are perfectly designed to meet. However, for travelers wanting to step outside of Cabos's tourist world and reach for something unexpected, the cape region has plenty to offer. Depending on just how adventurous you want to get, the cape is filled with places rich in history, intrigue, and culture. Furthermore, each region of the cape has a distinct personality created by geography and historical circumstances. For example, the towns along the East Cape provide amazing vistas and wonderful opportunities for sport fishing and diving. On the other hand, the town of Todos Santos is an oasis of art and enchantment, with famous surfing beaches located nearby and several boutique hotels devoted to relaxation and healing. Whether it's off-roading, windsurfing, or just getting into an RV and getting away from it all, the cape is an adventure waiting to happen.

Town square, Todos Santos.

Todos Santos

If you arrive in Todos Santos by bus, you may step off onto the street in front of the PEMEX gas station wondering why you took the time to come to such a rustic little town. To begin with, few of its dusty streets are even paved, and walking down

OPPOSITE: *Sunrise over the East Cape.* Jason MacBeth

115

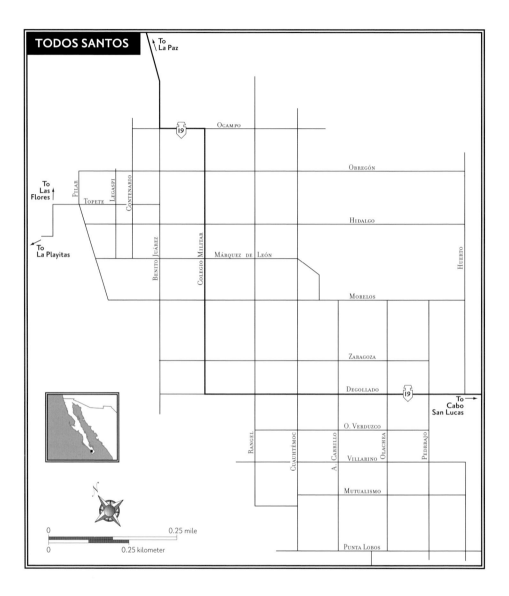

the roads off Degollado, where the bus drops you off, it's easy to feel as though you are lost in some back neighborhood. However, just under the surface (actually, just down the street on Benito Juárez) is a place filled with beautiful boutique hotels, interesting art galleries, and wonderful restaurants. With approximately 6,000 residents, this town, which sits on the Tropic of Cancer, is southern Baja's foremost artist colony where many prominent artists showcase their work.

ACCOMMODATIONS

Because Todos Santos is just an hour away from both Cabo San Lucas and La Paz, most people treat it as a day trip. However, if you do plan on staying over, be sure to make your accommodations in advance. There aren't a lot of hotels in Todos Santos, and they're spread out and tucked away. This means that they're not only hard to find but also they'd often be booked up once you got there. Many are actually large private residences owned mostly by expatriate Americans who have converted part of their property into vacation rentals or small, attractive boutique hotels that are perfect for relaxation.

ALEGRIA INN
612-145-0700
www.alegriainn.net
La Cachora
Price: Moderate to Expensive
Credit Cards: None
Special Features: Patio pool, massage therapist

Located in a Mexican hacienda on a large plot of land, this hotel has a small patio pool adjacent to an old mango grove. With just seven units, it is a rather intimate hotel with personal service. The rooms are nicely appointed with *saltillo* tile and hand-carved Mexican furniture. The daily maid service is accompanied by fresh flowers, and a massage therapist is available to provide you with a variety of treatments. Rates: average $200 per night depending on the room.

CASA BENTLEY
612-145-0276
www.casabentleybaja.com
Calle del Pilar #38
Price: Moderate to Expensive
Credit Cards: MC, V (through PayPal)
Special Features: Patio pool, convenient location

This rustic hotel with its blue-tile pool and quarry-stone walls has six attractive units, individually decorated with local art. They are furnished with king- or queen-size beds and fine Egyptian-cotton linens. The gardens that surround the pool area and trickling fountains create a relaxed atmosphere to enjoy after a long day of perusing the shops of Todos Santos or surfing the waves of the nearby Pacific beaches. The hotel itself is conveniently located off the main plaza, close to shops and restaurants and not far from the beach. Rates: $90–250 from October 16 through May 15 and $90–$170 from May 16 through October 15. Lower rates are available for stays longer than four nights.

CASA RAYO DEL SOL
612-145-0472
La Poza
Price: Expensive
Credit Cards: None
Special Features: Close to the beach, full kitchen, washer and dryer, satellite TV

This vacation rental is a three-bedroom, two-bath *palapa* house a short distance from the beach. The house has a large living room as well as a full kitchen and breakfast nook plus a washer and dryer as well as satellite TV. Bedrooms are furnished with king- or queen-size beds. Rates: $250 nightly and $1,500 weekly.

THE GARDEN CASITA
612-145-0129
Mutualismo
Price: Inexpensive
Credit Cards: None
Special Features: Wireless Internet

This guest house vacation rental combines the rustic feel of exposed brick walls and a thatched *palapa* roof with modern amenities such as a DVD player and wireless Internet. The bedroom is furnished with a queen-size bed while a separate loft area has a double bed. The property also features an enclosed patio courtyard with fruit trees and tropical gardens. Rates: $85 nightly and $395 weekly November through July 14; $55 nightly and $325 weekly July 15 through October.

HACIENDA TODOS LOS SANTOS
612-145-0547
Benito Juárez
Price: Moderate
Credit Cards: None
Special Features: Full kitchens in some units

This hacienda compound offers three guest houses, two equipped with full kitchens and all with a private garden terrace or patio and spacious bathrooms. Each house is well maintained and beautifully appointed. Bedrooms are furnished with either a queen- or king-size bed. A pool on the property is perfect for lounging on warm evenings. This

hotel is located at the south end of Calle Benito Juárez. Rates: average $122.

HOTEL CALIFORNIA
612-145-0525
Calle Juarez
Price: Inexpensive
Credit Cards: MC, V
Special Features: Convenient location

No, this is not the Hotel California made famous by the 1970 Eagles hit of the same name. However, that is one of the many rumors that surround this boutique hotel. After all, it is located off a dark desert highway around the corner from a mission. What is certain is that the Hotel California, which sits in the heart of downtown Todos Santos, is a luxurious retreat with 11 colorfully appointed rooms and plenty of desert ambience. Among these rooms is a large penthouse with a rooftop garden terrace offering ocean and mountain views. The

Hotel California.

hotel's La Coronela Restaurant also provides good food with a warm atmosphere. Rates: start at $85 for a standard room, double occupancy.

HOTEL SANTA ROSA

612-145-0394
Calle Agustin Olachea and San Vicente
Price: Inexpensive
Credit Cards: None
Special Features: Internet access, swimming pool, Jacuzzi

Located a block and a half south of Degollado, this attractive eight-room hotel may seem a little bit off the beaten path, but the town is so small that it isn't much of an issue. Rooms are nicely appointed and furnished with one or two queen-size beds and a hideaway bed as well as a fully equipped kitchen. The rooms face a good-size pool area that includes a Jacuzzi. The hotel is also equipped with wireless Internet access. Rates: start at $50. Discounted rates are available for stays longer than seven nights.

JARDIN DEL PILAR CASITA SUITES

612-145-0386
www.jardindepilar.com
Calle Pilar between Topete and Hidalgo
Price: Moderate
Credit Cards: None
Special Features: Wireless Internet

This hotel offers two privately gated suites located right off the historic district. These suites are actually small houses that are well kept and nicely appointed with colorful fabrics and original art. They are equipped with kitchenettes, CD stereo systems, and wireless Internet access. Behind them is a private patio area with lush gardens and a small pool that is perfect for relaxing. Rates: $105–125. Discounted rates are available for stays longer than seven nights.

LA ALIANZA GUEST QUARTERS

612-108-0436
www.bajaturtle.com
Km 19 Mexico 19 at El Pescadero
Price: Moderate
Credit Cards: None
Special Features: Close to the beach

This secluded six-room hotel is located 10 minutes south of Todos Santos. It overlooks vast orchard fields and is a short walk away from San Pedrito Point, one of the most popular surfing spots in Baja. The rooms are tastefully decorated with a blend of traditional and modern décor and are come with a king-size, queen-size, or two twin beds. The grounds provide views of both the mountains and the ocean. Rates: start at $95–110 from June through September, at $115–130 from October through May, and at $135–150 during Easter week and between December 15 through January 7.

LAS PALMAS TROPICALES

www.tropicalcasitas.com
Mexico 19, El Pescadero
Price: Inexpensive to Moderate
Credit Cards: None
Special Features: Close to the beach and sea turtle preserve

This hotel offers four secluded beachfront casitas overlooking San Pedrito Point, a sea turtle preserve and one of Baja's most famous surf spots. Getting to the beach from this hotel requires walking out your front door. The casitas are each individually decorated with a Mexican desert décor. Three have one bedroom, and one is a two-bedroom unit; all bedrooms are furnished with a queen-size bed. Rates: $75–140 depending on the casita.

TODOS SANTOS INN

612-145-0040
www.todossantosinn.com
Calle Legasi #33

Price: Moderate
Credit Cards: MC, V
Special Features: Garden patio pool, wine bar

Calling a hotel the most charming in Todos Santos is really saying something because there are several beautiful hotels here. However, it would be hard to beat the luxurious elegance offered at the Todos Santos Inn. A converted 19th-century sugar baron's hacienda, from the outside this hotel is a squat brick building that is only interesting because it looks so old. But this changes once you step inside the well-maintained courtyard with its brick arches and stone fountain. Follow the stone walkway down to the lush garden area, and you'll find a beautiful pool and the La Popa Wine Bar. This is also the setting for the daily colonial breakfast. The rooms are furnished with a large net-draped bed and heavy antique furniture. For extra-secluded comfort, check out the garden suites located down by the pool. Throughout, this hotel evokes the feel of colonial Mexico, a place with lots of history. This ambience is completed by the bullet holes found in the faded frescos of the lobby. Rates: $125 for terrace rooms ($165 December 20 through January 6). Junior suites and garden suites are more expensive.

RV Parks

EL LITRO TRAILER PARK
612-125-0121
Calle Olachea at Mexico 19, Todos Santos

These facilities offer RV spaces with electricity, water, and sewer along with flush toilets and hot showers. There are also tent spaces available with lots of shade. Rates: $15 per night for RVs and $4 for tents. First come, first serve. Guards are on duty 24 hours a day.

LOS CERRITOS RV PARK
Km 64 Mexico 19, Todos Santos

This is an old worn-down government campground located on one of the best beaches in the area. Facilities are only slightly primitive, with flush toilets, full hookups, and cold-water showers. Getting to the site is no meager feat, either. It is 1 mile down a narrow dirt road with exposed stones and potholes, and should be taken slowly. However, it is steps away from miles of wide-open beaches. Rates: $4–5 per night.

RESTAURANTS

Although the variety of food is limited in Todos Santos, the town has several good choices. The vast majority of food purveyors understandably offer Mexican food with plenty of seafood items on the menu. Eateries come in the form of street-side vendors, casual establishments, and elegant sit-down dining. For a change of pace, there are a couple of Italian restaurants in town—and, of course, there is always Shut Up Frank's, a beach-style sports bar and grill located at the west end of town.

CAFÉ SANTA FE
612-145-0340
Calle Centenario #4
Open: Wed.–Mon. noon–9 PM
Price: Expensive
Cuisine: Italian
Serving: L, D

This fine-dining restaurant features a full bar and elegant Italian dishes made with fresh seafood, organic vegetables, and homemade pastas. Meals are served in a lush courtyard setting. Closed parts of September and October.

FONDA EL ZAGUÁN
612-131-6769
Juarez between Topete and Hidalgo
Open: Mon.–Sat. 11:30 AM–9 PM
Price: Moderate
Cuisine: Vegetarian and Seafood
Serving: L, D

Located just east of the historic district, this Mexican restaurant serves delicious vegetarian and seafood specialties.

LOS ADOBES DE TODOS SANTOS
612-145-0203
Calle Hidalgo between Juárez and Militar
Open: Mon.–Sat. 8:30 am–9 pm; Sun. 8:30 am–5 pm
Price: Expensive
Cuisine: Mexican
Serving: B, L, D

This elegant restaurant located in an unassuming 100-year-old adobe building on the north side of town and is a gourmet take on traditional Mexican dishes. Meals are served on a shaded open-air patio that runs up against a desert garden. On the other end of the garden is a spa offering a variety of treatments.

PANCHO BANANO
612-145-0885
Hidalgo #11 between Juárez and Militar
Open: Daily 7 AM–9 PM
Price: Moderate
Cuisine: Mexican
Serving: B, L, D

Across the street from Los Adobes is Pancho Banano, and the contrast couldn't be more startling. This restaurant's owner can sometimes be seen standing out front drumming up business, declaring to the occasional passerby that "¡Pancho Banano es muy rico!" This down-to-earth restaurant serves standard Mexican fare and fresh-fruit drinks. Meals are served on plastic tables on a concrete patio facing the street. This establishment also doubles as a cybercafé, with several computers available for a nominal fee.

RESTAURANT LAS FUENTES
612-145-0257
Degollado and Militar
Open: Daily 7:30 AM–10 PM
Price: Moderate

Cuisine: International
Serving: B, L, D

A large menu of seafood and continental specialties are offered here as well as a full bar. Besides the usual menu items of fish, shrimp, and lobster, there are also such items as hamburgers and sandwiches, just in case you have grown tired of Mexican food. Meals are served on an attractive outdoor *palapa* patio. The rustic feel of the place is just reflects the ambience of Todos Santos perfectly.

SHUT UP FRANK'S
612-145-0707
Degollado and Rangel
Open: Mon.–Sat. 10 AM–10 PM;
Sun. 10 AM–8 PM

Artwork in Los Adobes de Todos Santos Restaurant.

Price: Moderate
Cuisine: Mexican and American
Serving: L, D

This sports bar and surf restaurant combines American flavor with Baja style. It is located a bit off the center of town, though if you are arriving by bus, this is one of the first restaurants you will see upon stepping off the bus. The menu includes steaks, burgers, giant burritos, and several vegetarian offerings. Come for the food and stay for the drinks. Show up for happy hour Monday through Friday 4 PM to 6 PM.

TEQUILA SUNRISE
612-145-0073
Benito Juárez across from Hotel California
Open: Daily 10 AM–9 PM

Price: Moderate
Cuisine: Mexican
Serving: L, D

Located just across the street from the Hotel California, this Mexican restaurant has a surfing and classic-rock theme. Sitting here among the pictures of Don Henley and Glen Frey, one gets the feeling that the restaurant staff would rather hang themselves than listen to *Witchy Woman* one more time. That said, this is a fun place with friendly service, good food, and a great chicken chimichanga. The walls are wall papered with dollar bills and the signatures of previous patrons. Be sure to try a margarita on the rocks, made with fresh squeezed limes.

NEARBY BEACHES

Todos Santos is located on a hill just inland from the Pacific Ocean. Although some beautiful beaches lie within a not-unmanageable walking distance, these beaches are not safe for swimming—though they are very good for strolling, whale watching, skim boarding, fishing, and other activities that don't involve you exposing yourself to heavy shore breaks and dangerous rip currents. Farther south along the coast, there are miles of beautiful white-sand beaches that are great for swimming, surfing, and just playing in the water. These beaches are accessible through rugged, unmarked dirt roads. Still, keep in mind that the Pacific Ocean can always be a dangerous place to swim, and there are no lifeguards around to save you if you get in trouble. Rip currents occur almost everywhere along this coast, and people drown in these waters.

TOWN BEACHES

You can access beaches within 20 minutes' walking distance from downtown Todos Santos. Heading northwest down Topete out of the historic district and down through a palm valley will bring you to La Cachora, a wide beach that is great for a stroll or watching the sun set. Farther down you will come to La Poza, a beautiful beach that has a freshwater lagoon inhabited by a number of birds. Neither of these beaches is ideal for swimming because of a heavy shore break and a strong undertow and rip tides.

Punta Lobos

This beach access road is at marker Km 54 on Mexico 19. The dirt road is clearly signed, and is the beach is about 2.5 km (about 1.5 miles) down the road. Punta Lobos is also sometimes referred to as Fisherman's Beach because local fishermen launch their *pangas* from this beach every morning and return in the afternoon with their catch. It's interesting to watch them negotiate the waves. If you are interested in going out with these men, you can often arrange it with them, though that requires a certain proficiency in Spanish. This beach is also a decent place to swim, but you should do so with caution, and keep in mind that there are no lifeguards to save you if you get into trouble.

Las Palmas (San Pedro)
This small stretch of beach is located down a dirt access road that's about 2.6 km from Km 57 on Mexico 19, across from the SAHR experimental station. It is secluded and surrounded by a palm grove with a freshwater lagoon. Las Palmas is good for swimming and body surfing, but you should do so with caution. Access to the beach is through private property, and the gates are open only between 6 AM and 9 PM; camping is not permitted. If you drive here, be aware that car break-ins have been reported at Palm Beach, so leave your valuables back at your hotel!

San Pedrito
Situated 3.1 km down a dirt road from Km 59 on Mexico 19, this beach has long been a favorite spot among surfers. The waves get pretty formidable here, and the area is not suitable for beginning surfers. A popular RV and camping park that was located here was recently sold to a developer with plans to build a resort hotel, so camping is no longer permitted, though day visits are.

Los Cerritos
Another popular camping and surfing spot, this beach is about 8 miles south of Todos Santos, off Mexico 19 at Km 64. The turnoff is easy to miss, so watch for the markers, and

Los Cerritos Beach.

follow the rocky dirt road 2.6 km down to the ocean. Despite its seclusion, the dirt parking area will likely be packed with RVs and tents. Set back from the beach there is even a *palapa* surf shop renting boards, though you would not describe this pristine crescent-shaped beach as crowded. The parking area opens onto miles of open sand.

SHOPPING

Todos Santos is Baja's art center, and as such, Benito Juárez and the streets of the historic district are some of the most interesting in Baja. Aside from fine art you'll find handmade textiles, surf shops, and *artesenía* from around Mexico and Latin America.

Cactus Folk Art (612-145-0771; Calle Juárez across from Hotel California, Todos Santos) This shop offers a variety of arts, crafts, and jewelry, including interesting pieces such as lamps and vases made of leather over clay with metal inlays.

Charles Stewart Gallery & Studio (612-145-0265; www.charlescstewart.com; Centenario and Obregón, Todos Santos) Charles Stewart was the pioneer who established Todos Santos as an artist's colony. This gallery located in the artist's refurbished home sells his oil and watercolor paintings.

Shopping in Todos Santos.

Curios Tony (612-145-0356; Juárez e/ Morelos and Zaragoza, Todos Santos) This shop has a good selection of Mexican arts and crafts, such as Talavera pottery from Puebla and *artesenía* from Oaxaca.

El Tecolote Libros (612-145-0295; Benito Juárez and Hidalgo, Todos Santos) An extensive selection of new and used books, including hard-to-find books in English.

Ezra Katz Fine Art Gallery (612-137-3473; Benito Juárez and Hidalgo, Todos Santos) Located next to the bookstore, this gallery carries works by a variety of artists.

Galería de Todos Santos (612-145-0500; www.galeriadetodossantos.com; Topete and Legaspi, Todos Santos) This gallery features several beautifully intimate pieces by numerous artists.

Galería Wall (612-145-0527; www.catherinewallart.com; Benito Juárez #4, Todos Santos) Pieces by artist Catherine Wall. Much of her art is inspired by Mexican culture and life in Baja California.

Jill Logan Galería (612-145-0151; www.jilllogan.com; Benito Juárez and Morelos, Todos Santos) Located in an attractively gated building, this gallery handles the diverse works of artist Jill Logan.

La Galera (612-145-0215; Obregón e/ Juárez and Centenario, Todos Santos) This shop offers a wide variety of custom-designed jewelry and home furnishings.

Los Cerritos Surf Shop (612-137-7343; Rangel and Degollado, Todos Santos) Rent surfboards and other gear here. They also offer surfing lessons and a variety of tours. A second shop is right off Playa Los Cerritos.

Mangos (612-145-0451; Calle Centenario e/ Topete and Obregón, Todos Santos) This shop offers a wide variety of *artesenía* products, including Mexican folk art, wood carvings, Talavera pottery, and Guatemalan textiles.

Los Cerritos Surf Shop at Los Cerritos Beach.

Events

February

TODOS SANTOS ART FESTIVAL
This weeklong festival showcases local artists, musicians, and craftsmen. Shows include Spanish guitar, classical music, films, and folk dancing as well as lectures and conferences on sea turtle conservation. For more information: www.todos santos-baja.com/todos-santos/art/art -festival.htm.

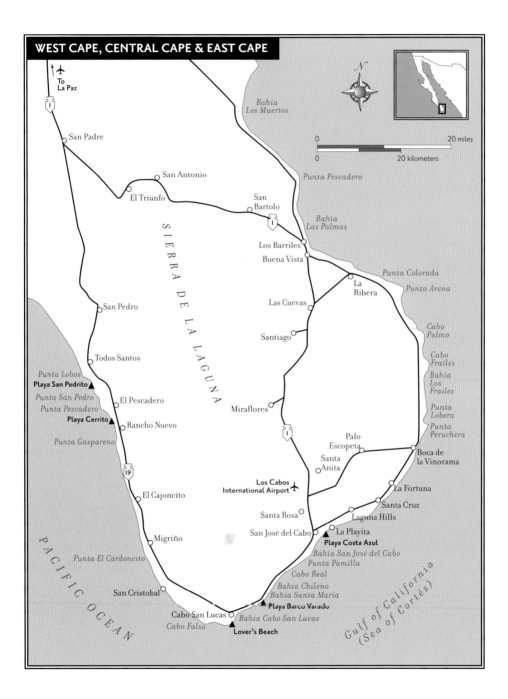

WEST CAPE, CENTRAL CAPE & EAST CAPE

To
La Paz

San Padre

San Antonio

El Triunfo

San Bartolo

San Pedro

Todos Santos

Punta Lobos
Playa San Pedrito
Punta San Pedro
Punta Pescadero
Playa Cerrito

El Pescadero

Rancho Nuevo

Punta Gaspareno

El Cajoncito

Migriño

Punta El Cardoncito

San Cristobal

Cabo San Lucas
Cabo Falso
Lover's Beach

SIERRA DE LA LAGUNA

Bahía
Los Muertos

Punta Pescadero

Bahía
Las Palmas

Los Barriles

Buena Vista

La Ribera

Las Cuevas

Santiago

Miraflores

Palo
Escopeta
Santa
Anita

Los Cabos
International Airport

Santa Rosa

San José del Cabo

La Playita
Playa Costa Azul

Bahía San José del Cabo
Punta Pamilla
Cabo Real
Bahía Chileno
Bahía Santa Maria
Playa Barco Varado
Bahía Cabo San Lucas

Punta Colorada
Punta Arena

Cabo
Pulmo

Cabo
Frailes
Bahía
Los
Frailes

Punta
Lobera
Punta
Peruchera

Boca de
la Vinorama

La Fortuna

Santa Cruz
Laguna Hills

PACIFIC OCEAN

Gulf of California
(Sea of Cortés)

N

0   20 miles
0   20 kilometers

West Cape

Despite the presence of Mexico 19—a well-maintained paved road that runs along the coast from Todos Santos all the way to Cabo San Lucas—the West Cape is by far the least developed area of the cape. The eastern side is dotted with small towns along the coastal dirt road, and several centuries-old villages lie along Mexico 1, which passes through the Central Cape. The western side is pounded by the tumultuous Pacific waves, and little is to be found here except turtle nesting grounds, a few small hotels, and a couple of campsites. However, this dearth of settled population may actually be what makes this area attractive to developers. After all, with a new resort going in at Playa San Pedrito in the north and the new Sunset Beach Pueblo Bonito timeshare facility towering near Cabo Falso in the south, the cape's Pacific coast seems to be teetering on development. Movements are gathering—particularly in Todos Santos—to resist such development and keep the beaches pristine and accessible to those willing to give a little in order to experience them.

Cabo Falso

About 2 miles west of Cabo San Lucas you'll come upon Cabo Falso, a wide strip of beach that is a protected nesting ground for sea turtles. Because of this, visitors aren't permitted within 165 feet of the surf. However, the nearby dunes have become a popular spot for adventure tourists on ATVs. In the hills above the beach is the El Faro Viejo lighthouse. Now abandoned, this lighthouse signaled ships off the coast of Cabo from 1895 until 1961. Not much of it remains, but it does provide spectacular views of the ocean, which makes it a popular ATV or horseback-tour destination.

Playa Migriño

Up over the Sierra de la Laguna foothills, at the turnoff at Km 94 on Mexico 19, you will come upon Playa Migriño. In the winter this is a popular surfing and camping beach, though the water here can be dangerous.

Playa Migriño.

La Candelaria

Up in the rugged foothills of the Sierra de la Laguna Mountains north of Cabo San Lucas is the small Indian pueblo of La Candelaria. This village is home to less than 100 inhabitants, but a local school draws children from nearby environs. This enigmatic village is known for its *curanderas* and its clay pottery. *Curanderas* are healers who purportedly wield "white magic," but in reality they've merely gained knowledge about medicinal herbs, which is probably necessary for living in such a remote area. The town's famous clay pottery is made from earth dug up from the local hillsides. This "ranchware" is popular among foreign collectors.

To get to La Candelaria, you have to take a dirt road that goes due north from Mexico 19 near Playa Migriño. This unsigned turnoff is less than a half mile north of the main Playa Migriño turnoff. The road is suitable only for 4WD vehicles and can be treacherous after it rains.

Central Cape

One irony of Todos Santos's ascendance as a tourist destination is that the towns of the central cape had a head start of more than a decade when the Transpeninsular Highway was completed in the early 1970s. Each of these towns has a unique history and definite charm that is genuinely Mexican. However, each of them has, for the most part, gone undiscovered while the rest of the cape's locations—accessible by paved roads—have boomed. This is fortunate for those looking for an authentic experience. And as places like Todos Santos become more "boutique-ized" with new resorts going up on nearby beaches, the towns of the Central Cape will surely have their day in the sun.

Desert blooms along the central cape.

Miraflores

Miraflores is a quaint, centuries-old village located approximately 25 miles north of San José del Cabo off Mexico 1 and about halfway to the coastal village of Los Barriles. This small ranching and farming community is well known for producing quality leatherwork, so if you're interested in purchasing leather goods such as saddles, this is the place for you. Another reason for making the short drive to Miraflores is the natural hot springs located just outside of town. This quiet, tranquil area is a good place to spend a half day relaxing in the lush hills and taking in a way of life that seems to belong to another era. For off-roaders, a popular dirt trail goes north from Miraflores through the village of Agua Caliente and on to Santiago, where it reconnects with the Transpeninsular Highway.

Santiago

About a 30-minute drive up the highway from San José, Santiago is the perfect place to get away from loud American tourists. This is the largest town on the Central Cape, with a population of nearly 3,000. Founded by an Italian missionary, Santiago is a colonial *puebla* that dates back more than 280 years. This authentic town sits on a hill a little more than a mile west of Mexico 1. It is known as a sleepy place, with fruit orchards, ranches, and, on the west side of town, the only zoo in Baja California Sur. It is also an important regional source for palm leaves used in making *palapa* roofs. Walking through Santiago's quiet streets, you won't help but be amazed that this place is in the same neighborhood as a tourist trap like Cabo San Lucas.

San Bartolo

San Bartolo is a picturesque tropical village of *palapa*-roofed homes in the hills 10 miles north of Los Barriles. This pleasant town owes its lushness to a spring-fed creek that runs along the nearby hills and provides San Bartolo with an abundant supply of fresh water. This is a great place to stop and buy avocados, mangoes, and homemade candy from the roadside stands.

San Antonio and El Trifuno

Located 20 miles north of San Bartolo, these two towns have plenty of history. Originally ranches were scattered through these hills before silver was discovered at the site of San Antonio in 1748, which soon became a minor mining town. The town's biggest distinction came in 1829, when Loreto was destroyed by a hurricane and San Antonio was briefly designated the capital of the Californias. However, the capital was transferred to La Paz the following year. Amazingly, San Antonio was once a city of 10,000. Today, the population stands at around a mere 800 residents. The unusual church, which dates to 1825, and the buildings that remain from the town's colorful past make for an interesting photo op to break the monotony of driving between La Paz and Los Cabos.

In 1862, gold and silver deposits were discovered 4.5 miles to the north, setting off a minor rush. Within 15 years, seven gold and silver mines had popped up around the new town of El Trifuno. The "triumph" for which El Trifuno was named lasted a little beyond the end of the last century. Then, in 1918, a hurricane flooded the mines, ending they heyday. In less than a decade, both towns were all but abandoned.

Today, El Trifuno is a town of only about 400 residents. Some of them are still involved in small-scale mining, though the local economy is now based on small-scale production of such wares as woven baskets that are sold to tourists.

East Cape

The East Cape retains the feel of what southern Baja California must have been like three decades ago, before developers turned Cabo San Lucas into a tourist Mecca. For the most part, much of this region is still only visited by off-roaders, yachtsmen, and deep-sea fishermen. More recently, other groups such as long-distance kayakers have begun to find adventures along Baja's East Cape. For adventurous travelers looking for a day trip, a graded dirt road that follows the coast out of San José del Cabo takes you along a series of small pueblos and secluded beach hotels. Keep in mind, though, that this road is in terrible shape, with certain stretches rutted and pocked with exposed rocks—and the seclusion that you set out to find can be a horrible burden should your vehicle break down. However, this treacherous stretch of road provides some of the most spectacular vistas to be found in all of Baja. The farther you dare to go, the more removed you become from civilization, and the closer you get to an isolated desert paradise. The road hits pavement between Punta arena and La Ribara and again about 10 miles north near Buena Vista, where it hooks up with Mexico 1. This region may represent the near future for the East Cape because here is where you will find new development and an influx of expatriate Americans. If and when this road along the East Cape shore is ever paved, this gorgeous stretch will surely see development. For now, it offers a view of what southern Baja used to be.

Cabo Pulmo

Since 1993 Cabo Pulmo Bay, including Cabo Frailes Bay, has been part of a marine preserve that is home to more than 350 different species of aquatic life. It is also the home to the only living reef in the Sea of Cortés—a fact that draws divers from around the world and

The East Cape draws deep-sea fishermen from all over the world.   Jason MacBeth

A fisherman show off the day's catch.   Jason MacBeth

diving tour companies from Los Cabos and La Paz. This environment is extremely sensitive, and care should be taken not to damage the reef in any way while visiting.

The bay acts as a natural shield to shelter the coral from the elements, allowing them to grow in abundance. The combination of clear water and a rich ecosystem results in one of the premier locations on the cape for scuba diving and snorkeling. Kayakers also come through for the opportunity for close contact with sea lions as well as great whale watching from January through March.

Los Barriles and Buena Vista

About an hour out of Cabo San Lucas along Mexico 1, the road skirts the Sea of Cortés before turning back inland until it reaches La Paz. This is where you will find the twin villages of Los Barriles and Buena Vista. This secluded stretch of beach currently seems to be in the process of becoming a booming beach town. Houses are popping up along the beach, and the word is out that this is one of the premier big-game fishing spots in the world. The waters here team with marlin, wahoo, dorado, and yellowfin tuna. Despite the development, the area retains the laid-back pace that made Baja famous in the first place. The calm, clear turquoise water here is a comfortable 70 to 80 degrees as is the air temperature during winter months, though nights do tend to be cool.

HOTEL PLAYA DEL SOL
877-777-8862 (U.S.)
Calle de la Playa, Los Barriles
Price: Inexpensive

Credit Cards: MC, V
Special Features: Pet friendly, swimming pool, two bars

This hotel is located right on Bahia Las Palmas and offers 26 air-conditioned rooms at very reasonable rates—amenities include three meals a day, and pets are permitted. Most of the hotel staff speaks English and are very helpful. The hotel features a bar inside and one next to a freshwater swimming pool that has a beautiful view of the sea. Rates: start at $65.

LOS BARRILES HOTEL
624-141-0024
www.losbarrileshotel.com
Calle de la Playa, Los Barriles
Price: Inexpensive
Credit Cards: MC, V
Special Features: Patio pool, RV hookups

This hotel has 20 rooms, each with two queen-size beds and a large bathroom. The rooms are attractively appointed and situated around a patio pool area. Internet access is available on the premises. The hotel also offers storage for boats and RVs. Rates: $49 for a room with one bed and $59 for a room with two beds.

PALMAS DE CORTEZ HOTEL
624-141-0050 or 877-777-8862 (U.S.)
Calle de la Playa, Los Barriles
Price: Inexpensive
Credit Cards: MC, V
Special Features: Located on the beach

This hotel is something of an unexpected oasis on the East Cape. Situated right on a beautiful beach, it has amazing views of the sea. It also has an impressive pool area that faces the Sea of Cortés. The hotel offers a number of condos and suites in addition to 28 regular rooms. Accommodations include three meals a day. Rates: $75 for a single room with one person and $120 for a double room, double occupancy.

MARTÍN VERDUGO'S RESORT AND RV PARK
624-141-0054
www.verdugosbeachresort.com
Playa Bahía de Palmas, 1 mile north of Los Barriles
Price: Inexpensive
Credit Cards: MC, V
Special Features: Laundry facilities, rooftop garden restaurant, cocktail lounge, pool

This attractive hotel and RV park is located right on the water and has 72 lots with full hookups as well as 25 tent sites, a few of which have electricity and water. The property has flush toilets, laundry facilities, and hot showers. If you prefer, stay in one of the 20 modern, air-conditioned rooms—some with kitchenettes. For diversion, there is a roof garden restaurant and cocktail lounge as well as a pool, a *palapa* bar, and steel mats for launching boats over the sand.

6

La Paz

On the surface, La Paz isn't much of a tourist town. After all, it doesn't have sprawling golf courses or resort-lined beaches. On first glance, it's more of a bustling port city with a few college kids mixed in and a bit of a graffiti problem. Located on a large bay on the Sea of Cortés, La Paz is the capital of Baja California Sur, and with a population of approximately 250,000, it's also the largest city in the state. Having such a population base, La Paz has trappings that are rare elsewhere in Baja, such as a theater, a number of museums, and a university—not to mention the best health care on the peninsula.

Even as the tourism industry in Baja has boomed over the last 30 years, La Paz has remained obscure to most visitors. For a brief period in the 1960s, this city seemed to be on the cusp of becoming the latest big resort destination south of the border. At the time, Puerto Vallarta and Acapulco were Mexico's chic tourist towns, bustling with sunbathers and high-rise hotels crowding the shoreline. However, La Paz's reputation for world-class sport fishing and tranquil coves was well known. Hollywood stars Bing Crosby and Desi Arnaz owned homes nearby, and John Wayne flew in regularly with friends for fishing trips. Yet when the Mexican government set about developing tourist centers in the 1970s, La Paz was passed over for Cabo San Lucas, a backwater town 90 miles to the south. This was perhaps because La Paz was already a busy industrial center: The town would likely have had a hard time developing a true resort identity in the midst of existing characteristics of local industry, such as the smoke-bellowing PEMEX refinery on the edge of town and the cargo ships that seem to be perennially docked in port. Although La Paz may not provide the prefabricated, easily accessible tourist experience of Los Cabos, it offers breathtaking beauty combined with the authentic feel of a provincial Mexican town to visitors willing to put forth the effort of exploration.

General Information

EMERGENCIES
Dial 066
Both public and private hospitals handle emergencies for foreigners. You'll need to pay for services when you're discharged, so get a receipt in case you want to collect on your insurance. Look in the phone book for specialists.

POLICE
612-122-6610
Boulevard Luis Donaldo Colosio Murrieta and Avenida Álvarez Rico

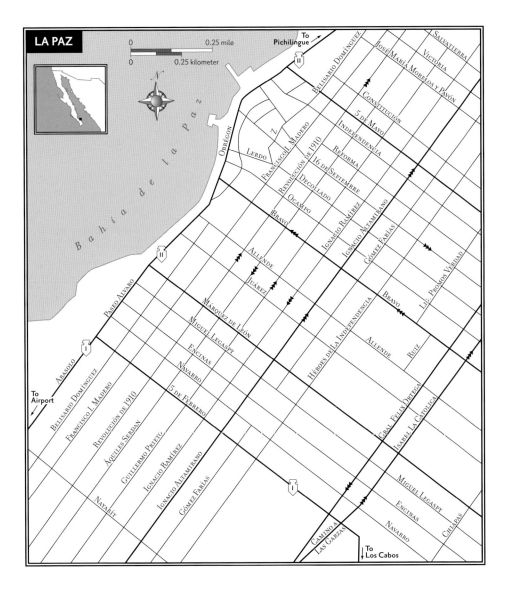

FIRE DEPARTMENT
612-122-0054
Corner of Isabel la Católica and Melitón Abáñez

POST OFFICE
Corner of Revolución and Constitución

TOURIST OFFICE
612-122-0199
Paseo Álvaro Obregón between Calle 5 de Mayo and Independecia

ACCOMMODATIONS

La Paz offers a wide variety of accommodations, from multibed hostels to secluded luxury resorts. For a beach town, however, it has a dearth of beachfront hotels. Only La Concha Beach Resort has beach access. There has been discussion in recent years of building a resort at Playa Balandra, though this has been fiercely opposed by local residents and environmental groups. Certainly a hotel at that location would take a lot away from what makes it special. Most of the hotels in La Paz are located along or near the *malecón*. What these hotels lack in beach access, they gain in convenience to restaurants and bars.

EL ÁNGEL AZUL

612-125-5130
www.elangelazul.com
Independencia #518
Price: Inexpensive
Credit Cards: MC, V
Special Features: Historic monument, wireless Internet, night guard.

Once the town's courthouse, this building situated in the heart of La Paz is considered a historic monument by the INAH (National Institution of Anthropology and History). Today, it is a tastefully renovated hacienda-style bed & breakfast hotel with a beautiful courtyard garden. The air-conditioned rooms, all with private baths, are decorated in a colorful Mexican décor. Three historical rooms are furnished with one queen-size bed and one single, while the hotel's six standard rooms are furnished with a double bed plus a single. The mini suite can accommodate up to five guests, as it is furnished with four beds, one of them queen-size. The main suite on the second floor is furnished with a queen-size bed. This hotel accepts only children older than age 12 and no pets. Breakfast is served daily, and a bar is available to guests. This is a great hotel for a relaxing stay as it is a quiet place despite its convenient downtown location. Rates: start at $90–100 for a standard room, double occupancy.

LOS ARCOS HOTEL

612-122-2744 or 949-450-9000 (U.S.)
www.losarcos.com
Paseo Álvaro Obregón 498
Price: Inexpensive to Moderate
Credit Cards: MC, V
Special Features: On-site masseuse, two swimming pools, sauna

This is one of the oldest and most popular hotels in La Paz. Along the *malecón*, this distinctive hotel is hard to miss with its 22 bay-view rooms jutting toward the street. It has 93 standard rooms along with 15 suites and 24 bungalow cabanas. Most of the rooms are a bit narrow and even a little cramped, though the suites do have plenty of space. There are also two pools on the property, one of which is in a private garden set aside for the cabanas. The on-site Bermejo Restaurant serves breakfast, lunch, and dinner. Additionally, a coffee shop is open for breakfast. The Los Pelicanos Bar offers live entertainment and nice sunset views. This hotel also has two conference rooms suitable for banquets or wedding receptions. Rates: $90–115.

ARAIZA INN PALMIRA

612-121-6200 or 877-727-2492 (U.S.)
www.araizainn.com.mx
Boulevard Alberto Aramburo s/n
Price: Inexpensive
Credit Cards: MC, V, AE
Special Features: Tennis court, gym, swimming pool, wireless Internet

This hotel offers five different accommodation packages, from standard rooms with two double beds to the master suite equipped with a queen-size bed in a separate bedroom, a 27-inch TV, and a refrigerator. The hotel also has a cafeteria that serves a buffet breakfast lunch and dinner as well as room service. The El Rollo Disco Bar is also located on the premises, complete with colorful lights and a giant-screen TV. If you're in the mood to check out the city, the hotel provides scheduled transportation to downtown La Paz. Rates: start at around $90 for a standard room, double occupancy.

LA CASA MEXICANA INN

612-125-2748
www.casamex.com
Calle Bravo 106
Price: Inexpensive
Credit Cards: MC, V (through PayPal)
Special Features: Deluxe continental breakfast, wireless Internet

A Spanish art deco inn located one block from the Sea of Cortés in downtown La Paz, this small hotel features five elaborately decorated rooms in a beautiful white stucco cottage. Each room has its own unique attributes, ranging from El Jardin, a secluded room decorated with vibrant Guatemalan fabrics set off a garden courtyard, to Vista Paz, an open suite decorated almost entirely in white with a private terrace and a view of the sea. Each room is air-conditioned and has wireless Internet access. A deluxe continental breakfast is included with the price of your stay and each room has a refrigerator in case you want to sneak up an extra helping for later. $75–105 depending on the room.

CLUB EL MORO

612-122-4084
www.clubelmoro.com
Km 2 Carretera a Pichilingue
Price: Inexpensive to Moderate
Credit Cards: MC, V
Special Features: Pool, satellite TV, Jacuzzi

This hotel features striking white Moorish architecture in a setting of landscaped gardens. Six different accommodation options are available, from a standard room with a king- or queen-size bed to a two-bedroom suite with queen-size beds. All rooms are equipped with air conditioning, satellite TV, and a private terrace. The Café Gourmet Restaurant serves a variety of breakfast specials as well as delicatessen sandwiches for lunch. The grounds also include a Jacuzzi, pool, and a *palapa* bar. Located just over a mile out of town, the hotel is slightly set apart from the action. However, buses pass on a regular basis during daylight hours. Rates: $80 for a standard room with one queen- or king-size bed.

CLUB HOTEL CANTAMAR SPORTS LODGE

612-122-1826
www.clubcantamar.com
Paseo Álvaro Obregón 1665
Price: Inexpensive
Credit Cards: MC, V
Special Features: Specializes in diving and other water sports, satellite TV

This hotel and diving facility is located near the ferry terminal at Bahía Pichilingue north of town. The four-story lodge has 35 standard rooms, four suites, and a four-unit apartment complex. These apartments are two bedroom, two bath with kitchenettes and private balcony. All rooms have a tasteful desert-themed décor with Mexican-tile floors, rustic furniture, and satellite TV. Other amenities include a swimming pool with a swim-up bar and a view of the sea, a dockside restaurant, and a 35-slip marina. The lodge offers diving packages for stays of 3 to 10 nights and includes lunch and transportation to and from the airport. Rates: $85 for a standard room, double occupancy.

LA CONCHA BEACH RESORT AND CONDOS

612-121-6161 or 800-999-2252 (U.S.)
www.laconcha.com
Carretera a Pichelingue Km 5

Price: Inexpensive
Credit Cards: MC, V, AE
Special Features: Swimming pool, Jacuzzi, sports bar, gift shop

This hotel is located right on Caimancito Beach 10 minutes from downtown La Paz. With 92 rooms and a slew of amenities, this old beauty does show its age a bit with missing roof tiles here and there in the hallway and rooms that are slightly less than roomy. However, the staff seems to constantly be doing upkeep, and it is a good option for travelers with kids on a family vacation as well as couples on a romantic retreat. The air-conditioned rooms have double or king-size beds and a small private balcony, the poolside bar is great for kicking back, and the palm-shaded patio has easy access to a beach with calm water. Caimancito Beach is usually clean and beautiful, though there are times during the spring when it is covered with algae. During these times the pool is especially appealing. You can also check out a kayak from the front desk to go exploring. The front desk can make reservations for island tours, but you would be much better served by going to Tecolote Beach and making reservations on your own so that you can choose the best tour company for you. The hotel restaurant is adequate but not great. Better food can be had in town for less money. Rates: start at $90 for a standard room, double occupancy.

GARDENIAS HOTEL

612-122-3088
www.hotelgardenias.com.mx
Aquiles Serdan #520
Price: Inexpensive
Credit Cards: MC, V
Special Features: Restaurant-bar, swimming pool

La Concha Beach Resort

This rustic hotel is located in the heart of La Paz, six blocks from the cathedral and three blocks from the *malecón.* It is an older hotel, which is apparent from the moment you step into the lobby whose stained-glass windows are definitely a throwback to seventies décor. However, it is clean and a good value for less than $50 a night. Each of the 56 air-conditioned rooms is furnished with two full-size beds and a color TV. Its restaurant-bar is open 7 AM to 10 PM, serving a nice menu of Mexican food. The hotel also has an old-style rectangular swimming pool with a diving board and plenty of on-site parking. Rates: start at around $55 for double occupancy.

HOTEL HACIENDA DEL CORTEZ
612-122-4011
Calle Nuevo Reforma
Price: Moderate
Credit Cards: MC, V
Special Features: Swimming pool, bar, laundry service, private parking

This hotel was previously the Posada de Engelbert, built by the pop crooner Engelbert Humperdinck in the 1950s as a resort for the Hollywood crowd. Today it is

A Few Words About Bathrooms and Toilet Paper

One of the less delicate issues that you will quickly face when you are traveling in Mexico, particularly in less tourist-centered areas, is the differences in bathroom etiquette. Toilet paper tends to clog most Mexican plumbing and septic systems to the point where it sometimes even requires digging up the pipes to clear them. Therefore, it is necessary to deposit used paper into the waste basket that is invariably placed next to the toilet. Many moderate and expensive hotels understand that this is more than a minor culture shock to their American guests and have gone to the trouble to equip rooms with plumbing that can handle toilet paper. However, you shouldn't assume this is the case unless there is a sign posted in the bathroom directing you to flush toilet paper. Part of the draw of small hotels in places like La Paz and Loreto is the ambience and many of these old buildings simply have not been brought up to the standards that you are used to. Quite often, there will be a sign explicitly asking you *not* to flush your used toilet paper. Also, women should never flush feminine products. You may find this unpleasant but it's better than dealing with a room with a stopped-up toilet.

There are other differences that you are likely to run into when you are out and about and discover that you need to use the public restroom. First of all, janitorial work is largely considered "women's work" in much of Mexico. Therefore, it is always possible that men may be surprised by an elderly female janitor entering the restroom while they are taking care of their business. If this happens, do your best to maintain a blasé attitude remembering that you're not doing anything she hasn't dealt with before. Also, you will likely find well-stocked facilities in high-end establishments that cater to tourists. However, you cannot always count on this. More often, public restrooms will cost a few pesos and an attendant will hand you a few squares of toilet paper when you enter. There are still other places where you will find no toilet paper at all and perhaps even the toilet seats will be missing. It's best to be well prepared, especially if you are traveling with children, who seem to have the habit of having to go at the worst possible moments. Be sure to pack a roll of toilet paper or—even better—a travel pack of baby wipes before you leave your hotel for the day. It is also a very good idea to carry a small bottle of disinfectant lotion, which you can pick up at any drugstore or pharmacy. This will go a long way toward making sure you don't pick up any of those nasty digestion problems that Mexico is so famous for.

a renovated colonial-style hotel located south of the *malecón* and the Marina de la Paz. It has 26 good-size, air-conditioned rooms decorated with heavy wooden furniture and Mexican fabrics. A garden courtyard features a swimming pool and a view of the Bay of La Paz. Adjacent to this is a restaurant that serves traditional Mexican fare. Rates: average $157.

HOTEL MARINA

612-121-6254 or 800-250-3186 (U.S.)
www.hotelmarina.com.mx
Km 2.5 Carretera a Pichilingue
Price: Moderate
Credit Cards: MC, V
Special Features: Swimming pool, Jacuzzi, tobacco store, wireless Internet, tennis court

This hotel is located on the west side of La Paz on the Marina Palmira, which is actually a bit of a walk to get to downtown. However, all rooms have a view of the marina, which provides nice sunsets, as well. The hotel's Dinghy Dock Restaurant is located in front of the marina and also offers views of the yachts and the sunset while you dine. The pool area has a bar and is shaded by palm trees in a very attractive setting. An on-site spa offers massages, body treatments, facials, depilation, pedicures, and manicures. Other amenities include a ballroom, laundry facilities, bike rental, and on-site parking. Rates: start at $105 for a standard room, double occupancy.

HOTEL MEDITERRANE

612-125-1195
www.hotelmed.com
Allende 36
Price: Inexpensive
Credit Cards: MC, V

The view of the sea from the Hotel Mediterrane.

Special Features: Rooftop terrace, restaurant

Where this intimate, Greek-themed family-owned hotel falls short with amenities, it makes up with character and convenience. This no-frills hotel may seem lacking to anyone looking for a four-star experience. The nine individually designed rooms are each named after a Greek island. While they are relatively small, each is equipped with a refrigerator and wireless Internet access. One room is located on the ground floor but most are upstairs, accessed by a narrow stairway, as is the rooftop terrace that overlooks the *malecón* (this hotel is not recommended for anyone in a wheelchair or who uses a walker). The hotel restaurant is not fancy but serves delicious Swiss and Italian cuisine at a modest price. Hotel Mediterrane is convenient walking distance from the center of the city of La Paz. Guests are offered the use of bicycles (and kayaks) at no additional charge. Those traveling by car must find parking on the street, which can be a bit of an inconvenience in this busy neighborhood. Rates: start at $75 for double occupancy.

HOTEL PERLA
612-122-0777 or 800-716-8799 (U.S.)
www.hotelperlabaja.com
Paseo Álvaro Obregón 1570
Price: Inexpensive
Credit Cards: None
Special Features: Swimming pool, Jacuzzi, kids' play structure, restaurant, nightclub

This hotel opened in 1940 and claims to be the oldest in La Paz. Conveniently located right in downtown La Paz, the hotel has 110 air-conditioned rooms, all equipped with cable TV and a minibar. Only about a quarter of the rooms have a view of the *malecón,* so be sure to request it when making reservations. The hotel's Terraza Restaurant opens for breakfast at 5 AM to accommodate guests heading out on fishing expeditions. It specialized in international cuisine but serves a buffet-style meal on some nights, consisting of seafood, chicken, and steak. A separate nightclub on the property called La Cabaña is open 9 PM to 3 AM. Rates: start at around $67 for double occupancy.

POSADA DE LAS FLORES
612-125-5871
www.posadadelasflores.com
Paseo Álvaro Obregón 440
Price: Moderate to Expensive
Credit Cards: MC, V, AE, D
Special Features: Convenient location, Mexican ambience

This boutique hotel is all about ambience. Located right across the street from the *malecón,* it offers great views of the sea as well as a romantic colonial Mexican atmosphere. The grounds have been carefully designed with stone fountains, colorful artwork, and plenty of handmade wooden furniture. All rooms are appointed in hacienda style with tile floors and Mexican furniture. They feature queen-size beds and colonial-style décor, with heavy wooden Mexican furniture, handwoven fabrics, and antiques. The tiled bathrooms include large marble showers and tubs. Rates: start at $150–180 for a standard room, double occupancy.

POSADA LUNA SOL
612-123-0559 or 800-355-7140 (U.S.)
www.posadalunasol.com
Topete 564
Price: Inexpensive
Credit Cards: MC, V
Special Features: Mexican ambience, views of the sea

This charming Mexican inn is located a short walking distance from the *malecón.* Decorated in Mexican colonial style with hand-painted tile murals, handwoven fabrics, and heavy Mexican furniture, the hotel has 11 uniquely decorated rooms, most of which provide a view of the sea. A *palapa* terrace is on the hotel's third floor, which provides a great place to relax and enjoy the sunset. Rates: start at $75 for a standard room, double occupancy.

RV Parks

AQUAMARINA RV PARK
Owners: Richard and Mary Lou Adcock
612-122-3761
Calle Nayarit 10, La Paz

This 5-acre RV park provides full hookups with plenty of water and electrical power, a swimming pool, and a boat ramp. It also offers large showers, a shaded terrace with tables and chairs, and a laundry room. Rates: $12–15 per night.

CASA BLANCA RV PARK
612-125-1142
Km 15 Mexico 1, La Paz

Facilities at the RV park include flush toilets, a lounge, and a grocery store. There is also a tennis court and swimming pool for recreation. Rates: $15–20 per night.

RESTAURANTS

Being a city of a quarter of a million people, La Paz offers a wide variety of cuisine. This is especially true along the *malecón*, where the city's largest concentration of restaurants is found. Unadventurous Americans can find several familiar fast-food joints here as well as an Applebee's that dominates its corner on Paseo Álvaro Obregón. However, you probably weren't attracted to La Paz for its familiar surroundings. And why get a fast-food burger when you can enjoy gourmet food for a fraction of the price of a similar meal in the United States? One of the great things to come out of the expansion of La Paz over the last decade is the emergence of some interesting and fine-dining establishments. Combine this with the fact that La Paz is not primarily a tourist town—which keeps prices scaled well below those at other tourist destinations. Travelers to La Paz will find a wealth of seafood obtained from the very waters that makes this place so beautiful. Additionally, you can dine on fine Sonoran beef, fresh chicken and pork, and vegetarian options. Furthermore, the city's wonderful atmosphere has drawn chefs from around the world, specializing in Italian, French, Asian, and other cuisines. This adds up to an abundance of great choices. The biggest problem is deciding which one to try next.

BISMARK II
612-122-4854
Degollado and Altamirano
Open: Daily 7 AM–10 PM
Price: Moderate
Cuisine: Steak and Seafood
Serving: B, L, D

This home-style restaurant has been a popular La Paz eatery for many years. It's a bit out of the way, but the generous portions and wide variety of dishes make it worth the trip. Seafood is the specialty here, starting with the fresh ceviche appetizer to fresh dorado or halibut and enormous grilled lobsters. Visa and MasterCard accepted.

BOUGAINVILLEA RESTAURANTE
612-122-7744
Malecón de Vista Coral 5
Open: Daily noon–11:30 PM
Price: Expensive
Cuisine: Steak and Seafood
Serving: L, D

Located on the west end of the *malecón* just behind Estella del Mar restaurant, Bougainvillea specializes in California cuisine in addition to steak and seafood dishes. The service is upscale, and the restaurant's location can't be beat. You can dine either in their hacienda-style dining room or the rear courtyard. Either way, this restaurant provides a romantic ambience for that special night out. The menu includes such items as baked red snapper in a tomato and basil salsa, T-bone steak served with a classic béarnaise sauce, and giant prawns marinated with a lime jalapeño sauce and sautéed with fresh ginger and mango. Live music is offered on some nights. Visa and MasterCard accepted.

CAFÉ CAPRI

612-123-3737
Malecón de Vista Coral, between Márquez de León and Topete
Open: Tue.–Sun. 7 AM–12:30 AM
Price: Inexpensive
Cuisine: International
Serving: L, D

This restaurant is situated on the north side of the *malecón* and boasts both a beautiful vista and a romantic atmosphere. On its international menu you will find crepes, pastas, salads, as well as an extensive list of drinks, and a variety of deserts. Patio dining is available, where you can catch a nice breeze and enjoy a light meal. Enjoy live music on Friday and Saturday nights.

CAFÉ EXQUISITO

612-128-5991
Paseo Álvaro Obregón e/ Tejada and Bañnuelos
Open: Mon.–Fri. 6:30 AM–11 PM; Sat.–Sun. 8 AM–midnight
Price: Inexpensive
Cuisine: International
Serving: B, L, D

If you're homesick for Starbucks, this is the place to come. You'll hardly know the difference, with its young baristas serving up Frappuccinos and pastries. They even have overpriced knickknacks to mull over while you wait for your order.

CAFFÉ GOURMET

612-122-6037
Esquerro and 16 de Septiembre
Open: Mon.–Sat. 8 AM–10 PM
Price: Inexpensive
Cuisine: International
Serving: B, L, D

This coffee shop is great place to come for dessert or to pick up a quick sandwich before heading out to the beach. The menu features a long list of light snacks and pastries. They also serve all types of coffee and espresso drinks, as well as Italian sodas.

CAFFÉ MILANO

612-125-9981
Calle Esquerro 15
Open: Mon.–Sat. 12:30 PM–11 PM
Price: Expensive
Cuisine: Italian
Serving: L, D

Authentic Italian cuisine is served in the comfort of a restored building that dates back more than a century. This fine-dining restaurant is located a block off the *malecón,* so it is near the city's nightlife. Meals are served in a large, elegant dining room with rough masonry walls and a vaulted ceiling. This is a great place to enjoy a meal with a date, as there is plenty of space and romantic lighting. The menu offers a wide range of wines to go with traditional favorites such as homemade sausages or fresh seafood tossed in fresh pastas. They also have a decent wine list. Reservations are recommended, particularly for large groups or on weekends.

CARLOS 'N CHARLIE'S

612-123-4547
Paseo Álvaro Obregón and 16 de Septiembre
Open: Daily noon–1 AM
Price: Moderate
Cuisine: International
Serving: L, D

This party-themed restaurant is brought to you by the same people who created Squid Roe and Señor Frog's. This restaurant provides a young crowd, a fun atmosphere, and a laid-back casual setting. And, oh yeah, they have food, too. The menu mostly features Mexican bar food, with such items as fajitas, quesadillas, and fish tacos. They also offer several steak dishes as well as a small selection of hamburgers. Decorated much like a TGI Friday's, there are musical instruments, automobile parts, and kitchen utensils hanging from the ceiling and waiters that double as entertainment guides. Be prepared to party when you're here, as guests are encouraged to cut loose among the comical skit performances, singing, and dancing on the chairs done by the staff. Although it feels a bit like a tourist trap, it's frequented by a good mix of tourists and locals.

THE DOCK CAFÉ
612-125-6626
Topete and Legaspi 3040, next to Marina de la Paz
Open: Daily 8 AM–10 PM
Price: Moderate
Cuisine: International
Serving: B, L, D

Casual and elegant at the same time, this small restaurant has street-side eating with a view of the marina. The extensive breakfast menu offers everything from chicken *chilaquiles* and ranchero eggs to French toast and bagels with cream cheese. The lunch and dinner menu is also quite extensive and heavy on the seafood. There are such diverse offerings as hamburgers and fish and chips as well as rib eye steak and fish fillet Veracruzano. There is occasionally live music in the evenings.

GULA
612-106-7001
Pueblo Marinero Local 43
Open: Tue.–Sun. 8 AM–10 PM
Price: Expensive
Cuisine: International
Serving: B, L, D

Gula, whose name means "gluttony" in Spanish, is located in the neighborhood of Pueblo Marinero about 3 miles north of downtown. It overlooks the marina, providing a wonderful sunset vista as you enjoy a meal at this fine-dining establishment. The restaurant's motto is, "This is where food becomes art," and the dishes are definitely presented that way with an amazing attention to detail. Additionally, the restaurant's chef has created some of the most interesting and elaborate dishes to be found in La Paz.

LA MAR Y PEÑA
612-122-9949
Calle 15 de Septiembre and Isabel la Católica
Open: Daily 9 AM–10 PM
Price: Moderate
Cuisine: Steak and Seafood
Serving: B, L, D

Located on a quiet street in downtown La Paz, this small casual-dining restaurant has a distinctly Mexican atmosphere. It is decorated with wooden furniture and white tablecloths, with air conditioning and ceiling fans to keep it bearable in the hot La Paz weather. The extensive menu is almost exclusively seafood dishes—and seafood is what this restaurant does well. From the ceviche to the Veracruz fish tacos to the lobster, seafood lovers are sure to find what they are looking for here. Visa and Master Card accepted.

EL PATRON BAR & GRILL
612- 165-5312
Márquez de León and Abosolo
Open: Daily 3 PM–12:30 AM
Price: Expensive
Cuisine: International
Serving: L, D

If you're looking for a distinctive meal in an elegant setting, this restaurant is probably a pretty good bet. Located at the south end of the *malecón*, this establishment has one of the finest waterfront views in La Paz. The best tables are outside on the patio, shaded by a *palapa* and several palm trees. The menu offers a wide range of interesting entrées with an international flair, including seafood, steak, and pork dishes, as well as lamb and veal. If you are in the mood for something a little more casual, they also serve great burgers made from 100% Angus beef. The bar has a good selection of wines and some of the finest margaritas and martinis in town.

LA PAZTA
612-125-1195
Allende 36
Open: Wed.–Mon. 7 AM–11 PM; Tue. 7 AM–3 PM
Price: Moderate
Cuisine: Swiss and Italian
Serving: B, L, D

This small restaurant is next to the Hotel Mediterrane, just off the *malecón*. Echoing the décor of that hotel, La Pazta is done up in striking Mediterranean white stucco with a black-and-white tiled floor. The menu serves mainly a mix of Swiss and Italian dishes, with pastas, pizzas, and fondues available. They also have a nice wine menu as well as real espresso drinks, a rarity in Baja. Breakfast offerings are sparse as it is mainly just a coffee bar at those hours.

PIZZA A PEZZI
Paseo Álvaro Obregón 1773
Open: Mon.–Sat. 6 PM–11:30 PM
Price: Inexpensive
Cuisine: Pizza
Serving: D

The Italian owners of this hole-in-the-wall pizza joint make the dough right in the restaurant. Standard pizza toppings are offered as well as some more interesting combos. There are a few tables inside as well as a few on the sidewalk out front. It seems to be a favorite with local college students.

EL QUINTO SOL
612-122-7274
Belisario Domínguez and Avenida Independencia
Open: Daily 7 AM–8 PM
Price: Inexpensive
Cuisine: Mexican and Vegetarian
Serving: B, L

Fruit salad isn't widely thought of as Mexican food, but it's a dish that has been perfected south of the border. This restaurant demonstrates this bit of trivia as well as other important but little-known staples of Mexican cuisine, such as fruit *licuados*, potato tacos, and *torta* sandwiches. This is also a well-stocked health-food store.

RESTAURANTE DRAGÓN
612-122-1372
16 de Septiembre and Esquerro
Open: Wed.–Mon. 1 PM–11 PM
Price: Moderate
Cuisine: Chinese
Serving: L, D

This is probably the most popular Chinese restaurant in La Paz. It's located in the heart of the city's small Chinatown, and while not particularly expensive, it's not a place to dine in shorts and a tank top. The menu is mainly made up of Cantonese dishes. You'll enjoy some of the best spicy shrimp you've ever had at a fraction of the price you're used to.

SEÑOR SUSHI
612-122-3425
Madero 1715
Open: Mon.–Sat. 2 PM–11:30 PM

Price: Moderate
Cuisine: Japanese
Serving: L, D

Fifty different types of sushi are featured at this sushi restaurant, which has a fun atmosphere. They are made with quality ingredients and fish fresh from the sea. There are also such Japanese specialties as tempura, *yakimeshi,* and *teppanyaki.* Free delivery is offered within the tourist corridor.

EL ZARAPE
612-122-2520
Avenida México 3450
Open: Daily 7:30 AM–midnight
Price: Moderate
Cuisine: Mexican
Serving: B, L, D

This brightly decorated restaurant provides the perfect ambience for a Mexican adventure. Come here to sample the tastes of Mexico, particularly on Saturday evenings when they feature a buffet dinner with choices from the country's heartland. The dining room is full of Mexican kitsch, with bright tablecloths and all manner of *artesenía* on the walls. Daily from 1 PM to 8 PM, they serve *cazueladas,* (traditional stews of all types, including vegetarian). This service is available in the restaurant or they will deliver it for between 10 and 300 guests. On Sunday evenings, the buffet offers choices from all over Mexico and an excellent breakfast buffet is offered Tuesday through Sunday.

BARS AND NIGHTLIFE

A great night in La Paz starts at a café at dinner and ends many hours later. After a great meal, fun-seeking travelers move along the *malecón* or sit in the bars that line it and enjoy the sunset over the Sea of Cortés. The bars and clubs of La Paz are conveniently located here and stay open late into the night.

CHATITO'S AND PLANCHA'S MARTINI BAR
612-128-7787
Paseo Álvaro Obregón at the corner of Lerdo de Tejada

Located upstairs in the Seven Crown Hotel, this bar tends to attract a younger crowd. Its terrace is a great place to watch the sunset. Open daily 7 PM to 2 AM.

LA CABAÑA
612-122-0777
Paseo Álvaro Obregón 1570

This nightclub located in the Hotel Perla features Latin rhythms, so come ready to dance. There is a $4 cover on the weekends. Open daily 7 PM to 2 AM.

TEQUILA'S BAR AND GRILL
612-121-5217
Ocampo 310 at the corner of Mutualisimo

Enjoy plenty of great appetizers such as nachos and ceviche as well as some great dinner entrées. Combine that with a fun atmosphere and a long list of tequilas, and you'd better be prepared to catch a cab back to the hotel. Open Monday through Saturday 8 PM to 3 AM.

LAS VARITAS
612-125-2025
Independencia and Belisario Domínguez

This is defiantly a nightclub for the Latin set, with Latin rock, ranchero, and salsa all being heard here. Open daily 9 PM to 3 AM, and there is a $5 cover charge.

Weather

La Paz has pleasant temperatures almost all year round. From December through March, average daily temperatures reach the high 70s whereas nightly lows average in the mid- to upper 50s. Temperatures climb into the high 80s in May and June, with nightly lows just lower to mid-60s. August and September are really the only uncomfortable months, as average daily highs creep into the mid- to upper 90s and nightly "lows" stay in the mid-70s. These two months are also considered the rainy season as it's the only time of year when precipitation gets much above an inch. Water temperatures tend to stay in the mid-60s from December through June and climb into the mid-80s from August through October.

Beaches

La Paz is an old working city that grew up around agriculture and industry rather than being designed for recreation and tourism. Consequently, the best beaches (and there are some good ones) are not really near town. This is not to say that the beaches near town aren't worth a visit. In recent years La Paz has worked to improve the quality of the beaches located near the *malecón* with daily cleaning crews, imported sand, and the construction of *palapas* to sit under. Unfortunately, the large cove where the city is located can create strong tidal currents, so most tourists choose to make the short drive—either in a rental car, bus, or taxi—to the outlying beaches north of town.

Get to the beach early to get a choice spot.

Pichilingue Beach.

El Coromuel
The first beach north of town, it's located within the harbor of La Paz and is therefore very convenient. Large *palapas* are available as are food and refreshment stands.

Caimancito
This beach is directly in front of La Concha Beach Resort near km 5 on Mexico 1. The best of La Paz's city beaches, it's lined with shade-providing *palapas*, and a rock reef within swimming distance offers decent snorkeling despite being so close to the city.

Tesoro
This calm beach situated 8 miles out of town along the Pichilingue road is a good beach for families and small groups. There is a small seafood restaurant here with plenty of *palapas* and moderate prices. If you're feeling active, you can also rent kayaks here.

Pichilingue
This beach is located in a tiny cove. A restaurant with a large patio area facing the beach is located right on the beach (612-122-4565). The beach offers a nice view of the ferry port and *malecón.* Three good-sized *palapas* offer shade, and on the north end of the beach, an abandoned *palapa* restaurant can be used as a shady area for a large group. Camping is allowed at this beach, which has clean bathrooms with flush toilets. However, these may not be stocked with toilet paper, so to be on the safe side (as is the case any time you're traveling in Mexico), you should probably bring your own.

Balandra Beach.

Balandra

If you were to ask around about which is the best beach in La Paz, your taxi driver, your waiter, and your tour guide are likely to reel off "Tecolote." This should be your first clue that Tecolote is *not* the best beach in La Paz. Even if Tecolote was not crowded with tourists, beachfront restaurants, and knickknack hucksters, it would still have a hard time beating out Balandra for beauty and tranquility. Balandra is actually a series of secluded beaches located in a small bay with rock formations that lend themselves to exploration. Decent snorkeling can be had here, and the water is shallow enough to allow an average-size adult to walk across the entire bay—though that would likely take an hour or so at its widest point. This beach has no bathroom facilities, and there is very little shade except the occasional *palapa*. Drive north of town toward Tecolote and watch for the sign to Balandra instructing you to take a left in the fork in the road. It is located about 5 miles beyond Pichilingue. Get here early to avoid crowds, particularly on weekends.

Tecolote

This is the largest and most popular beach in La Paz, located 18 miles north of the city on a paved road. The white sand and calm water make the beach ideal for swimming. Two seafood restaurants, El Tecolote (612-127-9494) and Palapa Azul (612-122-1801) offer good food and drinks as well as other beach necessities such as umbrellas and pay showers—keep in mind that you are expected to purchase something if you sit under a *palapa*. A large number of other vendors here offer a variety of refreshments and services such as parasailing and jet skiing. This beach also has facilities for RV camping. It's also where you will come to rent and board *pangas* to take you to Isla Espíritu Santo, which is clearly visible in the distance.

Península El Mogote

On a map, this 7-mile appendage of land looks like a thumb enclosing the bay of La Paz directly across from the city. The southern shore of the peninsula is outlined by mangroves, while the north side facing the open sea offers long, empty beaches and clear

Extending the Life of Mushroom Rock

Visitors to Balandra Beach north of La Paz have long been amazed by Mushroom Rock, located toward the north shore where the bay opens onto the Sea of Cortés. This 18-ton chunk of composite sedimentary rock has been sculpted by sea currents over the centuries into a 14-foot tall, 10-foot-diameter teardrop that sits precariously atop a rock reef. The rock has been photographed so often that it has become a symbol of La Paz itself.

You can imagine the waves that were kicked up among La Paz's beach-loving community when the forces that had shaped this landmark finally destroyed it.

In 2005 Mushroom Rock was discovered toppled from its pedestal. Although no one can be sure what happened, the most likely culprit was an unusually strong storm that brought powerful winds and waves from the west.

A local movement was quickly organized to remount the rock. This was a daunting task, as the spot where Mushroom Rock sat is surrounded by shallow water, sharp rocks, and no access roads leading to it. A scaffolding frame of steel pipe was constructed around the site to support the rock as it was hoisted into position. A 4-foot steel shaft was drilled into the base to support the rock, which was further supported by smaller support rods, and then small rocks were glued around the base to hide the support rods. This extraordinary effort ensures that you and generations of visitors who come after you will continue to enjoy one of Baja's most amazing landmarks.

Mushroom Rock.

Tecolote Beach.

water. The easiest way to reach this peninsula is by kayak since the access road is poorly maintained.

There is plenty to keep you busy at Tecolote Beach.

RECREATION

La Paz has been blessed with a seemingly unlimited assortment of natural resources that offer a number of recreational options. It has been a legendary spot for sport fishing for well over a half a century, and in more recent years snorkelers and divers have discovered it, as well. Whatever sport you're looking for, you'll find the city's tour agencies as well as your hotel staff to be more than accommodating.

Bike Tours

Southern Baja has long been a popular destination for biking enthusiasts. The 230-mile Cape Loop begins in La Paz, goes through Todos Santos down to Los Cabos, then turns north through Los Barriles, San Bartolo, and El Trufino. The longest distance between hotels is 70 miles, plus there are ample camping sites. Several tour companies offer guided tours. For mountain bikers, many single-track dirt trails on the Pichilingue Peninsula north of La Paz go along the coast or through inland canyons. Multiday routes come out of Los Planes in the south. You can rent bikes and arrange tours on the *malecón*.

Diving and Snorkeling

With its beautiful beaches and rocky offshore islands, La Paz is the ideal setting for scuba diving. The area has everything you could wish for in terms of underwater exploration, including shipwrecks, caves, sea mounts, and white coral reefs that are homes to more than 850 species of fish. Divers may also come across schools of hammerhead sharks, sea lions, giant manta rays, or even giant whale sharks. The beaches outside of town are great places for snorkeling, but the serious sea life is found offshore at Isla Espíritu Santo and other islands. For the best scuba diving, hook up with a local dive shop for a multiday trip. The warm months of May through November are when you'll find the clearest waters, with clarity down to 100 feet.

THE *SALVATIERRA* SHIPWRECK

In 1976 a cargo ferry named *La Salvatierra* sank after striking Swanee Rock, one of the few sites in the area with hard coral growth. The shipwreck victims were subsequently paid 50 pesos each in compensation, and *La Salvatierra* has become one of the most famous dive sites in La Paz. The ship now lies at a depth of approximately 60 feet and has become an artificial reef that attracts huge schools of fish, including baitfish, moray eels, and king angel fish.

ROCAS LOBOS

This dive site features several small caves and overhangs as well as a large number of coral heads. Here you'll immerse between corals and small coves, with depths that range from 20 to 100 feet. Rocas Lobos, which is very popular for night diving, was once home to a colony of sea lions. Although the sea lions have moved on, there is an abundance of life to enjoy here, including parrotfish and several species of ray.

GAVIOTA ISLAND WRECKS

The offshore isle of Gaviota was also once home to a colony of rare brown boobies, birds that have since disappeared from this area. This island is now the site of a 60-foot diving site in the bay of La Paz that features two sunken wooden boats. The ride from the city takes approximately 30 minutes, and for divers and snorkelers this island provides beautiful sandy beaches and a colorful abundance of sea life, including anemone, sergeant majors, and lobster.

ROCAS TINTORERA

Here, a series of underwater rock columns drop to 70 feet. Sea life commonly seen in this area includes octopus, king angelfish, parrotfish, and moray eels.

Fishing

The waters off La Paz are teaming with fish, particularly the waters to the south. Generally speaking, fishing in La Paz is done from standard 22- to 26-foot *pangas*. However, because La Paz is quickly becoming the location of choice among sportfishermen, larger boats are becoming more common at the city's three marinas. The two major fishing areas in La Paz

A fisherman shows off a dorado.

are the offshore islands of Isla Espíritu Santo and Isla Cerralvo. Here you'll find yellowtail from November to March; roosterfish and tuna in the spring; and dorado, marlin, and sailfish from March through September. Red snapper, pargo, and wahoo are also plentiful. While there is good fishing to be had nearly all year round in La Paz, some of the best fishing is done in the brutally hot months of summer. Don't forget to pack a big hat and sunscreen.

Kayaking

La Paz offers wonderful opportunities for kayakers of all skill levels. For beginners, Playa Balandra is hard to beat, though other beaches closer to town also offer pleasant experiences, particularly Playa Caimancito. More advanced kayakers will have an unforgettable adventure launching from the northern beaches and heading out to Isla Espíritu Santo. Another option is to hire a *panga* to take you out to the islands in the morning and arrange to be picked up in the afternoon. For the truly ambitious, packages to kayak from Loreto to La Paz are available.

Off-Roading

Sure, La Paz is best known for recreational activities centered on its crystal-blue water. But Baja is also famous for off-roading through its rugged desert terrain, and some of the best off-road trails in Baja lie along the corridor between La Paz and Loreto. In fact, La Paz has often been the final leg of the world famous Baja 1000. Day trips or multiday tours are available along these famous trails in ATVs or dirt bikes. When heading out to the course, be sure that your passport and driver's license is on your person in case of a medical emergency. There have been rare instances in which airlift to a San Diego hospital have been necessary and this evacuation could be delayed without a passport, due to new requirements.

Whale Watching

Whale enthusiasts from around the world come to La Paz for the chance to interact with the majestic gray whales that arrive yearly from January through March to bear their young. In addition to the gray whale, several other species are visible throughout the season, including the humpback whale, blue whale, fin whale, sperm whale, and orca. Schools of dolphins are also common throughout the winter months, and sea lions are present year-round. To learn more, visit the Whale Community Museum (612-121-1693; Navarro between Altamirano and Farias) open 9 AM to 2 PM.

OTHER ATTRACTIONS

MUSEO DE ANTROPOLOGÍA
612-125-6424
Calle 5 de Mayo and Altamirano
Open Monday through Friday 8 AM–6 PM, Saturday 9 AM–2 PM

This well-designed museum has three floors of exhibits that cover the anthropology of Baja California from prehistoric times through the colonial period and into modern times. For those interested in knowing more about the region's history, there are artifacts from the Native population as well as some dioramas depicting Native and colonial life. Although the labels are in Spanish only, you can't beat the admission fee: free.

CATEDRAL DE NUESTRA SEÑORA DEL PILAR DE LA PAZ
Calle 5 de Mayo and Revolución 1910

This structure is on the site of a mission founded in 1720 by two Jesuit priests from Loreto,

Kayaking near La Paz.

Tour Companies

As La Paz has grown as a tourist destination, servicing tourists has become a big business there. Consequently, all manner of guides are vying for your business. Although the businesses listed below have a certain degree of reputability, it's always best to discuss your expectations with the representative when making arrangements. This is particularly true when booking a trip from the *malecón* or your hotel. The last thing you want is to arrive at Tecolote Beach to find your captain cobbling together the *panga*'s engine right before you are to embark on an all-day tour. In the event something similar to this does happen, don't hesitate to back out and find another tour group. After all, there are plenty of 'em around.

Baja EcoTours

612-124-6629 or 877-560-2252 (U.S.)
www.bajaecotours.com
La Paz, Baja California Sur
U.S. office: 603 Seagaze Drive #732, Oceanside, CA
This eco-conscious company offers a variety of scuba diving and snorkeling trips tailored to your travel plans. Expeditions feature dives near the sea lion colonies at Los Islotes, at the Salvatierra shipwreck, and other popular locations.

Baja Expeditions

612-123-4900 or 800-843-6967 (U.S.)
www.bajaex.com
La Paz, Baja California Sur

Jet Skis head toward Médano Beach.

U.S. office: 2625 Garnet Avenue, San Diego, CA

Whether whale watching, diving, or hiking, this company offers a wide variety of tours and cruises. You may choose to whale watch from the deck of their 80-foot boat or rough it on a multiday kayak adventure. Likewise you can go diving for whale sharks based from your hotel, or live aboard one of their boats for a few days. Check their Web site for tour dates and availability.

Baja Outdoor Activities

612-125-5636

www.kayakinbaja.com

Centro, La Paz, Baja California Sur

This company offers multisport and combo trips: fly-fishing/sea kayaking or kayaking/remote hiking expeditions in May and October. In late January and February, they provide eight-day sea kayak expeditions to Isla Espíritu Santo with whale watching included. Trips are fully catered and hotel accommodations are included. Half- and full-day excursions are also available.

Club Hotel Cantamar Sports Lodge

612-122-1826

www.clubcantamar.com

Paseo Álvaro Obregón 1665-2, Plaza Cerralvo, La Paz

This is a fully equipped dive center and resort. Stay in their hotel and take a day trip on their 22-foot *panga*, or live aboard and dive from their 90-foot vessel. They also provide whale watching, kayaking, and sport-fishing excursions.

The Cortez Club

612-121-6120

www.cortezclub.com

Pichilingue Km 5 (at La Concha Beach Resort), La Paz

This is a full diving and water-sports center, complete with a private pier and a sunset bar. They offer everything from kayaking and windsurfing to jet skis and Hobie cats. Instruction for sailing, windsurfing, and water skiing is available. They also have a fully equipped dive center and are ANDI-, IANTD-, TDI-, PADI-, and DSAT-certified. Diving lessons are provided, and instructors are fully bilingual.

Fun Baja Diving

800-667-5362 (U.S./Canada)

www.deepdiscoveries.com

This Canada-based tour company offers multiday camping expeditions to the secluded bays of Isla Espíritu Santo. Trips include gourmet meals and three tank boat dives. They also offer whale-shark expeditions from June to November. Other package trips with various lodging options are also available.

Katun Tours

612-125-5636

www.katuntours.com

El Malecón in BOA's office, next to Hotel el Moro

This company specializes in mountain bike adventure tours, offering day trips as well as one- and two-week tours of Baja California Sur. Or just drop in, rent a bike, and ask for trail suggestions.

Mar Y Adventuras

612-123-0559

www.kayakbaja.com

Topete 564 (at Posada Luna Sol Hotel), La Paz

A variety of kayak expeditions, including combo snorkeling trips to Isla Espíritu Santos and whale-watching adventures, are offered by this company. Their tour guides are knowledgeable and professional and go out of their way to make sure you have a good time. They also rent to experienced kayakers.

The Moorings

888-952-8420

www.moorings.com

U.S. office: 19345 US 19 N # 4, Clearwater, FL 33764

This yacht-charter company offers boats from 38 to 50 feet. Typical weeklong trips for qualified sailors begin at La Paz and continue north about 75 miles to Puerto Los Gatos and back, stopping at points along the way.

Rama Jama Adventures

612-102-6175 or 760-346-3685

www.bajacharter.com

La Paz, Baja California Sur

U.S. office: 45405 Via Corona, Indian Wells, CA 92210

Enjoy a wide variety of activities with this water-adventure company . Explore hidden coves on kayak camping tours, dive beneath the surface to watch marine life, or sport fish from their 26-foot boat. Opt for scuba and snorkeling day trips or live-aboard multiday dive trips. They also rent scuba equipment, and their PADI-certified dive instructors offer lessons, as well.

Tailhunter International

626-333-3355 or 877-825-8802 (U.S.)

www.tailhunterinternational.com

Carretera a Pichilingue Km 5, # 205

This company specializes in sport fishing of all types, catering to traditional anglers as well as to fly fishermen and spear fishermen. They offer a variety of packages and have two fleets of *pangas*, one out of La Paz and one at Las Arenas on the northeast cape.

Ventana Windsports

612-144-0065 or 800-998-5500 (U.S.)

www.ventanawindsports.com

Topete 2730-A

Think of Ventana as a sort of a windsurfing bed & breakfast, located on the secluded La Ventana Bay 35 minutes east of La Paz on the other side of the Pichilingue Peninsula. They also have mountain bikes, plus yoga six days a week. However, windsports is the name of the game here, with windsurfing as well as kite-boarding equipment. Instructions are offered, as well.

Juan de Ugarte and Jaime Bravo. The mission was quickly abandoned and moved south to Todos Santos due to lack of water and a rebellious Native population. The present cathedral was founded in 1861 by Dominican monks. The square in front of the building, known as Jardín Velasco or Plaza Constitución, features a high eight-sided kiosk of wrought iron. This is an ideal location for a romantic evening walk.

MALECÓN

This three-mile sea wall is flanked by a wide promenade lined with statues, benches, and palm trees, making it one of the city's main gathering places. On warm evenings, the promenade is filled with couples and small groups of people enjoying the beautiful backdrop of the sea. Mornings find plenty of tourists and residents alike using the *malecón* for an early jog or bike ride. The only major drawback of the *malecón* is that it is difficult and at times even treacherous to access due to traffic on Paseo Álvaro Obregón, the busy street that parallels the promenade.

TEATRO DE LA CIUDAD

612-125-0207
Calle Farías and Calle Legaspy

This municipal theater is a 1,500-seat performing-arts facility that hosts musical, theatrical, and dance performances throughout the year.

MARINA DE LA PAZ

612-122-1646
Topete 3040

Marina de La Paz was the first floating marina in Baja California and only the second in all of Mexico. It began with only six slips but today can accommodate over 150 boats. It was remodeled in 2004 with all new docks and a Brazilian hardwood deck.

The Malecón in La Paz.

7

Islands of La Paz

The group of islands huddled north of the Pichilingue Peninsula is among the most important natural habitats in Mexico. These islands have the most pristine ecosystem in all of Baja California, providing a habitat for 500 species of fish, 31 species of marine mammals, and 210 species of marine and terrestrial birds. Additionally, this arid volcanic land rising abruptly out of the sea is home to 53 species of plants, including the world's largest cactus, which is endemic to the islands. Among the land animals found here (and nowhere else in the world), are a variety of lizards, snakes, toads, and the endangered blacktailed jackrabbit.

Needless to say, with biodiversity like this, found in a gorgeous and easily accessible setting, the islands off the coast of La Paz are bound to attract visitors. In fact, these islands attract about 30,000 visitors a year, 90 percent of whom are from the United States. Fortunately, the pressure exerted on this fragile ecosystem by tourism is now largely offset by a local conservation effort, though this has not always been the case. In 1976 Isla Espíritu Santo and Isla Partida came under the control of a communal landholding system known as an *ejido*. Despite their beauty, these arid islands provided few benefits to their owners, and in 1978 the entire area was designated a federally protected area, restricting activity and development. However, the *ejido* members continued to try to find ways to profit from their island parcels. In 1997 one member tried to build tourist cabins on his property, but Mexican environmental official ordered the rental cabins demolished. In 2003 some $3.3 million was given to buy out the *ejido* to transfer the islands to the federal government for formalized protection and conservation. Today there's a balancing act and sometimes a struggle over these islands between the tourists and the economy that they support and the environmentalists looking to protect and preserve the fragile ecosystem that exists here.

Getting There

Every year more tour operators appear offering adventures out to the sands of Isla Espíritu Santo, but the two companies that do most of the tour business in town are Baja Outdoor Activities (612-125-5636) and Mar Y Adventuras (612-123-0559). The types of tours that are offered vary widely, from four-hour *panga* trips around the islands to week-long guided kayak adventures. Whether you choose to book your trip through an agency in town, through the front desk of your hotel, or when you get to the beach, be sure to ask plenty of

OPPOSITE: *East side of the gulf islands is made up mostly of sheer cliffs.*

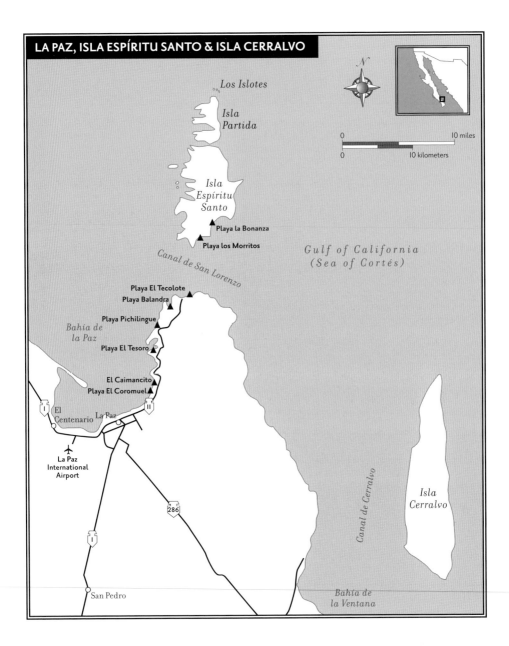

LA PAZ, ISLA ESPÍRITU SANTO & ISLA CERRALVO

N

10 miles

10 kilometers

Los Islotes

Isla Partida

Isla Espíritu Santo

Playa la Bonanza

Playa los Morritos

Canal de San Lorenzo

Gulf of California (Sea of Cortés)

Playa El Tecolote
Playa Balandra

Playa Pichilingue

Bahía de la Paz

Playa El Tesoro

El Caimancito
Playa El Coromuel

El Centenario   La Paz

La Paz International Airport

286

1

San Pedro

Canal de Cerralvo

Isla Cerralvo

Bahía de la Ventana

Isla Espíritu Santo.

questions so that you know exactly what you're getting. Most tours come with a lunch, so find out what that lunch entails. If it doesn't sound appetizing, consider bringing your own. Also, if you are taking a *panga* over to the islands, make sure that it is equipped with life preservers—not all *pangas* operating out of La Paz carry them. Even if you don't plan on getting in the water, you never know when something unexpected will happen.

If you're planning on going on an unguided kayak trip to the islands, it's best to make the trip with someone who has done it before. The 4.5-mile crossing to Punta Lupona on the southern tip of Isla Espíritu Santo is fraught with tricky currents and potentially treacherous winds. Playa Tecolote is the best place to set off. Despite there being two freshwater wells on the islands—one at Caleta El Candelero toward Isla Espíritu Santo's northwestern side and one at El Cardoncito on Isla Partida's southwestern side—you should bring your own water. If it is absolutely necessary to drink this water, treat it first with water purification tablets or boil it for at least 10 minutes. This water is perfectly suitable for bathing. However, it's likely that you will need your own bucket and rope to get at it.

The two companies mentioned above both rent kayaks—but only to experienced paddlers. They also rent other necessary gear such as butane stoves and portable toilets, which are required for camping. Rise early to take advantage of the low morning winds, and bring as much of your own gear from home as possible. Things like snorkeling equipment is surprisingly expensive to buy or rent here. Campers and independent paddlers must also obtain a permit from SEMARNAT, located Calle Ocampo 1045 (612-122-4414). The permit runs about $4.

Consider, though, the distinct advantages of going with a tour company, whether this involves a complete guided trip or just a *panga* ride to the island. These companies can speed you safely to the islands' western sides, where kayaking is a relative breeze. They also know the best snorkeling spots and carry your gear for you. Most importantly, they can evacuate you back to La Paz if you become ill or incur some other unexpected circumstance.

The best time to kayak is from March to mid-April. This skirts the end of the whale watching season when the air temperatures hang between 75 and 90 degrees and the water temperatures are in the 60s. Also, the El Norte winds that have been known to pin kayakers down for days during the winter begin to die down during this period. The biggest drawback of going in March and April is that this is also the busiest time of the year.

Isla Espíritu Santo

This 14-mile-long island is one of the world's top kayaking destinations. Even for nonkayakers, a trip to this island is an imperative when visiting La Paz. By far the biggest island in the chain that lies off the coast of Playa Tecolote, Isla Espíritu Santo is notched with bays and sandy inlets along its western and southern sides. Many of these areas are adorned with white sand and rock reefs that provide great snorkeling. Among these spots are Punta Prieta at the upper north end of Bahía San Gabriel, Caleta El Candelero, and Punta Bonanza on the southeast side of the island.

All along the way, florid volcanic rock rises out of the sea in soaring cliffs. The entire western shore is protected from the prevailing winds, and thus paddling here is generally calm. The same can't be said for the exposed eastern shore of the island, which is defined by soaring cliffs, sea caves, and strange rock formations. Depending on the wind conditions, *panga* captains are sometimes reluctant to venture over to this side of the island.

A ray glides into the air off Isla Espíritu Santo.

Making your way inland, several good day hikes can be taken from virtually every camp-site on the island. Follow the arroyos along the rocky bluffs but tread carefully due to the abundance of loose rock underfoot. These trails will lead you to unbelievable vistas and hidden inland lagoons.

Isla Partida

The larger Isla Espíritu Santo is separated at high tide from its northern neighbor, Isla Partida, by a narrow channel that can become an isthmus at low tide. There is a small fish-ing camp of indigenous fishermen here. Up the western side of the island, several coves cut out of the rock make for good anchorage. Toward the north you'll find the largest of these is the appropriately named Ensenada Grande, or "large cove." This is the best anchorage in this chain of islands, with crystal blue water and creamy fine-grain sand. The cove cuts deep into the island, and its walls provide protection from southerly winds. The beach here is backed by steep arroyos that invite hikers to explore what else the island has to offer. If you follow the craggy landscape to the northern tip of the island, you'll come to El Embudo, a precipice that offers stunning vistas. The eastern side of this island features sheer walls made of alternating layers of black lava and ruddy volcanic ash. This vicinity is pounded by winds and lapping waves that have created several sea caves and other unique formations.

Los Islotes

Perhaps the highlight of any trip to these islands is the opportunity to snorkel with the community of sea lions that inhabit the tiny rocks at the north end of this island chain. These guano-covered rocks called Los Islotes are home to the largest colony of sea lions in the Sea of Cortés. The water around these rocks drops to a pile of boulders at a depth of about 16 feet and beyond the boulders it drops to about 65 feet, making it an ideal place for scuba diving. In late spring sea lion pups will swim with divers and snorkelers, as will the females. However, always be wary of large, lone males, which can be dangerous if you get too close.

Isla San José

If Isla Espíritu Santo and its environs are a little crowded for your taste, perhaps a jaunt out to the secluded Isla San José is what your itinerary needs. Located about 15 miles north of Espíritu Santo, this remote island provides fine camping beaches and a real opportunity to escape the crowds. A few tour companies in La Paz make the 90-minute *panga* ride out to this island, where snorkeling sites are teeming with tropical fish. During the early days of La Paz pearl fishing, this island became famous for its pearl deposits. Today it is little more than a refuge for pelicans and osprey. However, there are a few human settlements on Isla San José and nearby islands. On the island of El Pardito (not to be confused with Isla Partida), between Isla San José and Isla San Francisco, a set-tlement of about 50 people is purportedly composed of the descendents of a single fish-erman and his nine wives.

Sea lion colony at Los Islotes.

Isla Cerralvo

About 20 miles southeast of Isla Espíritu Santo lies Isla Cerralvo, a 16-mile-long rock that juts out of the sea. For the most part, a lack of good anchorage keeps people off the island. However, drawing sportfishermen to the coast of this island is the abundance of deep-water fish such as marlin, sailfish, and dorado, which are conducted to the area by deep-water channels that abut the island.

El Bajo Sea Mount

While it's not actually an island, El Bajo is a popular deep-sea destination. The Marilsa Sea Mount, also called "El Bajo," is one of the best deep-sea diving locations in the Sea of Cortés. This is a group of three sea mounts rising up from the sea floor about 8 miles north-northeast of Los Islotes. The sea mounts top off at around 65 feet, and dives bottom out at 120 feet. This area is known for congregations of hammerhead sharks, though many other species of deep-sea fish also school and prowl in this locale, including marlin, Pacific manta, and whale sharks.

8

LORETO

On the surface, Loreto is a sleepy fishing village tucked between the indigo waters of the Sea of Cortés and the spectacular Sierra de la Giganta mountain range. This alone qualifies the town to be worth a visit. However, despite its rustic and unpretentious ambience, this is a town that is rich in history. As the oldest continuous town in all of the California's, it retains a certain secluded ambience. However, this rich beauty has not been continuous throughout all of that time. When John Steinbeck visited in the early twentieth century, he described a ramshackle community that was barely hanging on. The creation of the Transpeninsular Highway in the 1970s infused new life into Loreto and today it remains one of the best-kept secrets on the entire peninsula.

GENERAL INFORMATION

POLICE
613-135-0035
Paseo Nicolas Tamaral and Heroes de Independencía

CLINIC/MEDICAL SERVICES
613-135-0039
68 Salvatierra and Juarez

FIRE DEPARTMENT
613-135-1566

POST OFFICE
613-135-0647
Deportiva between Juárez and Salvatierra

TOURIST OFFICE
613-135-0411
Francisco I. Madero one block west of Salvatierra in the Palacio Municipal (City Hall)
Open: Mon.–Fri. 8 AM–8 PM

MARINA PARK OFFICE
613-135-0477
On the *malecón* next to the marina
Open: Mon.–Sat. 9 AM–3 PM

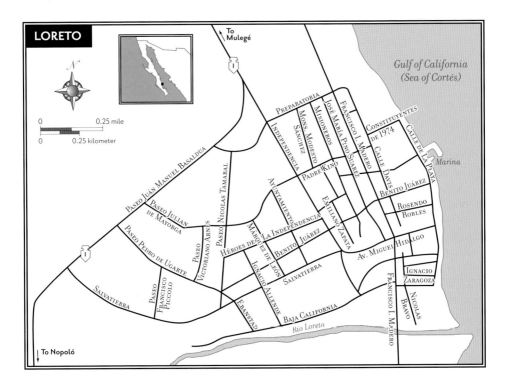

Laundry

LAVENDERÍA EL REMOJÓN
Salvatierra between Independencia and Ayuntamiento
Open: Mon.–Sat. 8 AM–3 PM

Bank

BANCOMER
Francisco I. Madero one block west of Salvatierra
Open: Mon.–Fri. 9 AM–3 PM

Supermarket

EL PESCADOR
613-135-0060
Salvatierra and Independencia
Open: Daily 8 AM–10 PM

Cybercafé

INTERNET SOLEDAD
Salvatierra between Ayuntamiento and Independencia
Open: Mon.–Fri. 9 AM–6 PM

Sporting Goods: Deportes Blazer

613-135-0911
Hidalgo #23
Open: Daily 9 AM—10 PM

Pharmacies

FARMACIA DE LAS CALIFORNIAS

613-135-0341
Salvatierra next to the El Pescador Supermarket
Open: Daily 8 AM—10 PM

FARMACIA FLORES

613-135-0321
Salvatierra and Avenida Calusio
Open: Daily 8 AM—10 PM

FARMACIA DEL ROSARIO

613-135-0670; Calle Independencia and Calle Juarez
613-135-0719; Salvatierra across from the El Pescador Supermarket
Both locations open daily 8 AM—10 PM

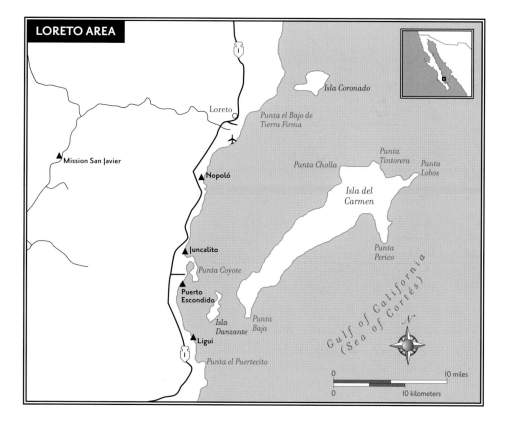

ACCOMMODATIONS

One additional benefit to Loreto never having been developed as a tourist center is that hotel prices are substantially less expensive than in Los Cabos or even La Paz. The few luxury hotels that are here offer prices that would qualify them as moderate hotels in other places, while budget hotels would be an absolute steal if they were in the tourist cities to the south. As is the case elsewhere in Baja, you will notice that many of the hotels here are run by expatriate American owners. These hosts can be a great resource for translation and travel advice.

BAJA OUTPOST
613-135-1134 or 888-649-5951 (U.S.)
www.bajaoutpost.com
Boulevard Adolfo Lopez Mateos
Price: Inexpensive
Credit Cards: None
Special Features: Diving tours

More than just a hotel, Baja Outpost is a certified full-service tour-guide operation. Although Baja Outpost offers many activities, including kayaking, horseback riding, and hiking, the specialty of the house is diving. The hotel has an excellent location close to the center of town and the beach. They offer seven good sized rooms and eight *palapas.* The rooms open up onto an attractive garden patio with several hammocks and an ocean view. A continental breakfast is included with the price of the room. Even if you don't stay here, Baja Outpost is a great resource for divers, offering complete equipment rentals and the capability to service up to 30 divers a day. Rates: start at $85 for double occupancy.

COCO CABAÑAS
613-135-1729
www.cococabanasloreto.com
Calle Davis
Price: Inexpensive

Hotel Posada de las Flores, Loreto.

Credit Cards: MC, V (through PayPal)
Special Features: Pool, barbecue area, kitchen, gated parking

This hotel offers eight cabanas that open up onto a palm-landscaped central patio with a small swimming pool. Adjacent to the pool is a fish-cleaning station and barbecue that you can use to grill up your catch of the day. Six of the cabanas have a double bed and a twin bed while the other two have a double and a set of bunk beds. Each room is also equipped with a full kitchen, including a small refrigerator, a stove, and a microwave. A free video library is nice for kicking back after a long day of exploring Loreto and its environs. There is also a gated parking area on the grounds. This hotel has a great location: one block from the waterfront at the north end of the *malecón* and two blocks from downtown Loreto. The American expatriate owners are more than happy to offer advice or make arrangements to make your trip more enjoyable. Rates: $89 for double occupancy.

LAS CABAÑAS DE LORETO
613-135-1105 or 707-933-0764 (U.S.)
www.lascabanasdeloreto.com
Calle José M. Moreles
Price: Inexpensive
Credit Cards: None
Special Features: Wi-Fi hotspot, outdoor barbecue area

Located on a gated property, this hotel is an easy walking distance from restaurants and shopping. It has four fully equipped cabanas, three of which have a queen-size bed and a twin bed while the remaining cabana—the Sailfish cabana—has two queen-size. The cabanas are located behind the main house, known as Casa de Loreto, and face an inner courtyard. Additionally, the property's main house has two master suites equipped with a single queen-size bed in each. The main house also has an upper-deck patio with a view of the *malecón*. The property is also furnished with an outdoor kitchen for barbecues, several hammocks, as well as a swimming pool and a hot tub. For travelers who can't leave their laptops behind, the hotel is set up as a Wi-Fi hotspot. This hotel also offers laundry service for $4 per load plus off-street parking. Las Cabañas de Loreto is one house away from the *malecón*, just a 5-minute walk from the public beach in front of the Hotel Oasis. Rates: start at $95 for double occupancy.

DANZANTE BAJA
408-354-0042 (U.S.)
Km 89 Transpeninsular Highway
Price: Expensive
Credit Cards: MC, V
Special Features: Eco-resort, all-inclusive rate

Situated 25 miles south of Loreto, this Mexican hacienda hotel sits on 10 seaside acres. This hotel was designed to harmonize with the natural surroundings and gets all of its power from solar energy. It is composed of nine suites built on a rocky, volcanic hill facing the Sea of Cortés. The buildings are made of handmade adobe bricks with ceilings of cactus wood strips and handwoven *palapa* roofs. The property is landscaped with desert vegetation, including many colorful bougainvillea, cordon and pitahaya cacti, and tall mesquite trees. Each suite has French doors that open onto a quarried slate terrace—an ideal place to relax in your hammock and take in the panoramic view of the mountains and the sea. There are no TVs or phones in the rooms and limited cell phone access on the premises. If you are looking for nightlife, this is not the place for you. However, there is plenty to do in the ecologically friendly resort. The beach fronting the resort is ideal for kayaking and snorkeling, and there are several hiking trails nearby. Guests are also invited to join guided horseback trips into the back country or just ride along the beach. After your strenuous day, relax your sore muscles with a therapeutic message in your room. Meals are served bed & breakfast style and typically feature seasonal seafood and local fruits and vegetables. However, the staff is more than happy to help you set up your own beach barbecue, where you can cook your own fresh catch of the day under the stars. Rates: $398 for double occupancy from November through April 15, and $360 for double occupancy from April 16 through October.

DESERT INN

613-135-0090 or 800-800-9632 (U.S./Canada)
Prolongación and Calle Davis
Price: Inexpensive
Credit Cards: MC, V, AE
Special Features: Restaurant, two bars, on-site parking, gift shop, laundry service

Unlike most of Loreto's hotels, La Pinta is part of a chain of hotels along the Baja Peninsula. On the beach just over a mile north of town, La Pinta is a two-story villa with 48 rooms facing the Sea of Cortés. All rooms have sliding-glass doors that open onto either a private balcony or a covered beach patio. Some rooms have fireplaces. An on-site restaurant—with a small bar—serves good Mexican food. The pool area is attractive and has a bar as well. A game room and a gift shop are also on the grounds. With its beachside location, fishing boats pull right up in front of your hotel room to take you out for the day. Rates: $79 for double occupancy.

HACIENDA SUITES

800-224-3632 (Mexico) or 866-207-8732 (U.S.)
www.haciendasuites.com
Salvatierra #152
Price: Inexpensive

Credit Cards: AE, MC, V
Special Features: Swimming pool, two bars, mini market, gift shop

This hotel offers somewhat of a hacienda ambience with the rooms built around a central courtyard that's dominated by a swimming pool. Arched entryways and *saltillo* tile give the courtyard a distinctly colonial feel to what otherwise might be reminiscent of a Best Western. The rooms are spacious and well kept, though the décor is definitely American budget hotel. The hotel is across the street from the bus terminal, several blocks from the beach, though the walk is manageable. There is room service and a restaurant that serves a good breakfast, as well as two bars and a well-maintained garden area. The staff is friendly and speaks English, and every Saturday night they put on a Mexican fiesta that features dances and music from around Mexico. Rates: $44.50 for double occupancy.

HOTEL OASIS

www.hoteloasis.com
613-135-0112
Calle de la Playa at Zaragoza
Price: Moderate
Credit Cards: V, MC, AE
Special Features: Pool, bar, restaurant, tennis court

Established in 1960, the Hotel Oasis is one of Loreto's oldest hotels. It also has one of Loreto's best locations: right on the beach at the south end of the *malecón*. It is a fairly large hotel by Loreto standards, with 40 rooms, each with a hammock strung outside the entrance. Not all rooms have an ocean view, so you should request one when making reservations. Rooms are furnished with two double beds, with TVs and phones on request. The rooms are clean, though they do show their age. The restaurant opens at 5 AM to serve guests heading out early on all-day kayaking excursions and fishing trips. At night, the restaurant occasionally offers seafood, chicken, and steak buffets. The food is well done, though the choices are limited. The Oasis also has a small bar and a good-size swimming pool that is advertised as being heated, though that hardly seems necessary. Rates: $115–144 for double occupancy.

HOTEL PLAZA LORETO
613-135-0280
www.loreto.com/hotelplaza
Avenida Hidalgo #2
Price: Inexpensive
Credit Cards: None
Special Features: Laundry service, travel agent service

Located in the center of downtown Loreto, this hotel is just one block from the mission and three blocks from the waterfront. It's a simple hotel centered around a beautiful courtyard that's ideal for meeting up with other travelers; a shaded terrace on the second floor overlooks the mission across the street. The 24 rooms are clean, comfortably air-conditioned, and attractively decorated in traditional Mexican style. However, the beds are on the hard and slightly lumpy side. Because of the Hotel Plaza's central location on the city's main street, noise can be a nuisance at times. If possible, request one of the rooms with a view of the mission. Rates: $51–73.

IGUANA INN
613-135-1627
www.iguanainn.com
Corner Benito Juárez and Calle Davis Col Centro
Price: Inexpensive
Credit Cards: MC, V
Special Features: Kitchenettes

This bungalow hotel is hands down one of the best deals to be found in Loreto. With four colorful and spacious bungalows set around an attractive courtyard, the Iguana Inn is a pleasant place to relax after a long day of exploring Baja. Tables and chairs outside each room facilitate conversations with fellow travelers. But if you'd rather stay in, movies and books are freely available, too. The courtyard is complete with a Spanish-style fountain as well as a barbecue pit where you can grill up the day's catch. Each bungalow is equipped with a small refrigerator and a kitchenette. The on-site owners, Mike and Julie, offer casually personal service and pride themselves on keeping the bungalows renovated and clean. They are also extremely knowledgeable about the area and more than willing to offer advice and information. Their kayak, kept in the driveway, is available to take out for a spin at the marina, which is a short walk away. Rates: $50–60.

INN AT LORETO BAY
800-507-6979 or 866-850-0333 (U.S.)
Boulevard Misión de Loreto, Nopoló
Price: Moderate
Credit cards: MC, V
Special Features: 155 rooms, handicapped accommodations, baby-sitting and concierge services

Formerly known as the Camino Real, the Inn at Loreto Bay is in Nopoló, 5 miles south of Loreto. It is situated on its own cove in front of a beautiful and spacious white sand beach, which is a perfect playground for kids and adults alike. With a great view of the Isla del Carmen, the beach is one of the best in the area for swimming, snorkeling, or just lounging around. Adjacent to the beach is an 18-hole, par-72 golf course that offers the same spectacular views of the Sea of Cortés and the Sierra de la Gingante mountains. The hotel has 155 rooms, each with a patio or balcony and most having a view of the sea—though you should request this, just in case. The tiled bathrooms are spacious and have granite countertops. Each room is furnished with

Inn at Loreto Bay.

air conditioning, a digital safe box, satellite TV, and a mini bar as well as a king-size or two double beds. The higher-end suites also have a private Jacuzzi on a large terrace. Facing the beach is a patio pool, which is beautiful but fairly small for the size of the hotel (however, with this beach, you probably won't even consider the pool). The restaurant and bar offer room service. Other services include baby-sitting, concierge, currency exchange, and laundry. Check the Web site for special packages, including an all-inclusive rate. If you'll be spending most of your time in the hotel, you should consider opting for the all-inclusive price as the food and drinks are expensive otherwise—although you can find much better meals and libations in Loreto for a fraction of the price. Rates: start at $125 for a standard room, double occupancy.

LORETO PLAYA BED & BREAKFAST
613-135-1129
www.loretoplaya.com
Calle de la Playa
Price: Moderate
Credit Cards: MC, V (through PayPal)

Special Features: Gourmet breakfast, discreet and personalized service, nonsmoking
Romance is the name of the game at this inn is located right on the beach on the north side of town, about eight blocks from the central plaza. Owners Roberto and Paulette have designed this small, tastefully decorated B&B to cater to couples. The first suite has a sitting room with a TV/DVD, a refrigerator, and a microwave. The separate bedroom is furnished with a king-size canopy bed, and off the bedroom is a private terrace as well as a large bathroom with a tiled tub built for two. A similar suite on the second floor has the addition of a

rooftop perch with an unobstructed view of the area and a hammock built for two. Adjacent to the main house is a smaller two-bedroom, two-bath beach house that sleeps up to six. A gourmet breakfast is included in the rates. Reservations are required. Rates: start at $145 for double occupancy.

MOTEL EL DORADO

613-135-1500 or 888-314-9023 (U.S.)
www.moteleldorado.com
Corner Hidalgo and Pipila
Price: Inexpensive
Credit Cards: None
Special Features: Pool, restaurant, sports bar, laundry service, Internet service

This is one of Loreto's newer hotels, located one block west of the *malecón*. The hotel provides several services, including laundry and Internet. It also offers the convenience of arranging fishing trips at the front desk. The 11 rooms are simple but spacious and clean. They are centered around a sports bar called Pelicano Loco that's a great place to hang out, but it's only open 1 PM to 8 PM because it borders a couple of residential properties. Rates: $50 for double occupancy.

POSADA DE LAS FLORES LORETO

613-135-1162 or 619-378-0103 (U.S.)
www.posadadelasflores.com
Francisco Madero just north of Salvatierra
Price: Moderate to Expensive
Credit Cards: MC, V
Special Features: Rooftop garden pool, laundry service, satellite TV, continental breakfast

This boutique hotel, designed in the tradition of an 18th-century Mexican hacienda, is located right in the heart of Loreto. The downside of this is that the rooms can be noisy, depending on the kind of night they are having at Mike's Bar down the street. The 15 units—10 standard rooms and 5 jun-

ior suites—all have satellite TV and safety-deposit boxes. Most standard rooms have a queen-size bed, though three of them have two twins. These rooms are beautifully furnished but rather small. Junior suites have one king-size bed. There is a glass-bottomed pool in the rooftop garden, which is itself a perfect place to relax with a cocktail from the rooftop bar and enjoy the sunset. The inner courtyard area of the hotel is elegantly and colorfully decorated, though the canned music adds nothing to the ambience. There are two restaurants on the premises. Vecchia Roma is an excellent Italian restaurant and has a good selection of wines. It is open Tuesday through Sunday 6 PM to 11 PM. From 8 AM until 10 AM, a delicious continental breakfast is included in the price of the room. However, it is served at Santa Lucía restaurant, at the south end

View of the street from Hotel Posada de las Flores.

of the *malecón* about five blocks away. Another quirky detail about this hotel is that children under age 12 are not allowed. Rates: start at $150–180 for a standard room, double occupancy.

EL SANTUARIO ECO-RETREAT CENTER
613-104-4254 or 805-541-7921 (U.S.)
Ensenada Blanca, Km 86 Transpeninsular Highway
Price: Moderate
Credit Cards: None
Special Features: Variety of healing arts, eco-activities, guided tours

This eco retreat center is located 25 miles south of Loreto on the bay of Ensenada Blanca. If you don't want to rent a car to get here, you can hire a taxi at the airport. (The cost of the trip will vary depending on the number of people in your party.) The property consists of six secluded bungalows, some situated on private white sand dunes whereas others face the beach. Simple living is the rule here, as the rooms are designed to be environmentally sensitive and contain no electrical outlets, TVs, or phones, though there is a cell phone and Internet access in case of an emergency. Showers and toilet facilities are located outside each bungalow. The toilets are designed for composting; the showers are solar heated and the run-off is distributed to nearby plants. Local materials were used to construct the bungalows as well as the outdoor kitchen and dining area. A local Mexican cook prepares the meals with fresh seafood and locally grown fruits and vegetables. If you prefer, you're always welcome to prepare your own meals or learn from the cook. This resort also offers healing retreats and a variety healing arts services such as yoga classes, private massage, and acupuncture. Although only several people are likely to be staying at the retreat at any given time, El Santuario is equipped to host group gatherings, including the availability of a 30-foot-diameter yurt, a tentlike structure ideal for music, dance, or group meditation. Or simply enjoy the natural surroundings with a horseback ride or guided hiking tour. Rates: $120 for double occupancy.

SUKASA BUNGALOWS
613-135-0490
www.loreto.com/sukasa
Calle de la Playa
Price: Inexpensive
Credit Cards: MC, V
Special Features: Private garden patios

This small waterfront establishment offers simple, personalized service. The three air-conditioned bungalows are spacious and decorated in a colorful Mexican style—including tiled floors—that is sure to put you in the right mood as soon as you arrive. The two smaller bungalows have a king-size bed, a living area with two twin-size sofa beds, and a small kitchen with plates and utensils as well as a refrigerator and microwave (no stove, though). The larger casita has all of these same amenities as well as a stove/oven in the kitchen. Bungalows are also equipped with small TVs—which only get three Spanish channels, so you're more likely to watch movies from the on-site video library. The bungalows open onto a tiled garden patio that is complete with a *palapa* and hammock. This is a great place to relax and talk about the day's adventures. Besides the bungalows, you can rent a two-story "main house" on a weekly basis. It is a one-bedroom, two-bath house with a king-size bed and a large balcony. Also available is a yurt. This 14-foot-diameter waterproof and air-conditioned tent is furnished with a queen-size bed, small refrigerator, and coffeemaker and has a private bathroom. A unique vacation experience! Rates: $55 per night for a yurt, $75 per night for a bungalow, and $85 per night for a casita.

LAS TROJES BED & BREAKFAST
613-135-0277
www.loreto.com/costa2.htm
Calle de la Playa
Price: Inexpensive
Credit Cards: None
Special Features: Internet, airport pickup,
Direct TV, outdoor hot tub

Just off the beach and a quarter mile away
from the center of town, Las Trojes is a nice
find for travelers looking for something a
little different. This hotel is made of actual
Trojes, or ancient granaries, from the
mountainous state of Michoacán. The
hotel's proprietor, Agustin Salvat, had the
structures shipped to Loreto a decade ago
and assembled by Tarascan Indians from
Michoacán. The result is one of Loreto's
more interesting hotels. Each of its eight
rooms has been uniquely designed with full
bath, air conditioning, and ceiling fans.
They are clean, well arranged, and the rates
are reasonable. Continental breakfast is
included, as is free use of bicycles. Group
discounts and long-term rates are available, and children are always welcome. This
hotel also offers airport pickup upon
request. Rates: start at $50.

RV Parks

EL MORO HOTEL AND RV PARK
613-135-1162
www.loreto.com/elmoro
Rosendo Robles No. 8, Loreto

This hotel/RV park is located only a hundred yards from the waterfront and near
the center of town. The facilities are a bit
cramped, but you can't beat the location.
The RV lots—which are either 20 by 36 or
30 by 36 feet—are all equipped with full
hookups. The hotel offers eight rooms with
private bathroom and showers. Rates: $15
per night for RVs full hookups and $5 per
night for tents.

TRIPUI HOTEL AND RV PARK
613-133-0814
P.O. Box 100, Puerto Escondido, 23880,
Mexico
Special Features: Twenty-four-hour secu-
rity guard

This large RV park/hotel—located in Puerto
Escondido, 15 miles south of Loreto—contains 31 transient spaces and 133 yearly
spaces to suit a variety of types of RVs. The
property also has a launch ramp and boat
storage, and supplies such as propane tanks
can be purchased at the local store. The
park is a half mile off Mexico 1, which
makes it convenient without being too
noisy. A swimming pool, gift shop, and a
restaurant are also on the premises. The
main office has Internet access for a fee. A
16-room hotel has recently been added to
the premises. The rooms are furnished
with a double bed and full bathrooms with
tubs and showers. The hotel provides
transportation to and from the Loreto airport. Rates: $18 per night for a site with full
hookups and $10 per night for tents.

Loremar RV Park
613-133-0711
Francisco Madero, Loreto

This RV park is situated on a 5-acre site
near the beach. Facilities include pool, lit
tennis court, and flush toilets. Rates: $18
per night.

RESTAURANTS

Loreto offers a variety of dining establishments. If you are the adventurous type,
some of Loreto's best food can be had for
less than $3 from such roadside vendors as
McLulu's, a taco stand on Salvatierra (open
10 AM to 7 PM).

If you are more in the mood to sit down
and be waited on, you'll find tempting
choices all over town. Breakfasts are nor-

mally inexpensive, with many restaurants posting their specials on a chalkboard out front. Choices include Mexican standards such as *pan dulce* (traditional sweet bread), huevos rancheros (ranch-style eggs), and *huevos a la Mexicana* (Mexican-style eggs). If you're craving something more familiar, you will have no trouble finding pancakes, omelets, or other favorites from north of the border.

Most restaurants in town are open for lunch as well as dinner. Lunch is generally casual, but if you do choose to eat in town, consider resisting the temptation to eat lunch in your beach attire—shirtless or in your bikini. While the proprietor may not say anything, local patrons seem to frown on this.

Once the sun goes down, restaurants fill up. Choosing where to eat can be almost as fun as eating. Many restaurants display sample entrées next to their menu. Keep in mind that few establishments take credit cards, with the exception of higher-priced restaurants and those located in hotels that accept credit cards. Furthermore, some may have restrooms that are not up to the cleanliness standards expected by some travelers. But they are still regulated by the health department and serve only purified ice and water.

ARMONDO'S PIZZA
613-135-0245
Benito Juarez at Tamaral
Open: Fri.–Wed. 11 AM–10 PM
Price: Inexpensive
Cuisine: International
Serving: L, D

This small restaurant is located across the street from the El Pescador Supermarket and offers good pizza at an inexpensive price. In the evening they also serve hamburgers. It is a little bit away from the main tourist area but it is a good option if you are looking for a quick bite. The restaurant has indoor as well as patio dining.

CAFÉ OLÉ
613-135-0496
Madero #14, one block north of Salvatierra
Open: Mon.–Sat. 7 AM–10 PM
Price: Inexpensive to Moderate
Cuisine: Mexican
Serving: B, L, D

This unassuming eatery may be the most popular restaurant in town. Located under a *palapa*, along a cobblestone street right off the city square, it serves breakfast, lunch, and dinner and specializes in Mexican fare, though the hamburgers and fries aren't half bad. With several indoor tables as well as a few streetside ones, there's perhaps enough seating for 30 diners.

EL CANIPOLE
613-133-0282
Pino Suarez #3
Open: Mon.–Sat. 8 AM–11 PM; Sun. 2 PM–8 PM
Price: Moderate
Cuisine: Mexican
Serving: B, L, D

Food is treated as art at this eatery, located one block west of the municipal building, which claims to be Loreto's oldest restaurant. The staff whips up all your food after your order, including the salsa. This adds to the prep time, but it's well worth the wait. For a real treat, try the chicken mole or the *carnitas* made with lamb.

LA CASCADA
Salvatierra and Zapata
Open: Fri.–Wed. 8 AM–10 PM
Price: Moderate
Cuisine: Mexican and Seafood
Serving: B, L, D

This restaurant is located along one of Loreto's prettiest historic streets and features homemade Mexican cuisine and seafood. The portions are large, and the fresh guacamole and tortillas remind you why you came to Mexico. A large covered patio is a great place to relax and enjoy a margarita. Come for breakfast, lunch, or dinner.

CHILE WILLIE

613-135-0677
Lopez Mateos and Padre Kino at the north end of the Malecón
Open: Daily 11 AM–10 PM
Price: Inexpensive to Moderate
Cuisine: Steak and Seafood
Serving: B, L, D

Located in a *palapa* on the beach just north of the *malecón*, this restaurant offers wonderful views of the Sea of Cortés as well as a competent steak and seafood menu. There is a full bar on site, as well, making it an ideal place to relax with friends old and new. MasterCard and Visa are accepted here, as are traveler's checks. This restaurant opens early for breakfast from October through April.

THE LOBSTER TRAP

613-135-0027
Located upstairs at the Quatros Altos
Open: Daily 2 PM–10:30 PM
Price: Moderate to Expensive
Cuisine: Seafood
Serving: L, D

This upstairs establishment has the same owner as El Nido Steakhouse. Situated two blocks west of the city square, it's a seafood restaurant that specializes in lobster dishes. With bare brick walls and mood lighting, this restaurant has a real cantina feel. It has a full bar with a large list of tequilas, wines, beers, and other selections. The staff strives to create an inviting party atmosphere that's great for getting together with friends.

LA PALAPA

613-135-0284
Madero and Hidalgo, next to La Terraza

Open: Daily 1 PM–10:30 PM
Price: Inexpensive to Moderate
Cuisine: Mexican
Serving: L, D

An open-air grill facing the street will lure you in to this casual restaurant, which serves Mexican food as well as seafood. Once inside, you'll be given a generous tray of chips and salsa while you wait for your order. The food is good, but a table can be hard to find on busy nights, and there is no host station to take your name. You may have to pull up a seat at the bar and jockey for a table. Bring your catch of the day, and they'll even cook it up for you.

MACAW'S

Malecón and Morales
Open: Daily 8 AM–10 PM
Price: Inexpensive
Cuisine: Mexican
Serving: L, D

This is bar/restaurant features a great view of the Sea of Cortés. It is located across the street from the *malecón*, two blocks south of Salvatierra. The food is good, particularly the guacamole, and the drinks are served stiff. Both indoor and outdoor seating are available. During football season, NFL games are shown on two small TVs all day Sunday and again for Monday Night Football. Overall, a good place to enjoy a drink and listen to music.

MEXICO LINDO Y QUE RICO

613-135-5004
Avenida Hidalgo and Colegio
Open: Tue.–Sun. 7 AM–10 PM
Price: Inexpensive
Cuisine: Mexican
Serving: B, L, D

The name of this restaurant means "Beautiful Mexico and How Delicious." The staff here approaches their food with the same enthusiasm. The menu features

Mexican classics such as *huevos a la Mexicana* and huevos rancheros for breakfast and *chiles rellenos* and tortilla soup for lunch and dinner. The portions are large, and the food is on the spicy side, so have a beer and take it easy.

MITA GOURMET
613-135-2025
13 El Centro Historico
Open: Wed.–Mon. 3 PM–10 PM
Price: Moderate to Expensive
Cuisine: Seafood
Serving: D

Located across the plaza from the municipal building, Mita Gourmet is a great place to go for Baja cuisine. Everything is prepared fresh, and the owners go out of their way to make sure you are taken care of. The menu has a variety of selections, though the seafood dishes are especially tasty.

EL NIDO
613-135-0284
Salvatierra #154
Open: Daily 2 PM–10:30 PM
Price: Moderate
Cuisine: Steak and Seafood
Serving: L, D

This restaurant is known for its Sonoran beef, seafood, and wine selection. It's also famous for its giant margaritas. The ranch-style atmosphere is complemented by gracious service. All dinners come with bean soup, salad, and a baked potato. Credit cards are not accepted here, though traveler's checks are okay. Reservations are recommended.

SANTA LUCIA
613-135-1332
Calle de la Playa and Fernando Jordan
Open: Daily 8 AM–10 PM
Price: Moderate
Cuisine: Mexican and International
Serving: B, L, D

This pleasant little restaurant is located across the street from the *malecón*. Its heavy wooden tables and handcrafted chairs are housed within a high-ceilinged *palapa* with large windows facing the water. This makes it the perfect place to enjoy breakfast and watch the sun rise over the Sea of Cortés. For breakfast, they offer a variety of homemade sweet breads, freshly squeezed juices, yogurt, and pretty decent coffee. For lunch and dinner, they offer traditional Mexican fare as well as sandwiches on freshly baked bread along with a full bar. You can also order delicious boxed lunches to take on excursions: a sandwich, a drink, and a homemade fruit pastry.

EL TASTE
613-135-1489
Benito Juarez and Zapata
Open: Daily 2 PM–10 PM
Price: Moderate
Cuisine: Steak and Seafood
Serving: L, D

This steak-and-seafood restaurant, formerly known as Caesar's, offers large portions in a distinctly Mexican atmosphere. Portions are often large enough to share, and the full bar makes some great drinks and they have wines to complement any selection. It's across the street from the gas station you pass on the way into town.

LA TERRAZA
613-135-0496
Madero and Hidalgo, upstairs from Café Olé
Open: Mon.–Sat. 1 PM–10 PM
Price: Moderate to Expensive
Cuisine: Steak and Seafood
Serving: L, D

A variety of fare is offered here, from Mexican food such as fajitas to styles from north of the border such as New York steak to more international cuisine such as shish kabobs. Located upstairs from Café Olé, La

Terraza is in a great location right in the center of town. Try to get a window seat, which overlooks the Loreto's main street, and do some people watching while you eat. Bring your catch of the day, and they'll cook it for you.

TIFFANY'S PIZZA PARLOR AND CAPPUCCINO BAR

613-135-0004
Avenida Hidalgo and Piño Suarez
Open: Wed.–Mon. 11:30 AM–9 PM
Price: Inexpensive
Cuisine: International
Serving: L, D

This small, home-style restaurant offers a change of pace from chips and salsa. Besides good pizza, you'll find hamburgers, organic coffee from the Mexican state of Chiapas, and real espresso drinks.

TIO LUPE'S

613-135-1882
Salvatierra and Madero
Open: Daily 11 AM–11 PM
Price: Inexpensive
Cuisine: Mexican
Serving: B, L, D

This is a classic Baja Mexican restaurant, complete with a full bar and plastic Corona chairs and tables. There are colorful murals on the wall and a *palapa* roof, just so you

don't forget where you are. The food is good, though the building is a bit run down. Then again, you won't even sit down in here if you're looking for fancy digs.

BARS AND NIGHTLIFE

To be perfectly honest, Loreto is not a place to come for lively nightlife. If that's your interest, head to Cabo San Lucas. Here there are really no clubs for dancing, and while several hotels and restaurants have bars, you can pretty much count on them closing early. When that happens, your choices are few and far between.

JARROS & TARROS

Paseo Hidalgo

This billiards bar is located on Paseo Hidalgo next to Deportes Blazer. Open Monday through Saturday 6 PM to 2 AM, although it is known to close around midnight on some nights.

MIKE'S BAR

613-135-1126
Paseo Hidalgo

This is the one place in town that really parties into the night. It doubles as a sports bar and a place for live music. Open Monday through Saturday 11 PM to 3 AM.

WEATHER

Loreto enjoys practically 360 days of sunshine. Winter weather is generally mild, with daytime highs averaging 70 to 85 degrees from November through June and evening lows dipping into the 50s only in January and February. Water temperatures also stay fairly warm through November, averaging in the 80s and dropping into the high 60s in January and February. In July and early August, daytime highs begin to creep into the 90s, and the air gets a bit humid. Evenings are warm, with temperatures remaining in the 80s. However, Loreto doesn't get truly uncomfortable until late August and September, when temperatures can get well above 100 degrees, and not even the sea provides respite from the heat, with water temperatures reaching an average of 90 degrees—the same as a warm bath. If there's a time of year to stay away from Loreto, September is it. Many smaller hotels and

Nopoló Beach.

businesses (of which there are a lot) close down, and those who can, spend the month on the Pacific side of the peninsula, where temperatures are relatively cooler.

BEACHES

Loreto is surrounded by miles of sandy beaches ideal for snorkeling, kayaking, sport fishing, or just enjoying their beauty. Along the waterfront in town, large boulders create a breakwater for the city. The beaches in town, west of the marina and on the other side east of the *malecón*, are made up of coarse brown sand and are not as nice as other nearby beaches but are safe for swimming.

Nopoló

Nopoló is a community 5 miles south of Loreto. This area has been the focus of tourism development since the 1970s, but it has only recently gotten under way in earnest. Currently, developers are building several condominium complexes and a wellness community along the beach here. Despite this, the beach at Nopoló continues to be beautiful, quiet, and easily accessible. With the Isla del Carmen visible in the distance, this beach offers good snorkeling or fishing as well as rocky coves to explore while watching pelicans dive bomb for their dinner. To get here, access Mexico 1 at 2 miles south of the airport, and take the exit for Nopoló. Follow the main road until it dead-ends in a cul-de-sac at the Inn at Loreto Bay. Parking on the street is not a problem. To get to the beach, walk around the hotel, or, if you don't mind acting like a guest, walk directly through the hotel lobby.

El Juncalito

Located 14 miles south of Loreto off Mexico 1, this beach is popular among campers. The beach is set in a protected cove that is rich with tropical fish. The gorgeous and isolated emerald waters and fine sand make it the perfect place for roughing it. You will have to keep an eye out to see the inconspicuous sign on the east side of the highway marking the turnoff to this beach. It is located about a mile north of the turnoff to Puerto Escondido. This leads you a half mile down a bumpy dirt road that comes out on the south end of Juncalito.

The view near Playa Juncalito.

Snorkelers at Nopoló Beach.

Puerto Escondido

Sailors know Puerto Escondido as the most well-protected anchorage in the Sea of Cortés, mainly due to the Sierra de la Giganta Mountains that come right down to the water. These rocky cliffs are perfect for exploring and offer wonderful views of the bay. Puerto Escondido, whose name means "hidden port," is actually made of two harbors, an outer harbor known as "the Waiting Room" and an inner, hidden harbor, that gives the town its name. Puerto Escondido was the planned site of a resort hotel. Construction was begun in the 1980s but was never finished. The ruins of this debacle remain and are themselves a point of interest. Puerto Escondido is 15 miles south of Loreto just east of Mexico 1. On the south end of the harbor, there's a beach that's ideal for camping. If you need supplies, the Tripui Resort & RV Park (613-133-0818; www.tripui.com) is just down the road near the turnoff from Mexico 1.

Playa Ligui

This small beach lends itself to exploration with several beautiful inlets that are excellent for snorkeling and scuba diving. Desert brush surrounds the beach, and vultures and pelicans circle the rocky hills that rise up in the near distance, which add to the feeling of seclusion. This beach is 21 miles south of Loreto on Mexico 1. Follow the dirt road 0.75 mile east of Mexico 1, and turn right once you reach the water; continue for less than a mile.

Relaxing on Coronado Island.

Relaxing at Playa Ligui.

Isla Coronado

The island of Coronado juts out of the sea with incredible rock formations on the eastern side where sea lions bask in the sun. The island is made up of huge volcanic pillars that create a rock wall that's 40 feet high in some places. Myriad sea life populates the island's waters, including moray eels, rock scallops, bumphead parrotfish, angelfish, and tigerfish, just to name a few. La Lobera, on the southeast side of the island, is popular with divers. On the west end of the island are several emerald coves with white sand beaches—wonderful spots to while away the day as you bask in the sun. You can get here by hiring a boat from one of Loreto's many tour companies. Keep in mind, some beaches are shallower and better for kids, some beaches are prone to be muddled by dead squid because of currents, and some beaches are more secluded than others. Specify what you are looking for to your boat captain so that he can select a spot that's just right for you.

Coronado Island offers wonderful vistas.

Isla del Carmen

At over 18 miles long, this is the largest island in the Loreto Bay National Park. It was once home to a large salt mining company, the remnants of which are now a ghost town. The boat ride to Isla del Carmen is a bit longer than the one to Isla Coronado, but this island has many great diving spots. A 120-foot fishing boat that was wrecked in the island's Salina Bay has become home to a variety of marine life and schools of fish, making it an ideal opportunity for divers. Some tour companies offer overnight camping trips that include hiking and sea kayaking.

Isla Danzantes

Danzante is a small island that lies south of Carmen. It's generally less traveled than the other, larger islands, and with its white sand beaches and rocky coves, Danzantes can seem like a paradise to those looking for an isolated experience. On the north side of the island lies Faro Norte, an underwater series of coral-lined cliffs that drop to over 100 feet. On the south end of the island is Piedra Submarino, or "Submarine Rock," named for its resemblance to a submarine from a distance. This rock formation provides a habitat for colorful sea stars and murex snails.

RECREATION

What Loreto lacks in nightlife, it more than makes up for in recreational activities—there's enough to see and do in Loreto during the day to get you into bed early. The main reason to come to Loreto is the calm, clear water and the nearby islands. Fishing, sailing, kayaking,

Snorkelers in the water off of Coronado Island.

diving, and snorkeling are all outstanding here. The nearby desert mountains also present opportunities for outdoor adventures.

Diving and Snorkeling

Loreto's offshore islands provide some of the best diving in the Sea of Cortés. Coronado, Carmen, and Danzante as well as the islands farther south in the Loreto Bay National Marine Park—Monserrate and Catalan—provide dozens of dive sites for divers and snorkelers of all levels. Because the islands are volcanic formations, they have characteristics that make them a sort of playground for fish and humans alike. Their rocky shorelines, coral reefs, and huge underwater rock formations attract schools of tropical fish and other sea life such as giant mantas and 40-foot whale sharks. The majority of the dive sites are fairly shallow and ideal for the novice, but there are also spots for divers looking to explore deeper sites. Access to these sites is determined by the ever-changing sea current as well as other water conditions.

BAHIA SALINA

Located near the old salt-mining operation on Isla del Carmen. The wreck of a 120-foot fishing boat sits in 35 feet of water, giving shelter to a variety of marine life. A great underwater photography opportunity.

PUNTA COYOTE

Located outside of Escondido Bay, Punta Coyote features an underwater drop of approximately 120 feet. Colorful reef fish populate the crevices and fissures of the rock, while sea fans and other, fingerlike gorgonians seem to reach out as you make your descent.

LOS CANDELLEROS

Five miles south of Puerto Escondido, this chain of islets juts out of the water like massive fingers and offers sheer vertical facades dropping to depths of nearly 200 feet. Deep crevices in the rock face provide cover for dozens of species of fish.

LAS GALERAS

Rocky outcroppings north of Isla Monserrate provide steep walls and large underwater boulders. This site is a great snorkeling spot. Just beyond it, the water drops to nearly 100 feet to an area filled with finger reefs.

LA LOBERA

On the southeast side of Isla Coronado. Intricate sea fans and black coral cover a rock wall that descends to a depth of around 100 feet. Small crevices provide cover for moray eels and pargo.

LAS TIJERATAS

Also located on the southeast side of Coronado, here a huge collection of boulders and giant pillars drop to around 75 feet. Myriad tropical fish and playful sea lions swim about as you dive.

Fishing

Although the Sea of Cortés offers many fine fishing spots, Loreto stands out as one of the finest. The town is located far enough north into the Sea of Cortés that the choppy water of the Pacific is not a factor. This allows Loreto fishermen to go out in smaller craft than are possible farther south at the East Cape and Los Cabos. Loreto fishing fleets are usually comprised of 22-foot open skiffs called *pangas.* These boats are perfectly suited for light-tackle and stand-up fly fishing. Loreto's waters offer some of the best fishing in the world—especially if you are hoping to hook dorado or yellowtail. Loreto has been called Baja's dorado and yellowtail capital. Dorado, which is among the most sought-after species in Baja, usually arrives in the waters off Loreto in June, swimming in schools and feeding on baitfish and squid. Their numbers don't taper off until early August. Then, through September, the large bulls are left to swim alone off Loreto's coast. Dorados weighing 50 pounds or more are not uncommon during this time. As the dorados disappear, yellowtail move in and populate Loreto's waters from November through April. Other species of sport fish in these waters include the Pacific sailfish (April through October), marlin (May through October), and yellowfin tuna (July through October).

Hiking and Mountain Biking

You will find many excellent opportunities for hiking or biking in the rugged mountains of Sierra de la Giganta to the west as well as in the winding canyons south of Loreto. There are no formal trails but the locals know many wonderful spots. For most of the year, mountain paths will lead you by hidden freshwater pools that are scattered throughout the area. Unique flora and fauna as well as rare desert animals live along these sparsely traveled trails, providing birdwatchers and other nature lovers a great opportunity to view unusual species. There are trails suitable for novice hikers as well as the experienced. You can rent gear and arrange hikes though Las Parras Tours and Juncalito Eco Tours (see the sidebar "Tour Companies").

Horseback Riding

Several local tour companies offer horse or mule excursions that take you along the beautiful back country leading to the San Javier Mission or other desert locales. Some of these trips are multiday affairs in which you eat and sleep at different ranches along the way. These outings last from three to five nights.

Kayaking

The calm waters off Loreto make kayaking the perfect way to explore. Several local tour companies offer a variety of kayaking adventures, ranging from two-hour tours to all-day excursions to Isla Coronado to overnight adventures to the Isla del Carmen, all the way to 10- day kayaking expeditions to La Paz. Most long trips are not available during the hotter summer months. If you are just looking to take a kayak out for a couple of hours, check with your hotel. Many have kayaks that you can use for free.

Whale Watching

With three major whale-watching locations nearby—Laguna Ojo de Liebre, Laguna San Ignacio, and Magdalena Bay—Loreto is an ideal place to see gray whales and their calves frolic in the Sea of Cortés. No other Baja lagoon can claim to be home to more than a thousand gray whales as they gather to mate and give birth. Local tour companies offer a range

Tour Companies

Loreto's tour companies offer a wide variety of services, making it important to discuss the particulars of your tour with the tour representative ahead of time so that you know exactly what to expect. Whale-watching trips are available from January through March. Many tour operators don't offer kayaking trips from August through October because of the hot weather. However, these hot months are the peak months for underwater visibility, so it's the best time for snorkeling and diving.

Arturo's Sport Fishing Fleet

613-135-0766

www.arturosport.com

Salvatierra, Loreto

Arturo's provides service in the full range of Loreto's recreational activities. They run a fleet of 12 boats between 22 and 27 feet. Additionally, they have 27 wet suits of various sizes and 50 diving tanks. They also offer snorkeling trips to Isla Coronado and whale-watching excursions of seven to eight hours for groups of three or larger. Arturo's also does guided tours of the nearby Mission of San Javier as well as hikes to the cave paintings near Mulegé.

The Baja Big Fish Company

613-104-0781

www.bajabigfish.com

Francisco Madero and Fernando Jordan

This tour company specializes in fishing expeditions. You can choose among the standard 20- to 22-foot *panga*, the 23- to 25-foot super *panga*, or the even larger deluxe *panga*, which carries up to four people. They also offer full vacation packages through several of Loreto's hotels. Check their Web site for more details.

The Baja Outpost

613-135-1134 or 888-649-5951 (U.S.)

www.bajaoutpost.com

Boulevard Adolfo Lopez Mateos, Loreto

The Baja Outpost is the only diving operation in Loreto that is a member of CMAS, FMAS, NAUI, and PADI. They offer a variety of diving packages that include a stay at their small hotel running anywhere from two to nine days. Other types of tours are also offered, including whale watching, mountain biking, and kayaking.

C&C Tours

613-133-0151

Paseo Hidalgo, Loreto

This tour company, run by Cecilia Haugen, a young geologist, takes guests on hikes through winding desert trails to see natural-spring water pools, citrus trees, and the ancient Mulegé cave paintings. They also offer tours of the San Javier Mission as well as a cheese-and-wine tour of Loreto.

Cormorant Dive Center

613-135-2140

www.loretours.com

Miguel Hidalgo and Misoneros, Loreto

Cormorant provides dive tours to the islands of Coronado, Carmen, and Danzante. They also have a scuba-diving training program. If scuba is not your thing, they do snorkeling trips to Coronado and Carmen. Additionally, Cormorant offers whale-watching tours, ATV tours, mountain-bike tours, and guided tours of San Javier Mission, and the Mulegé cave paintings.

Desert & Sea Expeditions
613-135-1378
www.desertandsea.com
Paseo Hidalgo between Colegio and Piño Suárez, Loreto

Desert & Sea specializes in eco-friendly tours of Loreto's environs. Five-hour tours of Isla Coronado include lunch and require a minimum of four people; tours of the nearby rock art and the San Javier Mission last approximately six hours and include nature guides. Whale-watching trips lasting approximately eight hours are available January through March. These, too, require groups of four.

Dolphin Dive Center
613-135-1914 or 626-447-5536 (U.S.)
www.dolphindivebaja.com
Avenida Juarez between Mateos and Davis, Loreto

This tour company has snorkeling trips to Isla Coronado and diving expeditions to Coronado, Carmen, and Danzante. The PADI-dive operation also provides a variety of diving certifications. Additionally, Dolphin offers guided whale-watching trips and tours of the Mulegé cave paintings and San Javier Mission.

Juncalito EcoTours
613-104-4030; fax 613-135-0240
www.loreto.com/josetorres/index.htm
Juncalito Beach, Loreto

This is a small outfit complete services for sportfisherman, scuba divers, and explorers. Owner José Torres has a fleet of three *panga* boats equipped with live-bait tanks. Juncalito is also a good source for hiking information.

Paddling South
800-398-6200 (U.S.)
www.tourbaja.com
P.O. Box 827, Calistoga, CA 94515

Although headquartered in California, this tour company—along with principal owner Trudi Angell—is based in Loreto. They offer sailing, kayaking, and mountain biking adventures. They also do multiday saddle tours through Loreto's mountain trails and to the Mulegé cave paintings. Check their Web site for trip dates and prices.

of whale-watching options. If you're a casual traveler, you can hire a *panga* to take you out for a few hours. If you're the adventurous type, some tour companies offer a more close-up whale experience by kayak. For more serious whale explorers, multiday excursions are available.

OTHER ATTRACTIONS

Misión Nuestra Senora de Loreto
Salvatierra between Misioneros and Piño Suarez
Established in 1695 by a Jesuit priest named Juan Maria Salvatierra, this mission was the first permanent establishment on the Baja Peninsula. The settlement surrounding the mission quickly became the religious and administrative capital of the entire peninsula. The Spanish had been trying to colonize this region since the conquistador Hernán Cortés had attempted to establish a settlement at the Bay of Santa Cruz (present-day La Paz) 150 years earlier. As Cortés and other Europeans had done elsewhere in the New World, the Jesuits who settled at Nuestra Senora brought diseases that the native inhabitants had never been exposed to. In less than a century, much of the region's indigenous population had been decimated by smallpox, plague, typhus, and measles. Out of an initial estimated population of around 48,000, only around 8,000 Natives remained by 1776.

Over the years the mission has been threatened by several natural disasters such as tropical storms and earthquakes, which took their toll on the structure. In an effort to salvage the edifice, it has been under almost constant reconstruction since 1955. Unfortunately, many of these efforts have failed to preserve the original artistry of the building. One alteration was the addition of the bell tower along Calle Savatierra. However, the mission's baroque stone façade remains an impressive monument to the region's history. A statue of Our Lady of Loreto rests on a pedestal above a small choir window. Below that, modest pilasters support a frieze with the inscription: HEADQUARTERS AND MOTHER OF THE LOWER AND UPPER CALIFORNIA MISSIONS.

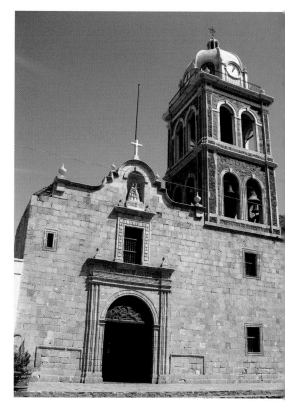

Misión Señora de Loreto.

MUSEO DE LAS MISIONES
613-135-0441
Salvatierra #16, Loreto
Open: Wed., Fri, Sat, and Sun. 9 AM—6 PM
Admission: $3
This museum highlights the history of the 18 Jesuit missions of southern Baja

California. It also has a modest anthropological collection that showcases the indigenous history of the region.

BAY OF LORETO NATIONAL MARINE PARK
613-135-1429
www.loreto.com/marinepark/index.html

This national marine park was established by a presidential decree in 1996. The protected area covers 1,283 square miles, from Isla Coronado south to Isla Catalana. In 2005, the park was added to the United Nation's list of protected World Heritage Sites. The park contains over 800 recognized species of marine life, many of them endangered . The goal of this park is the long-term protection of local fishery populations through the monitoring of fishing operations and the enforcement of park regulations. The marine park visitor's center features a marine conservation library and displays of the region's natural history and has become a meeting place for tourists, marine researchers, and students from around the world. Currently plans are in the works to add a sea and desert eco-center to promote the conservation of local flora and fauna in addition to local marine life.

CAMPO DE GOLF LORETO AND CHAMPIONSHIP TENNIS CENTER
613-133-0788 or 613-133-0554
www.gotoloreto.com/land-sport.html
Boulevard Misión San Ignacio s/n, Nopoló

This 18-hole golf course offers spectacular ocean and desert vistas. It has a par-72 rating, two beautiful artificial lakes with regulated water levels, numerous sand traps, and several desert plant species and a variety of palm trees that create obstacles to put your game to the test. Tee times are 7 AM to 5 PM Tuesday through Sunday. Reservations are recommended. Greens fees are $40 for 18 holes plus $40 for a cart and $25 for 9 holes plus $20 for a cart.

Adjacent to the golf course is find Nopoló's Championship Tennis Center, which features eight professional lit tennis courts with stadium capacity of 250. Facilities also include a restaurant/bar, a pro shop with men's and women's locker rooms, as well as a nearby children's pool. The tennis courts run $7 an hour ($10 per hour for lit courts), and pool access is $5. The facility is open daily 7 AM to 11 PM.

SHOPPING

To be honest, if you come to Loreto for the shopping experience, you'll probably go away disappointed. The town has a handful of shops on Salvatierra and within a block of the mission, where you can find some nice things, but the selection is limited relative to elsewhere in Mexico. A few boutiques sell fine handicrafts such as handwoven rugs, wrought-iron furniture, and silver jewelry. You'll also find a variety of sweatshirts, hats, beachwear, and T-shirts, as well as *artesenía,* which refers to the myriad handmade arts and crafts found throughout Mexico. In Loreto you'll find genuine silver jewelry, paintings, fine textiles from the mainland, ceramic and wood sculptures, blown glass and metal designs. Don't hesitate to ask questions about the art or bargain with the local vendors as this is a long-running and fun tradition in Mexico.

El Alacran (613-135-0029; Salvatierra 47, Loreto) Provides a wide variety of goods, including traditional Mexican *artesenía* and Taxco silver as well as T-shirts and beachwear.

La Casa de la Abuela.

Open Monday through Saturday 9:30 AM to 1 PM and 3 PM to 7 PM.

La Casa de la Abuela (613-135-3544; Salvatierra, in front of the Mission Museum, Loreto) Beachwear, Mexican *camisas,* leather goods, and handicrafts can be found in this shop. Prices are reasonable. Open Wednesday through Monday 9 AM to 10 PM.

Conchita's Curious (613-135-1054; Prolonación Misineros, Loreto) This shop offers rustic and wrought-iron furniture, colorful Mexican art, and traditional clothing. Open daily 9 AM to 8 PM.

Maria Teresa Mendoza Villa (613-135-0684; Salvatierra 47, Loreto) Located next to the Banamex, this small shop sells Mexican *artesenía* at reasonable prices. Open Monday through Saturday 9:30 AM to 7 PM.

Silver Desert Mexican Artwork in Silver (613-135-0684; Salvatierra #36, next to the bank, Loreto) Carries jewelry made from Taxco silver as well as a variety of arts and crafts. Open daily 8 AM to 2 PM and 3 PM to 9 PM.

9

Side Trips from Loreto

Loreto's environs offer travelers some of the best of Baja California. If you like Loreto's small-town feel, you'll love Mulegé, the oasis town 86 miles to the north. This town is also located near the best examples of Cochimí petroglyphs, which lie in the mountains east of town. (Don't show up in Mulegé with an empty wallet, however. The nearest bank and ATM are 38 miles to the north in Santa Rosalía.) Along the way to Mulegé, you will pass along Bahía Concepción and some of the most beautiful vistas in Baja. These beaches are great for enjoying the calm waters of the Sea of Cortés as well as for camping out. But they do lack amenities (which can be a good thing because it means fewer crowds), so come prepared. For an amazing look back in time at Baja's colonial period, the San Javier Mission, 23 miles east of Loreto, is one of the peninsula's best-preserved missions. Any of these excursions is great as a day trip out of Loreto or as a destination on its own with an overnight stay.

Mulegé

The village of Mulegé, 86 miles north of Loreto, is certainly one of the most charming towns in all of Baja. Mulegé is literally an oasis, one that has become a favorite destination for sportfishermen and travelers looking for rest and reflection. It sits in a valley along a freshwater stream that feeds the town's estuary before flowing into the sea. This stream—also called Mulegé—is what gives the town its lush landscape, with thousands of palm trees and twisted bougainvilleas filling this river valley that opens onto the Sea of Cortés. The town's close 7-mile proximity to the beautiful Bahía Concepción only adds to its draw. And if you're planning on beach camping, it's a good place to pick up provisions or get a hot meal.

Desert foliage east of Mulegé.

OPPOSITE: *Relaxing near Mulegé.*

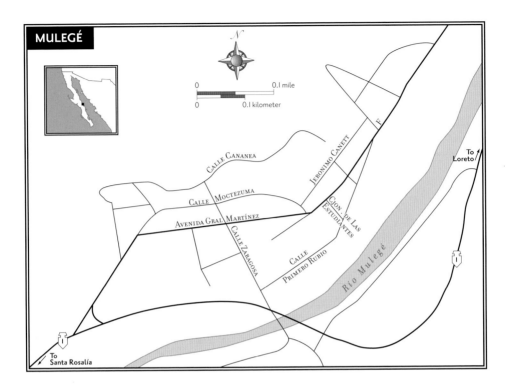

Unlike most Mexican towns, the government offices and old church are not located on the main square but are instead located several blocks to the east, as is the old state penitentiary that now serves as the regional museum. The penitentiary building itself holds interest not simply because it's a century old (it was completed in 1907) but also because it was built without bars. The prison operated this way until the 1960s, when it was closed. Inmates were allowed to work outside the jail during the day as long as they returned in the evening. Escape attempts were uncommon, but on the occasion that one did happen, the other prisoners were among those who pursued the escapees to bring them back.

ACCOMMODATIONS

Although limited, accommodations in Mulegé are extremely affordable and fairly wide ranging. Although most of the options are nothing too fancy, they are clean and comfortable. RV travelers, too, will have a lot to choose from when passing through this town.

CASA GRANADA
615-153-0688
www.casagranada.net
Estero de Mulegé#1
Price: Inexpensive
Credit Cards: None
Special Features: Located near airport

This small four-room hotel provides attractive views of the Sea of Cortés and the Mulegé estuary. With a classic colonial style and an almost tropical-island feel, the hotel is a short walk from the airport; pilots and their passengers can arrive and be in their rooms within minutes. All rooms are on the second floor and are therefore not wheelchair accessible. Rates: $75 for double occupancy.

LAS CASITAS
615-153-3023
Calle Madero #50, Mulegé
Price: Inexpensive
Credit Cards: None
Special Features: Convenient location, restaurant-bar, live music

Right in the center of town is one of Mulegé's quaint hotels from the 1960s. The building is also famous for being the birthplace of the Mexican poet and composer Alan Gorosave. The hotel has eight rustic but clean and colorful units situated around a central courtyard. The on-site restaurant-bar serves a buffet breakfast and traditional Mexican fare and seafood. Live music is also often featured, as are Friday night Mexican fiestas. Rates: start at $25.

CLEMENTINE'S BED & BREAKFAST AND CASITAS
615-153-0319
www.clementinesbaja.com
Km 131 Transpeninsular Highway just south of Mulegé
Price: Moderate to Expensive
Credit Cards: MC, V
Special Features: Continental breakfast

This hotel has four large Mexican-style rooms furnished with queen-size beds. The rooms rent from between $55 and $70 for double occupancy, depending on the room you choose. Weekly rates are also available. Continental breakfast is included. The hotel also offers three fully furnished casitas—

available on a weekly or monthly basis—complete with fully equipped kitchens, covered patios, and gas grills. Rates: $95–200, depending on the bungalow.

HOTEL SERENIDAD
615-153-0530
www.serenidad.com
Km 130 Transpeninsular Highway, just south of Mulegé
Price: Inexpensive
Credit Cards: None
Special Features: Airport

One of Mulegé's oldest and most famous hotels, Hotel Serenidad is also the location of the town's landing strip, making it a popular fly-in hotel since the 1960s. The hotel offers 50 rooms at $72 or $89 per night that accommodate two to three people. Also n the grounds are small, air-conditioned cottages at $128 per night, featuring a bedroom with two double beds, a fireplace, and a living room. For true luxury, a three-bedroom, two-bath riverfront villa is available for anywhere between five-day or month-long stays; daily rates vary from $250 for stays of 5 to 7 days, $200 for 8 to 14 days at, or $175 for 15 to 30 days. Another option is 15 fully equipped RV sites for $15 a night for two travelers plus an additional $2.50 for each additional person. For recreation, this hotel has a boat ramp onto the Mulegé River, as well as a good-size pool and a swim-up bar. The on-site restaurant serves good Mexican fare and is well known for its Saturday night pig roast. Rates: start at $70.

POSADA DE LAS FLORES
613-153-0188
www.posadadelasflores.com
Comicilio Conocida, Punta Chivato
Price: Expensive
Credit Cards: AE, MC, V
Special Features: Located on the beach

Located 15 miles north of Mulegé up Mexico 1 and 7 miles east off the highway at tranquil Puna Chivata, this exclusive hotel is affiliated with the hotel of the same name in down town Loreto. Sitting on 7.5 acres of beachfront property several miles from the nearest town, the hotel has 10 rooms and 10 junior suites at prices significantly higher than you will generally find this side of Cabo San Lucas. Rooms are furnished with either two twin beds or a single queen-size, while most of the junior suites feature king-size beds. Rooms have terraces; suites have porches overlooking the sea. Meals are included with the price of the room, which is good because the on-site restaurant is the only one within miles. The property also features a swimming pool and a tennis court. This hotel has its own private airstrip (frequency 122.8) and offers gas services. To drive to Punta Chivata, take Mexico 1 north out of Mulegé 15 miles, and turn right onto the graded dirt road just south of Palo Verde. Look for the sign that says Punta Chivato. Rates: start at $250–280 per night for a standard room.

RV Parks

CUESTA REAL RV PARK AND HOTEL
615-153-0321
www.bajaquest.com/cuestareal
Km 128 Transpeninsular Highway just south of Mulegé

Located off the Mexico 1 on the south side of the Mulegé Rive, this facility features 10 large RV sites with full hookups as well as a small hotel with a dozen rooms. The property has an on-site restaurant/bar, a swimming pool on a shaded patio surrounded by palm trees, laundry facilities, and a gift shop. Rates: $8 per night for an RV site with full hookup.

OASIS RIO BAJA
615-153-0425
www.oasisriobaja.com
Km 134 Transpeninsular Highway

This large RV park situated along the Mulegé River is mostly occupied by permanent residents, though there are generally 5 to 10 spaces available for short-term rental.

RESTAURANTS

LOS EQUIPALES
615-153-0330
Moctezuma, Mulegé
Open: Daily 8 AM–11 PM
Price: Inexpensive
Cuisine: Mexican
Serving: B, L, D

This second-story restaurant, located one block north of the town square, is perhaps the most expensive in Mulegé. But considering you can stuff yourself on shrimp and margaritas for about $11, that's not really saying much. The food here is very good and the service friendly.

BEACHES

There's a beach on the south side of the river just east of the Transpeninsular Highway that's very decent for relaxing, fishing, and snorkeling, and it's never crowded. However, well worth checking out are the beaches to the south, instead, along the beautiful Bahía Concepción. These are without a doubt some of the most beautiful and serene beaches in all of Baja. Or investigate the secluded beaches north of Mulegé, at Punta Chivato along Bahía Santa Inés.

Punta Chivato

Punto Chivato is one of Baja's best-kept secrets that's in the process of getting out. It's 15 miles north up Mexico 1 from Mulegé and east another 7 miles along a graded dirt road. (A 4,000-foot airstrip is located here at the Posada de las Flores Hotel.) The beach is found at the end of a 7-mile peninsula that reaches out into the Sea of Cortés and is the only south-facing beach on the east coast of Baja California. The result is a more temperate area during the peak fishing months of summer as cool prevailing winds flow right onto the beach. The Posada de las Flores (a newly refurbished hotel formerly known as the Hotel Punta Chivata) is the only hotel in the area. However, over the last five years there has been an explosion of homes being built along the beach here by homeowners from north of the border. Still, plenty of wide-open beaches are left that are great for walking and snorkeling. Dolphins often swim in the water not too far from shore. Closer in, along the white sand beaches and rocky shoreline, you'll find roosterfish, grouper, and cabrilla. The farther north you go past the hotel, the more remote the beaches become.

OTHER ATTRACTIONS

Cave Paintings

Just west of Mulegé in the foothills of the Sierra de Guadalupe Mountains are the most significant grouping ancient petroglyphs in Baja California Sur. Although their origin is not completely certain, they are thought to have been made by the Cochimí Indians who inhabited this region for many thousands of years before the arrival of Europeans in the 17th century. The mural-like paintings, in hues of red, white, black, and yellow, are believed to depict ancient rituals involving hunters and several types of animals, including deer, lizards, and fish. These paintings, which have been declared World Heritage Sites, appear on cave walls and ceilings as well as on rock walls exposed to the elements.

The finest group of petroglyphs is located in caves near Rancho La Trinidad, 18 miles west of Mulegé. Getting to this site is an adventure in itself. While most of the trip can be accomplished by SUV or on horseback, it also involves a hike of about 4 miles as well as several short swims. Another popular site is called San Borjitas, located near Rancho Las Tinajas. This site is much more accessible thanks to a new road that brings you within a mile of the cave.

Several tour companies operating out of Loreto offer tours of the cave paintings. However, Salvador Castro Drew, one of the most experienced and reputable guides, is found right in Mulegé. Contact him at Mulegé Tours: 615-153-0232; www.mulegetours .com.

Bahía Concepción

Along Bahía Concepción lie some of the most beautiful beaches anywhere. With calm water and secluded settings, this strip of land along the Sea of Cortés can provide you with some extremely memorable experiences. So alluring is the draw of this place that some people choose to spend entire seasons and even years along its shores.

Winter is the best time to visit due to the summer heat, though if you show up in late summer, you may be convinced that you have actually stumbled upon some lost Mediterranean shore, given the numbers of Italians who hang out here in August.

Beach camping along Bahía Concepción.

An entrance fee associated with these beaches generally runs between $7 and $10. You pay this either as you enter the beach, or someone will come around to collect. These fees help to keep the beaches clean, so don't fret. Someone paid that fee before you so that you could enjoy a pristine beach. Besides, services at these beaches tend to be minimal, with most featuring pit toilets and maybe a cold shower. Do not drink the water in the showers— it's untreated! Be sure to bring plenty of your own water; it's probably a good idea to pack at least a lunch, as well. Once you find yourself on the shore here, it can be hard to bring yourself to leave.

Playa Frambes

Located 8 miles south of Mulegé, this is site offers comforts that most beaches along Bahía Concepción don't. Look for the road sign, and follow the graded road to the beach. Although not the most isolated beach along this bay, it's still a serene place to while away the day. The calm waters here are ideal for kayaking, and you can launch a small boat over the sand. *Palapas* along the beach cost $7 a night beach and offer a majestic view of the sea. Restrooms and flush toilets are available, as well as hot showers. Casitas with private showers run $30 a night. These have solar power and two double beds.

Los Naranjos

This beach 10 miles south of Mulegé at Km 119 of Mexico 1 is easy to access (by Bahía Concepción standards), but you should still enter with care as the road has some soft spots. This beautifully tranquil beach has crystal-clear water and views of the mountainous

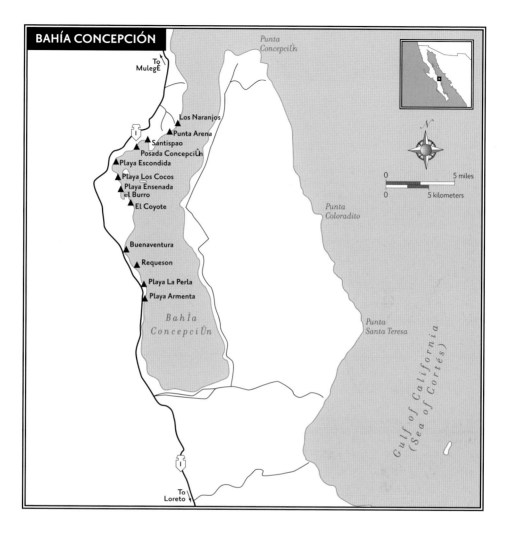

Punto Concepción Peninsula in the distance. Several *palapa* cabins are set up along the water, but tent campers are welcome, as well. Cabins run about $10, and campsites are $7. Restrooms with flush toilets and hot water are available for a small charge. There is also a small restaurant here that serves good eats for cheap. Be sure to bring your own water, though, and be aware that there is no security.

Punta Arena

You'll find this pristine, wide beach just south of Los Naranjos. Take the same exit as Los Naranjos, but stay to the left, and, as with Los Naranjos, watch for soft spots in the road. This beach has several permanent residences, though plenty of open beach is left over for tents and RVs. Some 50 campsites and a few *palapas* run about $7 a night. Minimal restroom facilities are provided but no security.

Playa Santispac

This beach is located at Km 114 of Mexico 1 about 12 miles south of Mulegé. The entry fee is about $7. It is blessed with an easy entrance that provides you with a nice panoramic view as you make your way down to the beach; just look for the road sign. The long, wide beach offers stunning vistas of offshore islands and the peninsula on the other side of the bay. It also has two small restaurants; an unusual convenience along Bahía Concepción. Playa Santispac is located in a protected cove, which is why many people spend the entire winter here. Arrive early if you want to get a good spot because this beach does tend to fill up.

Posada Concepción

This beach is largely taken up by a ten-site RV park. Located at Km 112 of Mexico 1, this beach is the perfect setting-off point with a kayak to explore the offshore islands that are in close proximity. Entrance here runs about $10. It has an outhouse and hot showers for a nominal fee, though it does tend to be crowded by the many year-round RV residents who have come to call this beach home. If you are looking for a choice spot on the water, forget it—the year-round residents have already taken them all up. The RV sites are set back from the beach are set aside for overnight visitors. However, there are plenty of other spots along this beach to be had in which you don't have to take a backseat to anyone.

Playa Escondida

This beautiful beach is nestled between two tall ridges along Km 111 of Mexico 1, which provide protection from the prevailing winds, making it an excellent place to camp in winter. The rough road in plus a lack of services make this beach much less congested than some of the others just to the north. It's a perfect place to while away the day kayaking or just relaxing in the warm, calm sea. The entrance fee runs about $6, and pit toilets are available.

Relaxing at Playa Escondido.

Playa Los Cocos

Located about a mile south of Playa Escondida, this beach is far enough away from Mulegé to be free of the year-round RV set, for you to be able to get a camp site right on the beach and enjoy the tranquility of your surrounding without having to worry about your neighbor two steps from your tent flap. It's a great place for camping out and enjoying the surroundings. The road in is a little rough, but the beach is suitable for launching small boats. Admission is about $6 and includes pit toilets.

Playa El Burro

This crescent-shaped beach, about 16 miles south of Mulegé along Km 109 of Mexico 1, is situated in a protected cove and is suitable for launching boats. Although certainly not the longest or widest beach along Bahía Concepción, it is undeniably beautiful. Pit toilets and several *palapas* are available, and tent campers are welcome. Arrive early to get the best spots because this beach does attract travelers. The entry fee is about $7.

Bahía El Coyote

Some 17 miles south of Mulegé along Km 109 of Mexico 1, this beach sits in a cove with a rocky shoreline at the south side, which both protects it from prevailing winds and provides good opportunities for snorkeling. This is a good beach for campers and RVs, though you should drive slowly along the access road coming in. If you're lucky, you can get a spot at the more secluded south end of the beach under a palm tree. An outhouse and cold shower are available. Entrance fee is about $7.

San Buenaventura

This pristine beach backed by steep hills is about 25 miles south of Mulegé at Km 94 of Mexico 1. It is home to the Hotel San Buenaventura (U.S.: 619-955-6278; www.hotelsan-buenaventura.com), the only beachfront resort along Bahía Concepción. This hotel has 18 rooms and 2 suites that feature hammocks and large balconies as well as a bar, restaurant, and a mini-market. Rates range from $69 for a standard room to $199 for a two-bedroom beachfront suite with kitchen, dining room, and private parking. For campers—both tent and RV—the hotel has a gated, secure campground in front of the hotel on the beach. Each camping space is furnished with a *palapa* for shade, and flush toilets are available for use in the hotel. There is also a concrete ramp along the beach for launching boats. Parking is $10, showers and trash disposal runs $20, and electricity bumps the price up to $30.

Bahía El Coyote.

El Requesón

Located 26 miles south of Mulegé, this beach is just about the most beautiful spot along Bahía Concepción—and that's really

Playa El Requesón.

saying something. It features two beautiful bays that bump up against each other and are separated by a narrow isthmus—submerged during high tide—that connects to a small island just offshore. The northern bay provides great opportunities for snorkeling and clamming, whereas the southern bay is shallower and perfect for wading and relaxing. Several *palapas* can be found along the beach, and tent campers are also welcome. Pit toilets are set back near the cliffs that rise up from the beach, but these toilets are not well maintained, and are actually downright nasty. Plus the road in is rather rough, though it is short. Access to this beach runs around $10.

Playa La Perla
This beach is off Km 91 of Mexico 1, just south of Playa Requeson. It has good access for RVs and offers about 10 *palapas* located along the shoreline. The camping area at the north side of the beach provides beautiful vistas of the Sea of Cortés. Minimal security is provided by the resident manager. Entry fee runs around $7.

Playa Armenta
Located 28 miles south of Mulegé off Km 90 of Mexico 1, this beach is situated in a wide cove with a rock reef that wraps around the south end. This provides protection from prevailing winds as well as good snorkeling. Pit toilets are available here as well as a few small *palapas,* making this beach good for tent camping. The access road is passable for RVs—just take it slow and realize that the fit is going to be tight in some places. Entry fee runs about $7.

Misión San Javier

One of Baja California's most historically important missions sits in an isolated canyon high above the Sea of Cortés, 23 miles west of Loreto in the Sierra de Gigante Mountains. This is Misión San Francisco Javier de Viggé Biaundó, commonly referred to as Mission San Javier. Considered one of the most beautiful and well-preserved missions in all of the Californias, San Javier is constructed of volcanic stone blocks and took more than 14 years to build. Atop the volcanic gray façade are domes and bell towers containing two bells, one dating from 1761 and another that arrived in 1803. Inside the mission, the unique baroque appearance is striking. The original golden alter is intact, with an 18th-century crucifix as well as several paintings, all of which were transported here from Mexico City by ship and overland in a caravan of burrows and wooden crates. There are also gilded 18th-century altars featuring statues of San Francisco Javier and Our Lady of Guadalupe, beautifully lit through stained-glass windows framed in wood, and 18th-century priestly vestments are displayed in a glass cabinet. This mission is often referred to as the jewel of the Baja California mission churches.

GETTING THERE

At Km 118 of Mexico 1, the Carretera Transpeninsular, about 4 miles south of Loreto, turn onto the dirt road heading east. This exit is clearly marked. This 23-mile stretch leads you along palm groves, remote ranches, and along the steep cliffs of the Sierra de la Gigante. There are also some marked trails that lead to some lesser-known Cochimí cave paintings.

Playing at Playa la Perla.

This road can be a little rough, but it's passable for most vehicles. Just take it easy. However, if it has been raining, you might want to consider taking the trip at another time.

San Javier is a small community of about 50 full-time residents. If the mission is locked, don't be afraid to inquire about gaining entrance from one of these folks. Also, as a courtesy be sure to slip a few pesos into the contribution box. This money goes to support the maintenance of the mission.

Road maps show another dirt road heading east out of San Javier and hooking up with Mexico 1 north of Ciudad Insergentes. This looks like a nice shortcut for anyone heading to La Paz or environs farther south on the peninsula. But don't even attempt to take this road unless you have a heavy-duty 4WD vehicle. And even then, road conditions will force you to drive so slow that it's not even worth it. Better just to head west to Loreto and take Mexico 1 from there.

ACCOMMODATIONS

Casa de Ana
613-135-1552 or 800-497-3923
www.casadeanaloreto.com/index.htm

The only accommodations in San Javier, situated in renovated 18th-century missionary housing, consist of five rustic adobe cabins. Bathrooms and hot water are available, though electricity is available only from dusk until 10:30 PM. Bungalows rent for $35 a night for a room with two twin beds.

RESTAURANTS

La Palapa
Just as San Javier has but one place to stay, it has but one restaurant, located near the mission. The owner, Señora Santana, cooks delicious traditional Mexican dishes on a wood-burning stove. There is no menu. You eat what *la señora* has cooked for her family that day—after all, it is her home. And you pay what you think the meal is worth.

10

General Information

Money and Money Exchange

American dollars are widely accepted and in some places even preferred in Mexico. However, your money will go further if you use pesos. For both convenience and the fact that you don't have much choice, prices are usually rounded off to equal 10 pesos to the dollar. This means that since the official exchange rate is currently fluctuating at more than 10.9 pesos for every dollar, you will generally be overpaying about 9 cents for every dollar you spend.

Mexican currency notes come in denominations of 20, 50, 100, 200, 500, and 1000. Breaking larger bills is a persistent problem in Mexico, particularly at smaller independent establishments. I once had to wait half an hour after finishing a meal while the restaurant owner ran around to nearby businesses trying to make change for a 500-peso note. The best strategy to avoid such a situation is to pay with larger bills when spending money at larger businesses and save your smaller bills and *monedas* (coins) for small establishments and street vendors.

The quickest and easiest way to get Mexican currency is simply to go to a Mexican ATM

Nopoló Beach.

and withdraw pesos. These machines generally offer cash at the wholesale bank rate instead of the less-favorable tourist rate, making ATMs not only convenient but also offering the best exchange rates. Once you withdraw currency in Mexican denominations, your bank will convert it back to the dollar amount and charge you that way. Additional transaction fees do apply. ATMs are usually accessible 24-hours a day. Like many banks north of the border, ATMs are located in an entrance area between the outer and inner doors to the bank. After normal business hours—as is the case in the United States—insert your card into the slot next to the outer door, and you will be buzzed inside to do your withdrawal.

It's probably not such a good idea to rely solely on ATMs as your source for money. In towns such as Loreto and Todos Santos where ATMs are rare (or in Mulegé, where there is no ATM at all), have a little extra cash on you in case of an emergency. Banks or *casas de cambio* (exchange houses) offer respectable exchange rates. Hotels offer the worst exchange rates. It's always a good idea to exchange at least $50 or $75 into pesos before leaving the U.S. so that you'll arrive in Mexico with pesos for your cab ride or a meal. If you are driving to Baja California Sur, some of the best exchange rates you will find are located near the border such as along San Ysidro Boulevard east of the 5 and 805 Freeways. A high concentration of *casas de cambio* means there is competition to offer favorable exchange rates. Traveler's checks are another good option. Although it can be time consuming to convert them into cash, banks don't charge extra fees for cashing traveler's checks. The rate of exchange will generally be less favorable than for cash, however.

Credit cards are widely accepted in Los Cabos and La Paz. However, outside of those areas, an acceptance of credit cards is less common. The benefit of using a credit card is that you will receive the more favorable wholesale rate. The drawback is that if you're spending money in a place that accepts credit cards, chances are that it's an establishment that is geared toward serving tourists—and thus you get less bang for your buck than at places that cater to locals.

MAKING HOTEL RESERVATIONS

Making reservations at hotels in Baja can be a tricky experience. Larger resorts accept hotel reservations over the Internet with the use of a credit card, but many smaller hotels—particularly ones owned by American expatriates—require a process that's a little less organized. Most will accept the initial hotel reservation via their Web site or by e-mail. However, to confirm the reservation, many require that you send a deposit check to a specified address, often inside the United States. In areas where the tourism industry is less developed, such as Loreto and Mulegé, many hotels require payment by cash only. You may find this to be an inconvenience. Still, the unique ambience offered at these smaller, independent hotels makes the extra effort well worth it. Note that the direct-dial prefix for Mexico from the United States is 011-52.

CALLING HOME

It isn't a good idea to dial direct long distance or international calls from your hotel room. Hotels often add their own surcharges, even to local calls. This also applies to bringing and using your cell phones while in Mexico. It may seem extremely convenient to take your phone out of your pocket and dial away, but you will likely wish you hadn't at the end of the month

Loreto retains a distinctly colonial feel.

when you get a phone bill packed with hefty international roaming charges. Even receiving calls on your cell can result in excessive charges. Public phones in the larger towns are provided by a company called Ladatel, which offers long-distance calls with a *tarjeta de teléfono* (phone card) issued through TelMex, the national phone company of Mexico. You can buy prepaid Ladatel phone cards in pharmacies, convenience stores, and supermarkets. Another option is to obtain a calling card though your own phone company back home.

INTERNET ACCESS

If you are bringing a laptop computer, many hotels offer wireless Internet access as part of their amenities. However, there is always added risk to traveling with a laptop. Several cybercafés throughout Baja California Sur offer travelers access to the Internet for a nominal fee. If you do use these machines, it's always a good idea to click on "Internet Options" and clear the cache before logging off. You don't want any of your personal information sitting on the computer after you have left. However, your best bet is to log into personal accounts sparingly on public computers since unscrupulous hackers have been known to bug computers in cybercafés and even hotels with software designed to gain access to personal information—especially banking and e-trade accounts.

Cybercafés

Cabo San Lucas

DR. Z'S INTERNET CAFÉ AND BAR
624-143-5390
Lázaro Cárdenas
Open: Daily 9 AM–8 PM

CAFÉ ON-LINE
624-143-7283
Cabo San Lucas Avenue, one block from Plaza Las Glorias
Open: Mon.–Sat. 9 AM–8 PM

SAN FRANCISCO COFFEE COMPANY
624-144-4387
Boulevard de la Marina #39
Open: Daily 8 AM–8 PM

San José del Cabo

CLUB INTERNET
Avendia Zaragoza in front of the medical clinic
Open: Daily 9 AM–10 PM

Todos Santos

PANCHO BANANO
612-145-0885
Hidalgo #11 e/ Benito Juárez and Colegio Militar Colonia Centro
Open: Daily 7 AM–9 PM

La Paz

BAJA NET
612-125-9380
Madero 430
Open: Mon.–Sat. 8 AM–9 PM

Electricity

Mexico's electrical system is the same as in the United States and Canada: 110 volts AC. The outlets are compatible with any electrical appliance, recharger, or extension cords you may bring. However, the outlets in older or smaller hotels may not have polarized plugs (in which one prong is slightly larger than the other). Pick up an adapter at any hardware or discount store.

Language

Spanish is the primary language spoken in Baja California. But tourism being what it is here, you will get along quite well speaking English in areas where there are lots of travelers. Particularly in Los Cabos, it is quite common for gringos to drop in for a week and go home without ever having spoken a word of Spanish. You will find that waiters, taxi drivers, tour guides, rental-agency clerks, and anyone else who deals with tourists for a living is quite adept at speaking English.

As you move away from tourist areas, you should not expect to get by on English alone. It is worth your while to make an attempt to learn at least the most basic Spanish phrases. Not only will this help you communicate better, it will also go a long way toward ingratiating you with your Mexican hosts. And that's never a bad thing.

FOOD AND WATER

Getting used to the food in Baja can sometimes take a period of adjustment, particularly if you are not used to the spices. A little common sense will go a long way toward making sure you don't get sick while you're enjoying yourself with sun and fun. Spend the first few days of your trip taking it easy. Many people go on vacation, suddenly find themselves free of the workaday hours

Beach vendor at Tecolote Beach.

and the social mores of home—and sometimes tend to cut loose and overdo it. Resist this urge—at least for a little bit. Give yourself time to adjust to jetlag, new cuisine, and the other strains traveling to a new place puts on your body.

Many larger resorts have purified water systems, and smaller hotels generally offer complimentary bottled water. Try to carry bottled water wherever you go so that you have it on hand to keep yourself hydrated. Be sure to brush your teeth with bottled water if you're staying at a hotel without a purified system. Restaurants serve ice made of purified water, so it's fine to have ice in your Coke. You may see street vendors selling flavored *aguas frescas* (fresh waters) with flavors such as *sandía* (watermelon), *limón* (lemonade), *melón* (cantaloupe), and *fresa* (strawberry). These are delicious and can be quite refreshing—but there is no guarantee that they are made with purified water. It's a good idea to ask just to be sure, though the answer is likely to be yes either way. The bottom line is that by consuming these refreshments, you are taking a calculated risk, and you need to be aware of that.

In fact, any time you consume peeled, raw fruits and vegetables, or eating from a small "locals" restaurant or street vendor, you are taking a risk of getting sick. You can help to prepare your body for these risks by eating plenty of yogurt for several weeks prior to your trip. Scientific studies have shown that the live active cultures in yogurt have properties that protect the intestinal tract from gastrointestinal infection.

Give yourself time to adjust before indulging in Cabo's temptations.

WHAT TO BRING

Obviously, if you are traveling to Baja California, you are going to want to bring a camera, a bathing suit, and some flip-flops. However, just because it's Mexico doesn't mean that you can buy certain items cheaper than you would in the United States. For example, if you plan on going snorkeling, it's a good idea to pick up a mask and snorkel before leaving for Mexico because you'll often find a much larger selection—and better prices—at your local sporting goods store or on the Internet than at the beach, where they know they can charge you exorbitant prices because you need the equipment.

Another item that you'll need if you plan on leaving the tourist zone for any length of time is a roll of toilet paper. Some off-the-beaten-path restrooms will charge you a few pesos and give you a couple of squares, but some places there just *isn't* any. Better to come prepared than find yourself in a situation where you have to improvise. Additionally, you'll want to have a tube or bottle of disinfectant hand lotion or disinfectant wipes to freshen up with. This comes in handy in a variety of situations.

One saying seems to have gotten truer in recent years: There are two types of luggage: carry-on luggage and lost luggage. We all know people who have taken trips and ended up spending days waiting for their luggage to arrive at their destination. It's best to pack light and carry all of your belongings aboard with you as you make your way south. But this is not always a possibility. A good trick is to make arrangements with your hotel and ship your belongings ahead. This costs extra, of course, but the peace of mind that it buys is really priceless.

Helpful Phrases

When it comes to conversation, Mexicans tend to appreciate formalities more than their neighbors to the north. When approaching someone for information, don't forget to greet them with the time-appropriate salutation (*buenos días, buenas tardes, buenas noches*), even if it's the only Spanish you can think of at the moment. Try not to say simply "*Hola,*" which comes across as abrupt.

Good morning—*Buenos días*

Good afternoon—*Buenas tardes*

Good evening (after 8 PM)—*Buenas noches*

Goodbye—*Adiós*

Please—*Por favor*

Thank you very much—*Muchas gracias*

You're welcome—*De nada*

Do you speak English?—*¿Habla usted ingles?*

I don't understand.—*No entiendo.*

How do you say . . . in Spanish?—*¿Como se llama . . . en español?*

My name is . . .—*Me llamo . . .*

Where is . . . ?—*¿Dónde está . . . ?*

To the right—*A la derecha*

To the left—*A la izquierda*

Straight ahead—*Derecho*

What is the rate?—*¿A cuanto es?*

Shower—*Ducha*

Towels—*Toallas*

Soap—*Jabón*

Toilet paper—*Papel higiénico*

Key—*Llave*

Order—*Orden*

Fork—*Tenedor*

Spoon—*Cuchara*

Knife—*Cuchillo*

Napkin—*Servilleta*

Food—*Comida*

Coffee—*Café*

Tea—*Té*

Beer—*Cerveza*

Wine—*Vino*

Milk—*Leche*

Juice—*Jugo*

Money—*Dinero*

Expensive—*Caro*

Cheap—*Barato*

Post office—*Correo*

Driver's licence—*Licencia de manejar*

Gas station—*Gasolinera*

Border—*Frontera*

Passport—*Pasaporte*

Tourists come and go at Lover's Beach.

TIPPING

Being a former waiter, I am all too familiar with the frustration of foreign tourists skipping out without tipping just because they aren't familiar with the local customs. That's just a bad excuse to be cheap. Many large, all-inclusive resorts uphold a no-tipping policy; in such cases where an exception has expressly been made, it's okay not to tip. Otherwise, be polite, and plan on tipping service personnel the customary amount.

Bellboys should be tipped based on the pieces of luggage they carry to your room. Restaurant servers are customarily tipped around 15 percent of the total bill; however, if you're dining with a large group, a service charge may be automatically added to the bill. The tipping of chambermaids is optional though highly appreciated. You should tip the gas station attendant about 50 cents and/or let them keep the change when it equals less than a peso.

If you take a tour, it's standard to tip the guide about 10 percent the cost of the trip. This is particularly important if you have a guide who goes out of his way to make sure that you are well informed and have a good time. Taxi drivers are generally not tipped in Mexico, except if they give special service or provide you with good advice. Even then, it is at your discretion since many taxi drivers will bend over backward to give you advice even if you're not looking for it.

HEADING TO THE BEACH

Baja has some of the most pristine and undeveloped beaches you will find anywhere. The drawback to this is that you will not have the security of a lifeguard. Even at hotel pools and crowded beaches like Médano Beach in Cabo San Lucas, there are no lifeguards to pull you

It's customary to tip your tour guides.

out of the water if you get into trouble. This should be of particular concern to anyone traveling with children. Even the calm water of Nopoló Beach present a dangerous environment for unattended kids. The crashing oceanic waters on the Pacific side of the peninsula are far more hazardous, though even the seaside beaches in San José del Cabo can have dangerous breakers and rip tides. If you are unfortunate enough to get caught in an undertow (a strong current under the surface of the water that can pull you away from the beach), swim parallel to the beach until you get out of it instead of swimming against it directly toward the beach.

Another amenity that is lacking from Baja beaches is easy access to convenience stores. Be sure to pack plenty of water and sunblock before you set out for the beach. You can also save yourself a few dollars by buying sunblock before your arrival in Baja. It is an absolute necessity and one that is generally sold at inflated prices in hotel gift shops.

Lost in contemplation at Balandra Beach.

BEACH ETIQUETTE

All the beaches in Baja California—in fact, all the beaches throughout Mexico—are federal property. Therefore, no hotel or homeowner can restrict access to the beach from the water or make their own guidelines as to what you can do on the beach. However, hotels can restrict you from crossing their property to get to the beach and they often set up private areas with *palapas* and tables for their guests. That being said, many people have no problem waltzing through the lobby of a beachfront resort as if they were a guest to get to a choice spot on the beach. Whether you choose to do so is entirely dependent on what you feel comfortable with.

Another aspect of Baja beaches is the amount of clothing that you're required to wear (or not wear) when playing along this beautiful coast. Mexico as a whole is a pretty conservative and traditional place, and decency laws prohibit going nude or even topless in public. Still, there are a few places in Baja where going topless is readily acceptable, such as the beach in front of the Whales Inn near Loreto. Also, keep in mind that Baja California Sur is a relatively empty place with miles and miles of vacant beaches, off-shore islands, and hidden desert arroyos. While it's not recommended that you go around violating decency laws, there is nothing to stop you from going around in the buff if you suddenly find yourself on a deserted beach with no one around for miles. Just be sure to keep your clothes within a reasonable distance in case someone should wander by.

A couple strolls along Tecolote Beach.

If you do find yourself on a deserted beach, resist the temptation to drive your vehicle along the shoreline. It is illegal to drive on the beaches in Mexico and doing so can result in stiff fines.

BAJA CALIFORNIA FOR GAYS AND LESBIANS

Generally speaking, Mexico is a fairly conservative and widely Catholic country. Particularly among the smaller towns in the lower Baja Peninsula, much of the population is traditional and provincial in their views. That said, while southern Baja in general and Los Cabos in particular have not developed the reputation for being attractive destinations for gay travelers that, say, Puerto Vallarta has, this region has plenty to offer gay and lesbian vacationers. There are many wonderful gay-friendly and even gay-owned businesses throughout Baja California Sur as well as tour groups that offer custom gay-friendly cruises, kayak adventures, and other excursions. The Rainbow Bar (624-143-1455) on Marina Boulevard in Cabo San Lucas is the only true gay bar in town, though most Los Cabos establishments are friendly and tolerant to all of their guests. Among the gay- and lesbian-friendly accommodations that exist here are:

CABO SAN LUCAS

THE BUNGALOWS BREAKFAST INN
624-143-5035 or 888-424-CABO (U.S.)
www.cabobungalows.com
Boulevard Miguel Angel Herrera

TODOS SANTOS

TODOS SANTOS INN
612-145-0040
www.todossantosinn.com
Calle Legaspi #33

LA PAZ

HOTEL MEDITERRANE
612-125-1195
www.hotelmed.com
Allende 36

LA CASA MEXICANA INN
612-125-2748
www.casamex.com
Calle Bravo 106

LORETO

BAJA OUTPOST
613-1351134 or 888-649-5951 (U.S.)
www.bajaoutpost.com
Boulevard Adolfo Lopez Mateos

The garden pool at the Todos Santos Inn.

SUKASA BUNGALOWS
613-135-0490
www.loreto.com/sukasa
Boulevard Lopez Mateo y Calle Fernando Jordan

Getting Married in Mexico

As "destination weddings" have become more of a popular practice in the United States, Baja California has become an increasingly popular destination to hold such an affair. Not only is Baja relatively close and stunningly beautiful, but it also makes for a great honeymoon. And if you're going to ask your guests to do some traveling, anyway, why not bring them to a place that resembles paradise?

As with any wedding (outside of Las Vegas), getting married in Mexico requires planning, coordination, and the completion of documents. One solution to make the process easier is to complete the legal paperwork in the United States and simply perform the ceremony in Mexico. However, if you want your ceremony to be more than symbolic, there are several requirements that you need to fulfill at the location in Mexico where you will be married.

Keep in mind that religious weddings are not officially recognized in Mexico and thus do not change your legal marriage status. Therefore, in order to have your wedding legally recognized in Mexico and back home, you'll need a civil ceremony performed by a Spanish-speaking judge who resides in the city where you are getting married. You can also arrange to have this ceremony performed at an outside site for an additional fee. In Los Cabos, the civil ceremony can be performed in the judge's chambers any weekday except for Tuesday at noon or 1 PM.

In addition to the judge, you'll need at least two witnesses who are 18 or older plus fulfill several other legal requirements that you'll have to get out of the way for your marriage to be legally binding. Completing these requirements will necessitate arriving in Mexico several days before the ceremony. You'll need certified copies of your birth certificates as well as passports and copies of your tourist cards. If you have been married previously, you'll need papers indicating that you have been legally divorced for at least a year. There is also medical lab work that needs to be performed in Baja California Sur.

With all of these ancillary details, it's probably a really good idea to hire a wedding coordinator to help you out, especially if you don't speak Spanish. Several wedding planners work out of Los Cabos, and many of the hotels in San José and the Corridor offer their own wedding planners. Check the hotel Web sites for more details. Or, check out the following wedding planners that operate in the Baja region.

BAJA WEDDINGS
624-105-3230 or 949-226-8320 (U.S.)
www.bajawedding.com
Plaza del Rey #3, Km 6 Transpeninsular Highway
Los Cabos 23400, Mexico

SUNSET WEDDINGS
624-143-5016 or 858-427-0658 (U.S.)
www.asunsetwedding.com
Boulevard Lázaro Cárdenas, Edificio Posada Local #7
Cabo San Lucas 23400, Mexico

Mexican Holidays

January 1
New Year's Day*

January 6
Three Kings Day

February 2
Día de la Candelaria (commemorates Baby Jesus being presented at Jerusalem temple)

February 5
Constitution Day*

February 24
Flag Day

Sunday before Ash Wednesday
Carnival

March 19
St Joseph's Day

March 21
Benito Juarez's Birthday*

Palm Sunday to Easter
Holy Week

April 30
Día de los Niños (Children's Day)

May 1
Labor Day*

May 3
Holy Cross Day

May 5
Battle of Puebla

May 10
Mother's Day

June 24
Saint John the Baptist Day

June 29
Saint Peter and Saint Paul's Day

September 1
President's State of Union Address

September 16
Independence Day*

October 12
Día de Raza (Discovery of America)

October 14
Saint Francis Day

November 1, 2
Día de Todos Santos and Día de Muertes (All Saints and All Souls Day)

November 20
Revolution Day (Revolution of 1910)*

December 8
Immaculate Conception

December 12
Virgin of Guadelupe Day

December 24
Christmas Eve

December 25
Christmas*

December 31
New Year's Eve
* Legal holiday—banks and government offices closed

Index